THE BUILDING OF CASTLE HOWARD

Ca: Campbell Delin:

Castle Howard in Yorkshire the Seat of the

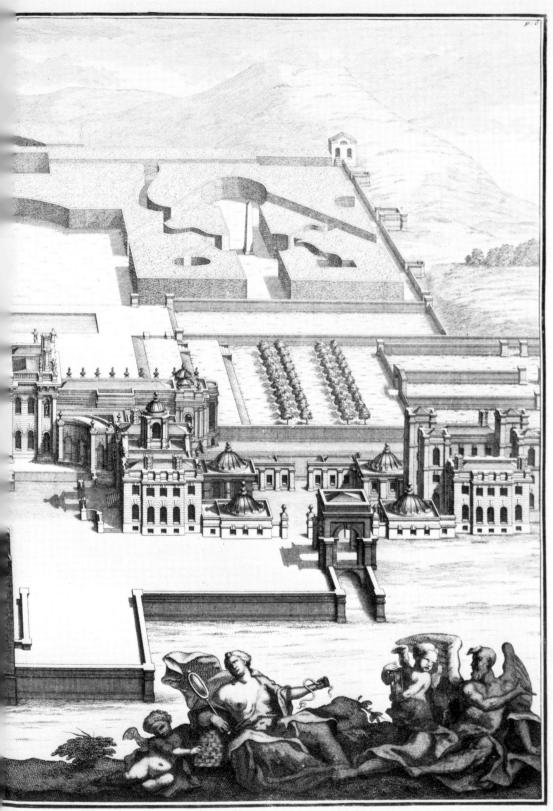

Honourable the Earl of Carlisle &c :

H. Hulsbergh Sculp:

# THE BUILDING
# OF
# CASTLE HOWARD

CHARLES SAUMAREZ SMITH

The University of Chicago Press

Charles Saumarez Smith is Assistant Keeper
at the Victoria and Albert Museum
with special responsibility for the V&A/RCA
MA Course in the History of Design.


The University of Chicago Press, Chicago 60637
Faber and Faber Limited, London

Printed in Great Britain
99 98 97 96 95 94 93 92 91 90   5 4 3 2 1

International Standard Book Number: 0–226–76403–6
Library of Congress Catalog Card Number: 89–052015

This book is printed on acid-free paper.

PLATE I

The aerial view of Castle Howard published in the third volume of
*Vitruvius Britannicus* provides the best image of Castle Howard
as it was originally intended by Vanbrugh.

*For Romilly*

# Contents

# Illustrations

## FIGURES

## PLATES

The author and the publishers are grateful to the following photographers, sources and other owners of copyright material for their permission to include illustrations: the Castle Howard Archive, the British Library, the National Portrait Gallery, the London Library, the Victoria and Albert Museum, A. F. Kersting, *Country Life*, Keith Gibson, the National Monuments Record, Mrs Olive Smith, Mayotte Magnus, Ben Johnson, the Warburg Institute and the Courtauld Institute. John Flower drew the maps.

In addition, we are indebted to the following for financial assistance towards the cost of illustrations:
   Christ's College, Cambridge
   The Erasmus Prize Fund
   The Hawksmoor Committee
   The Victoria and Albert Museum

# Acknowledgements

I first became interested in the history of Castle Howard when, as an undergraduate, I wrote a dissertation on eighteenth-century mausolea: the mausoleum at Castle Howard was much the most significant, as well as the best documented. At that time, I received much help and encouragement from Nicholas Penny, Hugh Honour and Howard Colvin; and Angelo Hornak kindly gave me notes he had assembled on the subject.

In the autumn of 1978 I visited the archive of Castle Howard, where, for the first time, the enormous body of family papers was being systematically catalogued. On examining a few tantalizing fragments of manuscript relating to the life of the third Earl of Carlisle, including his original library catalogues and the *Essay on God* which he composed, and on discovering how little was known about him, I became interested in the subject of how and why he had built Castle Howard, what had influenced him, and what part it played in his career. I devoted my PhD. thesis to this subject, under the direction of Professor Michael Baxandall. I am enormously indebted to him for the amount of time and care he devoted to reading and commenting on the thesis. At Castle Howard, I was given freedom of access to the archive by the late Lord Howard of Henderskelfe and was greatly assisted by the then archivist, Judith Oppenheimer, and by Richard Robson; more recently, the Hon. Simon Howard and his archivist, Eeyan Hartley, have both been extremely helpful. The majority of the thesis was written while I was Christie's Research Fellow in the History of the Applied Arts at Christ's College, Cambridge. I received much moral support from the former Master of Christ's, Professor Sir John Plumb, and I remain grateful to him, to the Fellows for electing me, and to Hugo Morley-Fletcher of Christie's, who arranged the terms of the Fellowship.

In rewriting my PhD. thesis for publication, I have been helped by the comments of my examiners, John Newman and Professor Christopher Clay, and of several publishers' readers, including Howard Colvin and the writer of an anonymous report for Chicago University Press. A number of people have read chapters in draft and I have been saved from many errors by their criticisms: they include John Cornforth, Eveline Cruickshanks, Wendy Hefford, Professor Geoffrey Holmes and Natalie Rothstein. In addition, friends have read large parts of the manuscript at different stages and I am especially grateful to them: Malcolm Baker, Rupert Christiansen, Adrian Forty, Paul Greenhalgh, Richard Hewlings, Elizabeth McKellar and John Styles. Andrew Duncan, Eeyan Hartley, John Dixon Hunt, Christopher Ridgway and Richard Wilson generously provided detailed comments on the final draft. Gillian Varley kindly helped with proof-reading. Last, I should record my debts to Maggie Hanbury, my literary agent, to John Bodley, Ron Costley and Robert McCrum at Faber's, and to Romilly, to whom this book is dedicated.

# Introduction

Anyone who has visited Castle Howard, the swaggering mansion which lies across the top of a line of hills north-east of York, will have been aware of the extent to which the surrounding landscape has been manipulated into a strange, hyperreal environment. As soon as one leaves the flat plain of the vale of York and climbs the first hill off the main Scarborough road, following the road as it straightens and descends towards the Carrmire Gate, which marks the entry into the estate, then up the steep hill on the other side towards another and more formidable gate, the realization begins to grow of the scale and ambition whereby nature has been coerced into an intense architectonic order.

This approach to the house has been deliberately contrived to induce a dual sense of awe and anticipation of the magnificence which is to come, of a carefully controlled stripping of consciousness as one enters underneath the narrow gates through an architecture which is larger than expectations. The Carrmire Gate consists of elaborately overarticulated machicolations, a fantasy version of medieval fortifications, more bristling than the real thing. The Pyramid Gate is, again, a narrow gate, compressed by the huge weight of an Egyptian pyramid, which it carries above it.

Standing beside the Pyramid Gate, with its massive stonework structure towering above, and looking eastwards along a line of pseudo-medieval walls, complete with imaginary watchtowers, it is possible to see in the distance a small pyramid and, beyond, a domed building surrounded by columns. It is an evocative landscape, with the elements of the Roman *campagna* translated into the rolling and manicured hills of an English parkland, each building expressing a powerful historical reminiscence through its architectural form.

Passing through the Pyramid Gate, not far beyond along a broad avenue, is a great obelisk, a feature of Roman town planning, at which point the visitor turns sharp right towards the immediate approach to the house. This lies along the edge of the hill, so that to the north a distant view opens up towards the North York Moors. It is a lateral and unexpected approach through a series of switches in direction to the full-blown main entrance to the house, which consists of a series of façades swooping out towards the spectator, and a proliferation of gates and towers, of turrets and statuary, which are impossible to encompass at a single glance and which invite exploration while at the same time diminishing the human scale by their extent.

Everywhere at Castle Howard, whether it is in the house or in the parkland, there is an overwhelming feeling of control, of assertion, of the orchestration of the physical elements of landscape and building; but the nature of the historical and architectural consciousness which exerts this control is not clear. In most English houses, the meaning of the architecture is clear. There is a known history. But at Castle Howard the meaning of the architecture is elaborated and extended and, to some extent, subverted, so that it is not evident what the spectator is supposed to be viewing, nor what message is being conveyed.

This book is an attempt to decipher the message, to examine the meaning of the building by an intensive examination of the original circumstances of production. Whenever one is looking at a building there is a tendency to interpret or intuit the original purposes that it served, purposes which extend beyond the physical use to which it was put, into the moral dimension of the lives of the people for whom it was built. In the conventional discourse of academic architectural history it is normal to ignore this extended meaning of a building and to concentrate on the immediate reading of its form and structure; but beyond the form and structure lies the concealed nature of the intention, which challenges explanation. Lurking behind the superabundance of architectural forms are critical questions: who built Castle Howard and for what?

CHAPTER ONE

# The Patron

## EARLY LIFE

Charles Howard, third Earl of Carlisle, was born in 1669 at Naworth, a small fortified border castle close to Hadrian's Wall and near Carlisle, a territory which was as far as it possibly could be from the culture and urbanity of Restoration London. Apart from the monumental presence of the local Roman remains, which had been studied by the third Earl's scholarly ancestor, Lord William Howard, in the early part of the century and fragments of which had been assembled in the garden at Naworth, the local neighbourhood was unpromising, consisting of small farmholdings and a few local gentry. Its architectural language was of a continuing vernacular and it was only in the second half of the seventeenth century that Cumberland began to witness the occasional importation of a classical motif in a doorway or window surround. Life at Naworth in 1649, as described by Lady Anne Halkett in her autobiography, was immune from outside influence and, apart from the suggestion of domestic scandal, humdrum.[1] So it is difficult to imagine that the third Earl of Carlisle absorbed very much from his childhood except perhaps an exaggerated craving for more sophisticated company than the tenants and the resident chaplain, and an urge to escape the constricted horizons of north Cumberland.

The third Earl is said to have been educated at Morpeth Grammar School in a town where the earls of Carlisle had a dominant political influence.[2] The first time he surfaces properly to historical view was in 1688, a year racked by the threat of rebellion against James II's autocratic policies, when, at the age of nineteen, he married Lady Anne Capel, daughter of the first Earl of Essex, who had been imprisoned in the Tower for his involvement in the Rye House Plot and committed suicide in mysterious circumstances. It was an arranged marriage. Lady Anne was aged only thirteen and it was claimed that *'through the greenness of their years, [they] do not yet cohabit together'*.[3]

PLATE 2

The bust of the third Earl of Carlisle's ancestor, Lord William Howard, which was placed in the pyramid at Castle Howard.

Soon after the wedding, which took place in July, the third Earl of Carlisle, or Viscount Morpeth as he then was, set off on a long Grand Tour, which was beginning to be the standard mode of education for the nobility. It was a convenient time to be out of the country. A warrant was issued to all admirals '*to permit Charles, Viscount Morpeth, his governor Alexander Rasigad, and his servants, to embark in any port and sail for Flanders without hindrance*' on 17 November 1688, twelve days after the landing of William of Orange at Brixham in Devon and while James II was on his way to join his forces on Salisbury Plain.[4]

The details of Viscount Morpeth's Grand Tour are not known. His movements may have been impeded by the outbreak of the Nine Years War: French troops had moved across the Rhine to lay siege to Philippsburg in southern Germany in September 1688, and Hanoverian, Saxon, Bavarian and Austrian troops had been sent to defend the frontier states of the Holy Roman Empire. It may be presumed that Viscount Morpeth spent some time in Holland, which was regarded by the English as a model of civic order and a necessary part of an education in the values and beliefs of Protestantism. It had become a place of retreat for the exiles from James II's regime and, since the Whig peerage had vested their hopes in William of Orange's abilities to restore political order and their power, it would have been wise for the future third Earl of Carlisle to familiarize himself with the forms of

Dutch cultural life. From Holland, he probably took the normal route for the Grand Tour down through the German principalities to Vienna and so, across the Alps, to Venice and Padua, where he signed the visitor's book '*ye first day of ye year 1690*'.[5] Since he visited Padua, he is likely also to have seen the nearby town of Vicenza, which was described in 1685 as '*a place worth the seeing, by reason that Palladius hath here shown great skill in Architecture in his Rotunda, in imitation of the Pantheon at Rome, in his Theater exactly proportioned to the strict Rules of Building and other fair Houses in the Town*', although other contemporary guidebooks disagreed with this favourable verdict.[6]

The principal evidence of how Viscount Morpeth spent his time in Italy appears in two small commonplace books he kept while he was in Rome. The first of these is called *Remarks out of several Books in Latin, French, & English*.[7] This contains long extracts of books which he was reading, including passages about Raphael, Leonardo da Vinci, Holbein and Titian, interspersed with improving quotations from classical authors such as Cicero, Seneca and Martial. The second is a further book of notes which principally records items of social information about the most important families in Rome; but it also includes observations on painters, as, for example, that '*Charles Maratti is counted ye most famous Painter now of Europe, Gordian at Naples is also very much esteemed*', that '*Il Cavalier Bernino Napolitain was very much esteemed for his works in painting, sculpture, & Architecture*', and that '*Chevalier Fontana is counted one of ye most famous sculptures at Rome*'. This indicates that he was finding out which contemporary painters were well regarded, and inspecting their works. He also mentions the fact that '*John Piter Bellori Antiquario del Papa, a great vertuoso, he hath a very good closet*', suggesting that he was aware of the writings and views on art of the influential collector, Gian Pietro Bellori; and that '*Mon sig. Fabretti a vertuoso at Rome is about puting out a book of all ye Triumphal arches at Rome*'.[8]

The cumulative impression of these two volumes of notes kept while Viscount Morpeth was in Rome suggests a young man who was taking his education seriously, reading widely in classical authors, and interested in what information he could glean about art and antiquities. Unfortunately they do not reveal the tremendously powerful impact Rome must have had in forming the third Earl's architectural taste and sensibilities. It is clear from the way that Castle Howard was built that he must have visited and been deeply impressed by the pyramid of Gaius Cestius and the tomb of Cecilia Metella, known as the Capo di Bove, on the side of the Appian Way; he must have admired the many obelisks and the way that they were used to articulate the great schemes of urban design. He returned to England with a memory formed at an impressionable age of the symbolic power and evocative landscape setting of the great monuments of classical antiquity, and of the intense visual excitement and architectural complexity of the churches and palaces and piazzas of seventeenth-century Rome.[9]

Viscount Morpeth returned to England from his Grand Tour in February 1691 and succeeded to the title on the death of his father in April the following year. After his return, he spent most of his time back at Naworth in a life of comfortable domesticity: having children, breeding horses, corresponding with the Duke of Somerset about the races at Newmarket, buying occasional books from Mr Chapman, a bookseller in London. There is no evidence of any great political ambitions or of his participation in affairs of parliament. He was more interested in hunting.

Yet, from about 1695, the tenor of Lord Carlisle's life changed. He decided to spend much more of his time in his London house in Soho Square, at the centre of a fashionable area of recent urban development. Carlisle House was on the east side of the square, according to the rate books, No. 20A. Other titled residents of Soho Square in its early years included a Yorkshire neighbour, Thomas Bellasyse, first Earl of Fauconberg and, according to John Macky, Lords Foley, Mansel, Gainsborough and Berkeley *'with many others of the first quality'*.[10] In the middle of the Square were tree-lined walks and a statue of Charles II: in its original form, it was one of the most elegant examples of Restoration town planning.

At the same time that the third Earl of Carlisle began to spend much more of his time in London society, he demonstrated a forceful interest in political matters during the toughly fought parliamentary election of 1695. He was able to influence the elections both in the Cumberland county constituency and in Carlisle, where he had been appointed governor in 1693; and he attempted to extend his influence into the neighbouring constituency of Westmorland, despite the fact that he owned no estates there. On 12 March 1695, he wrote a letter to Sir Daniel Fleming, a Westmorland landowner:

*Considering it may be of dangerous consequence ye admitting Mr. Graham to be a Parliament man every body being acquainted with his fathers principalls, I do think it is absolutely necessary for every well wisher to this Governement to keep him out, if they can, therefore I must take ye liberty to presse you heartyly to espouse Mr. Lowthers interest.*[11]

This presumably referred to Henry Grahme, the son of James Grahme of Levens

PLATE 3

The third Earl of Carlisle painted by Sir Godfrey Kneller as a member of the Kit-cat
Club, at the time Castle Howard was being built, *c.* 1705.
(National Portrait Gallery).

Hall; Henry Grahme was, indeed, an unsuitable candidate as he was a well-known Jacobite in exile at the court of Saint-Germain.

Lord Carlisle acted in the same high-handed way in Carlisle, where he decided to cooperate with Sir John Lowther of Lowther Castle to exclude the Musgraves, an old-established local gentry family, who had traditionally divided the seat with a nominee of either the Howards or the Lowthers. As William Gilpin, the Lowthers' agent in Carlisle, reported to Sir John Lowther in Whitehaven,

*On Wednesday last Mr Chr. Musgrave came hither, and I am told desired my Lord Carlisles Interest to recommend him to this City upon ye next Election for Parliament. My Lord told him he designed to propose his Brother. Mr Musgrave desird to joyn. My Lord reply'd, He had another Friend to whom he was already engaged: Upon wch Mr M[usgrave] has declared he will stand upon his single Interest.*[12]

Understandably this was bitterly resented. Differences of political opinion broke down along lines of local prejudice and a gap emerged between the families with metropolitan tastes and large estates and those who were loyal to the traditions, as they saw them, of their county. An attempt was made at the October sessions in Kendal to reconcile the two parties.

*Great interest was made to unite them, but in vain. Sir John [Lowther] proposed that Sir Christopher [Musgrave] should, in the presence of the Bishop of Carlisle, Sir George Fletcher, and Sir Daniel Fleming, declare that he will without disputing vote such a supply as shall be demanded for carrying on next year's war. Sir Christopher offered a general declaration in favour of the Established Church and his present Majesty, but he thinks that to confine himself in particulars is such an infringement of the liberty of a commoner as no man ought to agree to who undertakes the service of his country in Parliament.*[13]

Tough, bellicose and prejudiced, Musgrave was staunch for the Church and opposed to continental war. Lord Carlisle, on the other hand, had demonstrated his allegiance to the political principles of the Whigs, his opposition to any form of Jacobitism, and his loyalty to the interests of the post-Revolution monarchy. James Lowther and Lord Carlisle's brother, William Howard, were eventually elected, at a cost of at least £1,000 each.

It is evident both from the third Earl's decision to spend more of his time in London and from his interference in Cumberland politics that he had powerful social and political ambitions which could not be satisfied by the limited scope of life at Naworth. He wanted to move in fashionable court society, and to have access to the pleasures of London. There was an enormous gap between social life in London, which acted as an intense magnet for the whole life of the nation, the centre for politics and all the luxury trades, and the deep provincialism of north Cumberland, where many forms of entertainment were not available to be purchased, where local life was constrained, and where the highest form of sociability was to meet as a pall-bearer at a local funeral.

During the second half of the 1690s, Lord Carlisle began to exercise the taste and artistic discrimination which he had learned in Rome. The ceiling of the main staircase at Carlisle House was painted by Henry Cook, a gentleman artist, who had travelled in Italy and been a pupil of Salvator Rosa. Cook had spent a further period in exile for murdering a man who paid court to his mistress but, during the reign of William III, he was much employed by the peerage and was commissioned by the King to restore the Raphael Cartoons. He was paid £28 by Lord Carlisle's agent on 23 May 1698. Several other artists received commissions. The French Huguenot artist, Louis Cheron, was paid £12 18s. *'for 2 pictures'* on 29 April 1699; like Henry Cook, he too had studied in Rome, before being commissioned by the Duke of Montagu to come to England, where he embarked on a career as a history painter in the currently fashionable dark Marattesque manner. Thomas Highmore, the Serjeant Painter, was employed to paint portraits of the family.[14]

Lord Carlisle did not confine his commissions during the late 1690s to painters. Richard Osgood, the sculptor, was paid £14 15s. on 15 June 1697 and a further £12 10s. on 30 January 1699. He had previously been employed at both Kensington Palace and Chatsworth, where he had produced lead ducks for the garden; and the third Earl's neighbour in Soho Square, Lord Fauconberg, had paid him for the statues of Mars and Minerva for his country seat in Chiswick.[15] Lord Carlisle's accounts for this period also include payments to joiners and cabinetmakers, including Joel Lobb, who had worked at Hampton Court. On 25 April 1698 *'Mr Johnson ye Cabinettmaker'* received £66. This was Gerrit Jensen, who had premises nearby in St Martin's Lane and supplied the Royal Household from 1680 onwards with extremely ornate, inlaid furniture.[16]

Lord Carlisle had clearly set himself up in style in Soho Square and was spending considerable sums of money on luxuries. He bought expensive china and delftware and *'a rich Indian quilt'*. He purchased large numbers of books from a Mr Harding, five books for Lady Carlisle *'covered with green vellum and gilt'*, and commissioned a man *'yt help'd in ye Library and writt ye Letters and Catalogue of ye books'*.[17]

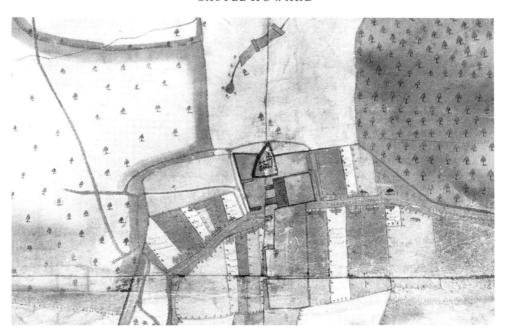

PLATE 4

The early estate map of 1694 provides the only evidence of the physical appearance of Henderskelfe.

It is evident that, in the late 1690s, the third Earl was developing a taste and appetite for works of art and furniture; by 1698, this may not have been satisfied by expenditure on his London house alone.

Towards the end of July 1698, Lord Carlisle travelled from his house in Soho Square to a small village, Henderskelfe, north-east of York. The village consisted of about twenty small houses, each with its own strip of land, a parish church, and the remains of a medieval castle which had had improvements made to it in the 1680s by Lord Carlisle's grandfather, the first Earl, but which had been burned down in March 1693.[18] Its situation was cold and bleak, exposed to the wind which blows from the North York Moors (*Plate 4*).

On 31 October 1698 the third Earl took out a lease for life on the '*Castle and Manor of Henderskelf*' from his grandmother, Anne, the Countess Dowager of Carlisle, widow of the first Earl.[19] By 15 November he was back in London.[20] On 21 February 1699 it was reported that '*My Ld. [Carlisle] has bin hunting in Sussex & Hampshire, but has some thoughts of going for Yorkshire after a while but not so soon as he intended.*'[21] He set off for Henderskelfe on the morning of 6 March, returning to London again at the end of the month.[22] On 9 May it was said that '*My Ld. intends to goe to Yorkshire this Summer designing to build.*'[23] Between the summer of 1698 and May 1699, he had conceived the idea of building one of

8

the most grandiose and flamboyant private houses in Europe. Yet neither then nor since has anyone investigated why he took this decision, why a not particularly well-remembered member of the late seventeenth-century peerage thought of building on such a scale.[24]

## FAMILY ORIGINS

The first piece of evidence as to why the third Earl of Carlisle chose to build Castle Howard is contained in the architectural form of the buildings. One of the most striking features of a visit to Castle Howard is the way the different buildings evoke a sense and presence of the past. This manipulation of imagery is not accidental. The buildings were intended to produce in the mind of the spectator an awareness of the lineage of the Howard family and of its place in history. The third Earl himself composed the inscription on the pyramid in front of the house which read:

O THEE, O VENERABLE SHADE
WHO LONG HAST IN OBLIVION LAID,
THIS PILE I HERE ERECT;
A TRIBUTE SMALL FOR WHAT THOU'ST DONE,
DEIGN TO ACCEPT THIS MEAN RETURN,
PARDON THE LONG NEGLECT[25]

The wording suggests a strong sense of family pride, and a feeling of deliberate and self-conscious authentication. One of Lord Carlisle's actions late in his life was to commission his portrait from the Scottish artist William Aikman and, at the same time, arrange that portraits of his grandfather and father, the first and second Earls of Carlisle, should be lengthened and inscribed, so that they could be hung together to show the continuity of the line (*Plate 53*). It is not unreasonable to suggest that a first and powerful motive towards the desire to build Castle Howard was a desire to provide an appropriate physical emblem of the status of the Howard family. It was not called Henderskelfe Castle, but Castle Howard.[26]

The third Earl's attitude towards his family can be understood in terms of his slightly ambiguous relationship to the Howards. On the one hand, they were a great and ancient dynasty stretching back in a direct continuum to a powerful medieval past, a legitimate source of pride;[27] on the other hand, the third Earl himself came from a junior and relatively undistinguished branch of the family.

The third Earl's direct ancestor, Lord William Howard, who was responsible for the acquisition of the family's estates in the north of England, had been a younger son of the fourth Duke of Norfolk. He was betrothed at the age of nine to his stepsister, Lady Elizabeth Dacre, to enable him to inherit a portion of the Dacre estates, thereby adding to the landed wealth and power of the Howards. Yet this piece of blatant territorial and political ambition was one of the factors which caused the fourth Duke of Norfolk to be executed, and much of the early part of Lord William Howard's own life was spent in various legal disputes about his wife's inheritance. It was only in 1603, twenty-six years after their marriage, that they were finally able to settle in Naworth Castle, close to the Scottish border at Brampton near Carlisle.

Lord William Howard was a remarkable figure, hard-bitten yet scholarly.[28] He occupied himself with local recusant politics and with policing the borders, but also with assembling a library and collection of antique remains. Lord Carlisle had good reason to be proud of this ancestor, but also slightly embarrassed. Lord William Howard, like the rest of the Howard family, was known principally for Catholicism; the third Earl's own religious sympathies were latitudinarian. Lord William Howard collected a great library; the third Earl allowed medieval manuscripts to be sold to John Warburton, the herald and antiquary. Lord William Howard's great love was Naworth Castle; the third Earl abandoned it to build Castle Howard and, according to William Stukeley, allowed the antique fragments in the garden to fall into decay.[29] It is perhaps not surprising that the third Earl felt some form of reparation was in order.

Equally, Lord Carlisle's attitude towards his grandfather, the first Earl, cannot have been one of unalloyed pride. Lord William Howard's great-grandson, Charles Howard, was born in 1628 and brought up by his aunt, Lady Alathea Fairfax.[30] In June 1645 he was sent to France, but, following a shipwreck, his party was captured by parliamentary troops and he was fined £4,000. After a spell in the United Provinces, he returned to live at Naworth. Apparently he served with distinction at the Battle of Worcester as one of Cromwell's guards and subsequently became an Independent, assuming '*a high profession of religion, to the pitch of praying and preaching in their meetings*'.[31] For his loyalty to parliament he was rewarded with a number of offices: high sheriff of Cumberland; governor of Carlisle; a member of the Council of State and of the Barebones Parliament; in 1657, aged twenty-nine, he was created Baron Gilsland and Viscount Morpeth. Yet, following the death of Cromwell, he turned against the army, was imprisoned in the Tower, and was assumed to be in touch with the exiled Court through his brother-in-law, William Howard. According to Gilbert Burnet, '*He loved to be popular, and yet to keep up an interest at court; and so was apt to go forward and backward in public affairs.'*[32] After the Restoration, he changed religion again, declaring: *'As monarchy had been so long interrupted by rebellion and faction, so had episcopacy by schism and heresy, and that no one that spoke against episcopacy offered anything better.'*[33] On 30 April 1661 he was made Earl of Carlisle. Thus not only was the third Earl's title to his estate derived from a disputed inheritance through the female line, but his title to nobility was of recent origin, and he owed it to his grandfather's opportunist shifts of allegiance.

Following the Restoration, the first Earl of Carlisle is said, again by Burnet, to have *'run into a course of vice'.*[34] Among his subsequent distinctions were acting as ambassador to Russia and the invention of the ante-supper,

*the manner of which was to have the table covered at the first entrance of the guests with dishes as high as a tall man could well reach, filled with the choycest and dearest viands sea or land could afford, and all this once seen, and having feasted the eyes of the invited, was in a manner throwne away, and fresh set on to the same height, having this advantage of the other that it was hot.*[35]

By 1683 the first Earl was described by the Duke of Ormond as *'the decrepidest man that ever I saw out of a bed'.*[36] He died on 24 February 1685. Although there was not a skeleton in the family cupboard, it cannot be said that the third Earl's ancestry was of the utmost distinction. It can be understood why he may have felt the need for an exaggerated display of family aggrandizement through building.

The third Earl's interest in his own ancestry was not confined to its statement in his schemes for building. His library catalogue records a passionate interest in heraldry: Sir William Segar's *Honor, Military and Civill, contained in foure Bookes* (London, 1602); Ralph Brooke's *Catalogue of the Succession of the Kings, Princes, Dukes, Marquesses, Earles, and Viscounts of this Realme of England, since the Norman Conquest* (London, 1619); John Selden's *Titles of Honor* (London, 1631); James Yorke's *The Union of Honour* (London, 1640); Elias Ashmole's *The Institutions, Laws & Ceremonies of the most Noble Order of the Garter* (London, 1672); Sir William Dugdale's *The Baronage of England, or an historical account of the lives and most memorable actions of our English Nobility* (London, 1675); and, most recent, Robert Dale's *An Exact Catalogue of the Nobility of England, and Lords Spiritual, according to their Respective Procedures* (London, 1697).[37] In 1695 the funeral of his daughter was conducted *'with heralds of his own creation'.*[38] Among his few surviving private papers is the manuscript title page of *A Book of Coates & Crestes* by Charles Carlisle dated 1699.[39] When the seventh Duke of Norfolk died in April 1701, leaving an heir who was a minor, the third Earl became acting Earl Marshal, responsible for organizing and orchestrating all aspects of court ceremonial, the order of precedence on royal occasions, and the ranking of the peerage at coronations and funerals.[40] Prominent in the carved decoration of the entrance front at Castle Howard is the cipher CCC, standing for Carolus Comes Carleolensis, under the coronet of his earldom. It is an appropriate emblem of his intentions.

Although the evidence is indirect, it suggests that there was a conjunction in Lord Carlisle's mind between heraldry and the idea of building: Castle Howard was a way of articulating three-dimensionally his family ancestry and lineage. There are analogies between heraldry and architecture: both are a form of ceremony established according to exact rules of decorum; both are concerned with the visible demonstration of social status; both involve display.[41] Like so much heraldry, the act of building may have been a means of masking a sense of uncertainty, for the holder of a title of relatively recent origin. In 1698 the third Earl of Carlisle may have decided to employ architecture as a language of dynastic legitimation.

## POLITICAL CAREER

It is not easy to differentiate the third Earl's desire to promote esteem for his family from a similar ambition for himself. Clearly the two are closely associated. Just as he wanted his family to be glorified by the construction of a great house, so, too, he wanted to be remembered himself.

In 1698, when Lord Carlisle first made plans to build Castle Howard, he was aged thirty and on the threshold of a short-lived, but prominent, involvement in politics as a minister of William III and, briefly, first Lord of the Treasury. At this stage of his political career he was able, energetic and ambitious.

The political implications of the decision to build Castle Howard are made clear by what happened subsequent to the plans being drawn up. Lord Carlisle began to assume much greater power and prominence at Court. On 20 June 1700 the model of what was proposed at Castle Howard was taken to Hampton Court for inspection by the King, who was well known to have an interest in building and gardening. On 24 June the third Earl was appointed one of the Gentlemen of his Majesty's Bedchamber at a salary of £1000 per annum.[42] If the idea of building was conceived as a stake in a game for royal favour, then it rapidly began to pay off.

The third Earl revealed the strength of his allegiance to the monarchy and the political ideals of the Whigs in the parliamentary election of January 1701, which was fiercely contested and acrimonious.[43] On 27 July 1700 he received a letter from the Jacobite, James Grahme of Levens Hall, again requesting his support for the election of his son, Henry Grahme, as in 1695. The tenor of Lord Carlisle's reply was unequivocal:

*I have received yours of ye 16th., where in you acquaint me with your design of recommending your son, to serve ye County of Westmoreland as theire representative in Parliament, in ye room of Mr Fleming, & you hope, it will meet with my approbation. I do not pretend to have any interest in yt County, therefore can be but of little use, or service to any one in an affair of this nature, but I will deal plainly & ingeniously with you. I could wish to see your son rathere in any othere place, than where you have thoughts of sending him, or serve you, upon any othere occasion than in what you now desire. As far as I am able to influence, I will endeavour all I can, yt no violent man of any oppinion shall come within ye walls of ye Hous of Commons, but such shall have my assistance, who will make it theire equal concern to preserve ye Government, & serve theire Country.*[44]

Two months later, in September 1700, Lord Carlisle travelled to Penrith to draw people into the Whig party. Understandably, his conduct was bitterly resented and James Grahme wrote to a freeholder that

*A letter is handed about in the name of the Earl of Carlisle in favour of Major Lowther. It is a new thing for any man who has no lands in a county to concern himself in elections there. The Earl's grandfather and father enjoyed the posts he has in these northern parts, yet never meddled with elections in Westmoreland.*[45]

Meanwhile, Lord Carlisle was similarly involving himself in electoral affairs in Cumberland. On 19 September 1700 he wrote to the Duke of Somerset:

*If your Grace has not already engaged your interest, I beg yt you will be pleased to favour Mr. Lawson, Mr. Wilfred Lawson's son of Drayton, with it, who at a meeting of several Gentleman of ye Country was unanimously pitched upon, & recomended by them to ye Freeholders of ye County of Cumberland to be their Representative in Parliament & I do not doubt but ye Gentleman will answer ye good oppinion ye County seems to have of him. I must let your Grace know, yt.*

*Sr. Christopher Musgrave has engaged his interest for another Mr. Musgrave, Sr. Richard Musgrave's son, so possibly there may be a contest. I thought it proper to acquaint your Grace with this, yt you might afterwards be under no surprise, for I have given your Grace a true account how matters stand at present in this County in relation to ye next Election. If you please to favour us with your interest it will be of extraordinary service to Mr Lawson.*[46]

By December 1700 Lord Carlisle's activities were clearly unpopular; it was reported that he was losing interest in the county; ill health compelled him to be in London; and he wrote much more guardedly to Gilfrid Lawson:

*It is very confidently reported, yt wee shall have a New Parliament, if it so happens, I should be glad to know what you, & ye Gentlemen, yt have espoused your interest, judges most proper to be done in relation to ye County Election. As I have always declared, yt I will endeavour as much as I am able to maintain a good corrispondency amongst ye Gentlemen of ye Country, so I will lay hold of this occasion to make it further appear, for it is my oppinion yt in case Mr. Musgrave stands singly, yt you should doe ye same, & by yt means unite ye differences, yt have been Made amongst ye Gentlemen of ye Country upon this occasion, but if another is taken in to support Mr. Musgraves interest with a design to exclude you, it is then my oppinion, yt wee must also doe ye same. But altho this is my present thought, I will resolve upon nothing till I have your advice, & ye advice of those Gentlemen, yt have espoused your interest, and whatsoever you together shall think most adviceable to be done for ye Countrys Service, I shall most readily agree to it; therefore I desire you would give yourself ye trouble to communicate this to ye Gentlemen of your interest; & to let me know their thoughts. I would have writt to them severally upon this occasion, but yt objections have been made to my former letters & so much noise made concerning them, which I do not apprehend, tho by ye by, they can any way make use of to your prejudice yt I will rather choose to let you & ye rest of my friends know my thoughts by this single letter, for fear in a greater number some one may miscarry.*[47]

When the new Parliament met in February 1701, James Lowther reported that a great many complained

*of Lds medling at Elections & there was a Vote pas't Nem: Con: That for any Ld Lieutts or Peer of the Realm to concern themselves at any Elections of Commoners to serve in Parliamt is a high infringement upon the Liberties & Priviledges of the Commons of England. This gave Occasion to Sr. Chr. Musg[rave] to take notice of my Ld Carl. writing Circular Letters for the Gentlemen to stay for his coming down to consult about a Knight of the Shire & of his calling the Justices together for that purpose when he came down.*[48]

Although the third Earl's autocratic attempt to dominate elections in city and county caused him to be deeply distrusted at the level of local gentry politics, it brought him further into the favour of the King. In the following June 1701 Lord Carlisle was made a member of the Privy Council and, soon afterwards, accompanied William III on a visit to Holland, where he stayed at Het Loo, the King's great country estate, with its sophisticated gardens and interiors designed by the Huguenot architect, Daniel Marot.[49]

In the autumn of 1701 Lord Carlisle was one of the leaders in the campaign to secure the dissolution of parliament, on the grounds that it was dominated by Tories with Jacobite sympathies who were unlikely to provide support for heavy expenditure on another continental war.[50] In the election which followed he was determined to keep out Gilfrid Lawson, whom he had supported at the previous election, since Lawson had consistently voted against the Whig interest. On 13 November 1701 James Lowther reported,

*My Lord Carl. has writt to his Friends for George Fletcher & for Sir Edwd Hasell if he will stand which is very much to be desir'd & then my Ld fears not but they will both carry it, if Sr Edwd refuses then for Mr. Carlton. Sr Wilfd Lawson & Mr Lawson waited on my Ld C. this morning to desire his assistance for the latter of them but my Ld let them understand that he was engag'd & that he could never be for one that differ'd from him in opinion so much in voting.*[51]

Two days later he continued,

*My Ld Carl. D. of Sommersett & Ld Wharton have aggreed to oppose the two last Knts Mr Musg. & Lawson with all their power. The Duke of Sommerset was one of the most forward for the Dissolution of the Parlt the City of London is mightily pleas'd with it, & we have great Reason to hope for another kind of Parlt than the last which the King plainly saw wld have fallen into the same heats with the House of Lords which would have bin of dangerous consequence at this time.*[52]

At the election, Sir Edward Hasell and George Fletcher were voted in for the county seat, thanks to Lord Carlisle's support. In Carlisle, Captain Thomas Stanwix, an army officer, stood against the sitting members, Philip Howard, a cousin of Lord Carlisle's, and James Lowther. The ill feeling engendered by the election led to rioting and Lord Carlisle thought that Stanwix ought to be prosecuted *'with those disorders in Court & the insulting & threatning & abuseing the Mayor & Alderman'*.[53]

In December 1701 the third Earl of Carlisle was rewarded for his loyalty to the King by being appointed first Lord of the Treasury, the most important political post in the realm.[54] Following this appointment, even the Lowthers grew disillusioned by his arrogance and his attempts to interfere with electoral affairs in Carlisle and Cumberland. On 3 January 1702 James Lowther wrote,

*In a little time he may grasp both in town and country at more than he can hold. Very likely he will find himself overloaded with business here and my Lady Lonsdale may find fault in a little time that he is endeavouring to engross the Pt. Men for the 2 countys.*[55]

On 17 January, he went further:

*It is plainly to be perceiv'd that his aim is to bring all the elections of the 2 counties to his own nomination and I can see that he will do nothing to help any bodies interest in the county but his own.*[56]

Yet Lord Carlisle's career at the centre of national politics was short-lived, because of the death of William III on 8 March 1702. Queen Anne had very different political and religious sensibilities from William III. She was a staunch High Anglican with a detestation of political faction and a leaning, at least at the beginning of her reign, towards the Tories as 'the Church Party'. She regarded the Whigs as potential republicans and enemies to the Church of England. She especially disliked the so-called Junto, the alignment of prominent Whig peers, whom she referred to as 'the five tyranising lords'. In her first speech to parliament on 11 March 1702 she appealed to Tory and nationalist sentiment, against the advice of Lord Carlisle. Following her coronation in April, she turned for political guidance to Lord Godolphin and the Earl of Marlborough. They constructed a ministry which was deliberately moderate, including a substantial number of prominent Tory leaders. In May 1702 the third Earl of Carlisle was dismissed from office.[57] During the rest of the reign he played only a minor part in national politics, an associate of the Whig political interest group known as the Junto, but not admitted to their innermost councils.

The trajectory of the third Earl's brilliant, but brief, political career as a minister of William III indicates that the plans for Castle Howard were made at exactly the moment when he was looking for promotion at Court. Building a great house was a means of drawing attention to his capabilities, of demonstrating his potential usefulness as an ally of the King. The evidence suggests a man of strongly autocratic disposition, who used architecture as a means of social and political aggrandizement.

## COURT ARCHITECTURE

So far, the decision to build Castle Howard has been represented as a private decision deriving from an intense dynamic rooted in political and dynastic ambition. But, of course, the third Earl of Carlisle did not operate independently of broader social and political movements. The precise historical resonance of his decision cannot be understood outside the context of the politics of aristocratic country-house building in the late seventeenth century.

In the decade following the return of Charles II, the peerage was not sufficiently confident of the political climate to embark on major building projects. Country-house building was dominated by designs of the architect-cum-country gentleman, Sir Roger Pratt, who had travelled in France and Italy in the 1640s and returned to establish the classic type of Restoration house – self-contained, unostentatious, strictly rectilinear and astylar. The most significant new building for a member of the peerage was a town house, Clarendon House in Piccadilly, designed by Pratt for Edward Hyde, first Earl of Clarendon and Charles II's Lord Chancellor; but Clarendon House was regarded by its owner as a major error of judgement when it came to symbolize all the defects of his political policies. By 1664 it was already known, according to the French ambassador, as the new Dunkirk – a reference to Clarendon's part in the sale of Dunkirk to the French, reputedly for £40,000 on the grounds that it was anyway indefensible.[58] In 1665, according to Burnet, Clarendon had 300 men at work during the Plague and the Dutch War, '*which he thought would have been an acceptable thing, when so many men were kept at work, and so much money, as was duly paid, circulated about. But it had a contrary effect. It raised a great outcry against him.*'[59] By 1667 public animosity was so far inflamed that the populace cut down the trees in front of the new house, smashed the windows, and erected a gibbet on which were the words '*Three sights to be seen, Dunkirke, Tangier, and a barren Queene*' – Tangier because it was part of the dowry which Catherine of Braganza brought on her marriage to the King and which was regarded as an expensive white elephant, and the gibe against her infertility because it was supposed, totally unjustly, that the Chancellor had

17

arranged that she should be barren in order that the heirs of his daughter, who, against his wishes, had married the Duke of York, should inherit the crown.[60]

During the 1670s the pattern of aristocratic country-house building began to change, with several members of the peerage deciding to make major alterations to existing houses or, in a few cases, constructing completely new houses in an architectural language which derived not so much from geometry and strict classicism as from a more vigorous idea of Italianate monumentality and display. At Euston in Suffolk, Henry Bennet, Earl of Arlington, an able and effective politician and member of the Cabal, reconstructed an existing house in an extremely grandiose manner. According to Roger North, Euston

*fell into a profuse courtier's hands who must needs make the place fitt to entertain the King, to whom court was made by treats, and administering pleasure. But to be frugally profuse he did not take downe the house, and build another with the aid of the old materialls, but would compass his designe by altering and vamping the old.[61]*

At Cliveden in Buckinghamshire, another member of the Cabal, George Villiers, Duke of Buckingham, commissioned the military architect, William Winde, to design a four-storey brick mansion overlooking a garden, which reminded John Evelyn of Frascati.[62] At Nottingham, William Cavendish, Duke of Newcastle, began in 1674 to construct an impressive palace with prominent columns and heavy, mannered window surrounds in place of the old castle, which he had purchased from the Duke of Rutland.[63] And at Ragley in Warwickshire, Lord Conway, one of Charles II's secretaries of state, employed Robert Hooke, whose drawing for the main façade contains a richly ornamented central section with three prominent circular windows on the first floor draped in carved ornament.[64]

During the 1680s the evidence of major new building projects suggests that the peerage had recovered its confidence and several members of the nobility indulged in remarkable displays of wealth and ostentation. Four great houses in particular, all dating from the 1680s, are likely to have served as partial models for the idea of building Castle Howard.

The first of these was Thoresby in Nottinghamshire, which the third Earl of Carlisle is likely to have visited and known well, since he was '*the most intimate*' friend and political associate of its owner, Evelyn Pierrepont, fourth Earl and subsequently first Duke of Kingston; they shared political beliefs and membership of the Kit-cat Club.[65] Thoresby was a large, square, brick house with elaborate pediments over the windows on the ground floor, a balustrade along the roof-line

– comparable to Cliveden – and a grand central section flanked by Corinthian columns. According to Nicholas Hawksmoor it *'never was good, and was burnt down as soon as finished'*; but it was greatly admired by the Duchess of Marlborough for the quality of the outhouses, which were *'put so near the back of the house that the meat may be brought into it as easily as from wings; which prevents all stink and noise of every kind.'*[66]

The second significant great house designed during the 1680s was Boughton in Northamptonshire, belonging to Ralph Montagu, Duke of Montagu, the father of Lady Anne Popham, with whom Lord Carlisle was rumoured to have had an affair in 1698.[67] Boughton was in a much more sophisticated architectural idiom than any of the houses so far mentioned, a remarkable and self-consciously French house, with a horizontally rusticated basement storey, a grand first floor articulated by flat Doric pilasters, and a mansard roof with prominent dormer windows; it was described by Defoe as *'built at the Cost, and by the Fancy of the late Duke, very much after the Model of the Palace of Versailles'*.[68]

The third great house, begun during the 1680s, which certainly influenced the plans for Castle Howard, was Chatsworth in Derbyshire (*Plate 5*). William Cavendish, Earl and first Duke of Devonshire, for whom Chatsworth was built, was, like the Duke of Kingston, a close friend and political associate of the third Earl of Carlisle.[69] In July 1685 the Earl of Devonshire, while standing at the door of the King's bedchamber, was accused by Colonel Colepepper of being a member of the Exclusion party; a fight ensued, in which the hot-tempered Earl punched Colonel Colepepper to the ground, for which he was prosecuted by the King's Bench and fined £30,000. Legend has it, in which there may be a measure of truth, that the Earl retreated to his estates in Derbyshire and built Chatsworth as a gesture of aristocratic defiance. As Bishop White Kennet wrote in a letter to the Reverend Samuel Blackwell of Brampton in September 1707:

*Under these Straights and Confusions He laid the Design of Building, like a Merchant that was to make the greatest show when nearest to breaking; or a desperate Gamester loosing so much that he would throw at all. He treated immediately with workmen to pull down the south side of the Old House, and gave them the Plan of a new Wing to front his gardens so noble and grand, that it lookt like a Model only of what might be done in future Ages.*[70]

Chatsworth established a new standard of aristocratic flamboyance and was much visited and admired throughout the 1690s. As Bishop Kennet said, *'it looks too*

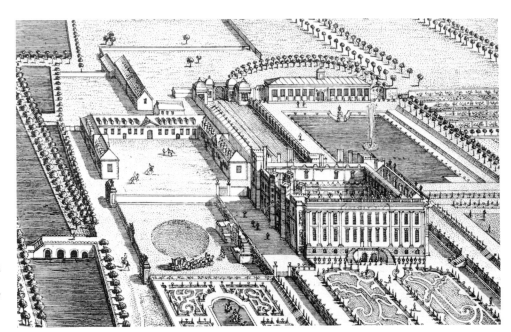

PLATE 5

A view of Chatsworth
drawn by Leonard
Knyff, engraved by Jan
Kip, and published in
their *Nouveau Theatre
de la Grande Bretagne*
(London 1707).

*great for the design of a Private subject, it seems rather the Model of a Palace
becoming the greatest Prince, and the effect of a Publick Fund.*'

The fourth great house begun during the 1680s, which Lord Carlisle also knew
and visited, was Petworth in Sussex, belonging to Charles Seymour, sixth Duke
of Somerset, the most absurdly arrogant member of the peerage, known as the
Proud Duke of Somerset.[71] Like Chatsworth, Petworth appears to have been
begun just before the advent of William III at a time when Seymour was out of
favour at James II's Court for refusing to organize the ceremonies for the visit of
the papal nuncio. Like Boughton, Petworth was built in an architectural style of
fastidious monumentality, long and low, with a central section of horizontally
banded rustication, surmounted by a balustrade and with urns and statuary along
the roof-line.[72]

The tendency of the peerage during the late seventeenth century to indulge in
extravagant architectural displays of power and social position was reinforced
during the reign of William and Mary by the interest of both the King and Queen
in architecture and gardening. William III has traditionally been represented as a
man who was not interested in culture, but, rather, too preoccupied with
government, the army and international affairs to bother much with the arts of
peace. As Abel Boyer wrote soon after his death, '*His Ear was tun'd to no other*

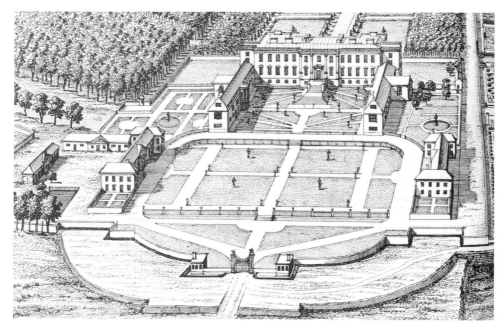

PLATE 6

A view of Lowther Castle, Westmorland drawn by Leonard Knyff, engraved by Jan Kip, and published in their *Nouveau Theatre de la Grande Bretagne* (London 1707).

*Numbers than the Clangor of the Trumpet, or the Rattle of the Drum. As for fine Musick, and good Poetry, He scarce had any Relish for them. He admir'd excellent Pictures, but never encourag'd Painters: or, indeed, any other Artists.'*[73] Certainly, it is a convenient fiction, this image of a man who was too busy on the battlefields of Europe to enjoy the pleasures of his home, too preoccupied in the council chamber to consider art or poetry or music. Yet there is plenty of evidence to suggest the contrary: that William III was well aware of the propaganda value of architectural display, particularly in competition with the court of Louis XIV; that an interest in buildings and gardens was one of the few recreations that he allowed himself; and that, during his reign, his Court emulated his example by constructing a series of remarkable private palaces.

Ten days after their proclamation as King and Queen on 13 February 1689, William and Mary visited Hampton Court; and soon afterwards, Narcissus Luttrell was to write in his *Relation of State Affairs* that *'Their Majesties go frequently to Hampton Court, taking great delight in that place.'*[74] Already, by 2 March 1689, it was reported in a newsletter that *'The bed of state is removed from Windsor to Hampton Court, and Sir Christopher Wren hath received orders to beautify and add some new building to that fabric.'* Between 1 April 1689 and 31 March 1691, a total of £54,484 was spent on improvements, despite the fact that, according to Bishop Burnet, *'the entering so soon on so expensive a building, afforded matter of censure to those who were disposed enough to entertain it'*.[75]

As if improvements to Hampton Court were not enough, on 18 June 1689 Narcissus Luttrell reported that *'The King hath bought the Earl of Nottingham's house at Kensington for 18,000 guineas and designs it for his seat in the winter, being near Whitehall.'*[76] A rapid programme of works was undertaken in order to convert the existing rectangular villa into a palace suitable for the reception of the King, by the addition of four pavilions at the corners of the house and the construction of a grand new entrance court to the west. By April 1690 the account stood at £26,049 11s. 4d.

The example established by the monarchs was followed by their subjects, anxious to demonstrate their political allegiance through a knowledge of, and interest in, continental architecture. During the 1690s, in spite of difficult political circumstances, there was a rash of major new building projects on the part of the peerage: great prodigy houses of the late seventeenth century. At Lowther in Westmorland, John Lowther, Viscount Lonsdale, Lord Carlisle's political ally and rival in the north, built Lowther Castle, with a thirteen-bay main façade, two projecting pavilions and offices on either side of an enormous entrance court (*Plate 6*).[77] At Chippenham Park in Cambridgeshire, Edward Russell, Earl of Orford, an Admiral of the Fleet, who had collected the signatures to the invitation to William of Orange and been in charge of the first ship to land at Torbay, made extensive improvements to an existing house, which allowed him to entertain the King on a visit in 1698 and several times the following year.[78] At Kiveton in Yorkshire, Thomas Osborne, Earl of Danby and first Duke of Leeds, built a grand eleven-bay house with a temple portico and two flanking pavilions.[79] And at Burley-on-the-Hill in Rutland, Daniel Finch, second Earl of Nottingham, constructed a great stone house, described by Sir John Perceval, later first Earl of Egmont, in the summer of 1701 as

*a new built Seat of the Earle of Nottinghams the body being but just erected, & the Yards and Gardens not finish'd. it is built of Stone design'd to last Some ages as well as to be bewtyfull. It is very regular & long being 197 feet in Front and it is as convenient on the inside as bewtifull on the out, & has a great deal of Room.*[80]

Although it would be simplistic to claim that all these houses were built for the same reason, and certainly not all their owners can be described as Whigs, they do in aggregate give the impression of an extremely powerful and self-confident landed elite attached to the Court interest, which erected striking monuments to the consequences of the Revolution Settlement. The political role of these great aristocratic houses is indicated by the extent to which they were used for political meetings, particularly by members of the Whig Junto. For example, in 1693 it was reported that *the town, in love of mystery, having talked of a so-called Congress at Althorp, has now changed the scene to Petworth, upon the Earl of Rochester, the Earl of Ranelagh, and some others going to meet Sir Edward Seymour at the Duke of Somerset's*.[81]

In October 1695 William III went on a tour of England, during which he took the opportunity to inspect several of the great houses of his subjects. He began with a whole week at Althorp, the country house of Robert Spencer, Earl of Sunderland, before moving on to Boughton.

*Here his Majesty was splendidly Entertained, and was attended with a great Number of the Nobility and Gentry of this Country, whom his Majesty received very kindly, and told them, 'Their Country was, in his Opinion, the finest in England, and, perhaps, in the whole World; that nothing made a Gentleman look like a Gentleman, but living like one'.*

From Boughton the King went on to Burghley House, where, on learning that the Earl of Exeter was away, the King could not restrain his curiosity to see it: *'Then, says the King, I'll go and see it; which his Majesty did twice, that night and the next morning, being extremely satisfied with it.'* From Burghley the King proceeded to Welbeck Abbey, where he was entertained by the Duke of Newcastle, and then returned to London by way of Oxford, where a lavish entertainment was provided by the Vice-Chancellor and the conduits ran with wine.[82]

When, therefore, the third Earl of Carlisle began to nurture political ambitions, he must have felt that the old border castle at Naworth, where he had been living, was too far removed from the circuit of political meetings, too old-fashioned architecturally ever to contemplate entertaining the King, inadequate to his status as a courtier and a peer. He must have been aware of the recent trajectory of country-house building towards ever more extravagant displays of competitive ostentation. He decided to enter the arena with a great monument of his own.

## TASTE FORMATION

The emphasis so far in this account of the decision to build Castle Howard has been upon the socio-political factors which are likely to have been in Lord Carlisle's mind at the time that he travelled to Yorkshire to consider plans in the summer of 1699: the desire for aggrandizement of family and self; the political environment which is likely to have provided an impulse towards architectural display and ostentation. This is in line with traditional sociological accounts of the formation of taste, which are inclined to stress the desire for status, either in terms of imitation within a social group, of emulation of a superior social group, or differentiation from one below, as the most powerful motivating force in culture.[83]

The problem with this type of cultural analysis is that it relies on a reading of subconscious motivation. Few individuals are so brazen as to admit, even to themselves, that they buy art or build great architecture out of a straightforward desire to provide visible bulwarks to their social or political position. There is almost always – and there certainly seems to have been in Lord Carlisle's mind – a more conscious and more positive motivation, a desire to participate in, and contribute to, a cultural tradition learned through education and the experience and enjoyment of art.

During the late seventeenth century the nobility did not regard their role as artistic patrons merely as a pleasure and recreation, a welcome diversion from the late nights and debauchery demanded by politics and the Court; nor is it fair to view their investment in culture in a purely instrumental way as a means of indulging in vainglorious ostentation and competitive display. Instead, there is ample evidence to suggest that they saw the purchasing and commissioning of works of art as a duty and responsibility of their rank.

This idea of artistic patronage as a hereditary responsibility, appropriate to a particular rank in the social hierarchy, emerges clearly, for example, in the various biographies of the first Duke of Devonshire, for whom Chatsworth had been built. As John Griffith wrote in *A Sermon occasion'd by the Death of the late Duke of Devonshire*, '*he has, by the building of Chatsworth, made many an ignorant Man a knowing Artist, and upheld a sinking and poor Neighbourhood, and it is but the least piece of Gratitude they can repay him for all these obligations, to preserve his Memory sweet and embalm him in their Minds.*'[84]

This theme is also evident in contemporary descriptions of Petworth. Instead of being disgusted by the insane arrogance of the sixth Duke of Somerset, who was well known for his refusal to give precedence at court and who is said to have cut off his daughter from her inheritance for sitting down in his presence, many contemporaries appear to have accepted that this might be an appropriate form of behaviour for a great peer of the realm. As John Macky wrote of Petworth, '*This Palace is every way answerable to the Grandeur of its great Master, whose*

*Family hath always made one of the brightest Figures in the English Court, ever since the Reign of Henry VIII.'*[85] Or, as the anonymous author of the *Memoirs* of the sixth Duke of Somerset wrote,

*He always delighted to live in Magnificence, Delicacy, and Splendor; constantly preserving that Respect and Dignity which was due to his Rank; and, like a Man of Birth and Fortune, ever moved in a Sphere above the Vulgar, thereby maintaining that just Order and Regularity which proceeds from a Distinction of Persons, without which a State could not look comely, nor Government subsist. — His House was always kept with that Grandeur and Decorum, as formerly was used by the English Kings and Men of Quality: Not as now-a-days, when very little Distinction appears between a King's Palace, and a private Gentleman's House; and often the latter is conducted with more Regularity in Appearance.*[86]

The façade at Petworth, presumably like that at Castle Howard, was specifically intended to represent a strong sense of social as well as architectural order.

The clearest document of the intentions of the late seventeenth-century nobility in commissioning grandiose new architecture appears in an unpublished letter of instructions written to his son by John Lowther, Viscount Lonsdale, Lord Carlisle's political associate and neighbour in the north-west. He wrote,

*The Next thing you will observ in the Estimate is my Buildings; and in this I confesse that in my own Judgement I think I have committed an Excesse; Thoe much is to be said ffor it; As that Our Estate had Exceeded our hous, and that a Good hous is a Debt owing to a ffamilie; That perhaps the Disagreeablenesse off the Hous and Scite might have inclined you to have lived att London than which nothing can be more destructive to yr Welfare, Estate and Happinesse, that besides my own satisfaction and Eas I was apt to think it could not be done att a more reasonable time, nor with lesse Expence than I was capable of performing it; That some Expence was even Necessary more than I cared to be att in Magnificent liveing to redeem the ffamilie ffrom Envie and Objection; That this therefore was likelie to be a lasting advantage to my ffamilie. That I was willing that my Posteritie should participate in the advantage off the Expence, and that it might not be consumed in my own Luxurie; Nothing could be a greater relief to the Poor in the Neighbourhood, Not even so much money given them would have done them so much good.*[87]

The third Earl of Carlisle did not leave any comparable document of his conscious intentions in building Castle Howard, apart from the house itself. It is likely that he entertained the same slightly confusing mixture of ideas and ideals as expressed by Viscount Lonsdale: believing that he was doing it not for his own good, but for that of his family; that it was a better and more lasting way of spending money than employing it in luxury or in gambling; that it was expected of him as a way of demonstrating his rank in society; and, besides, that it kept the poor usefully employed, which was preferable to other forms of charity.

Although sociologists may question these motives as a mere masquerade concealing different and more venal purposes of self-aggrandizement and status differentiation, such ideas have a long history. Perhaps the closest Lord Carlisle got to recording the thinking behind the building of Castle Howard was when passages from Leoni's translation of Palladio were transcribed into the great vellum-bound 'Account Booke of All the Mason And Carpenter Work don att Hinderskelfe'.[88] As Palladio had written:

*an Architect must chiefly observe, what Vitruvius recommends in his first and sixth books, viz., that when he builds for persons of quality, and more especially for those that are in publick employment, he must Build their Palaces with Portico's, Galleries and large stately Halls richly adorn'd: that those who come for business, or to pay their respects to the owner, may be receiv'd commodiously, and delighted and amus'd whilst they wait for him.*[89]

## CULTURAL GEOGRAPHY

Up to this point, the decision to build Castle Howard has been interpreted from the viewpoint of the nobility, in terms of the ideas which are likely to have motivated the third Earl of Carlisle at both a conscious and subconscious level to undertake a major and remarkable building project on the hills of North Yorkshire. It is worth attempting to shift the viewpoint in order to document the way the decision may have been seen outside the network of interest and ideas which bound the peerage to the Court.

During the course of the 1690s English society became progressively factionalized around a series of key political and social issues. The first major issue was the degree of loyalty to the Revolution Settlement and to William III, combined with the vexed question of the succession. William III never commanded a strong personal loyalty and many continued to think of, and some actively to conspire towards, the restoration of the exiled James II to the throne. William had no heir besides Princess Anne, who was frequently ill, her son, the Duke of Gloucester, who died in 1700, and, following the Act of Settlement in 1701, the electoral family of Hanover. Second, there was conflict round the idea of toleration and the growth of dissent, which led many to believe that the established Church of England was in danger. Third, there was the debate about the extent to which England should allow itself to be involved in William's war on the continent, which led to high taxation and the government's dependence on money raised in the City. These issues provided the high ground of argument around which different political groupings clustered.[90]

The conflict of political ideology was exacerbated by extremely adverse economic circumstances. Up until 1699 there was a succession of seven disastrously bad harvests, which led to unprecedented corn prices and severe shortages. The cost of war in Ireland and on the continent required a sharp increase in the land tax, which doubled to a rate of four shillings in the pound. The coinage was clipped and the national debt established. The fighting made trading conditions difficult up until the signature of the Treaty of Ryswick on 10 September 1697, and merchants either lost the capital profits of the previous decades to French privateers or invested them in the fever of speculation. There was a widespread feeling in the countryside, which appears to have been justified, that the burden of taxation was falling most heavily upon those who were dependent for their income solely on their landholdings, the lesser gentry and farmers, while those who had government office or who were in some way involved with government contracts and finance were growing rich on the profits of war. There was a polarization between the countryside, where smaller landowners were having difficulty in raising credit, and the City, where the monied men were investing their capital in paper assets.[91]

These conflicts in the political, economic and social sphere inevitably entered the cultural domain and meant that any activity, including country-house building, was charged with political, economic and social connotations. Building a great country house was not a value-free activity at a time when money was scarce, when the majority of landowners were feeling the pinch of high taxes, low rents and mounting debts, and their tenants and labourers were in acute difficulties. This was particularly true if the style in which the country house was built spoke clearly and unequivocally of French and Italian taste, of government money, and of allegiance to a Dutch monarch and a metropolitan court.

Fierce opposition to the policies and ideas of the third Earl of Carlisle is most clearly evident in a manifesto issued on 10 December 1701. This reads as follows:

*In the Name of God Amen.*

*Wee the Gentlemen of Ancient Families & substantiall Freeholders of the County of Cumberland, finding ourselves insensibly falling into a Lethargic Number, but yet of perfect and sound Memories, That we have not wholly forgot the transactions in Forty one, praised be to God for ye: same, Do make Ordain and appoint this our Last Will & Testament in Manner and form following.*

*First and principly we commend our dying Liberties, Properties, Priviledges, and Immunities into the hands of the Noble Peer the Lord C[arlisle] to be disposed of according to his discretion for ye supporting & Maintaining his Grandeur at Court, hoping by the Merits and Mediacon of the Trienial Bill they will have a Joyfull resurrection at the three Years end or sooner.*

*Item we give up our Sences to be Manag'd by the friends of the impeach'd Lords whose business it was to procure a dissolution of the last Parliamt: and to endeavour to procure another of their own Kidney.*[92]

*Item we give up our understandings, Wils and Affections to be gulled and bubled by the Pr: W[illiam's] faction who we trust will make use of them to pull down the Churches, and build up ye: Meeting Houses.*

*Item we give and bequeath all our Estates, Scituate, Lying & being in Cumbld: aforsd. to Country-fd-King Esqr. and Sr Henry Presumption Knt: the latter of wch: will dispose of them by Vote according as the noble P–r aforementioned will think fitt to direct.*

*Lastly for all the rest, residue & remainder of our reason &c. (if we have any Left) We give and bequeath unto the Lord W[harton] and the Lady L[onsdale] who we appoint Execurs: of this our Last Will and Testmt: which we intend to revoke at another dissolution, hoping in the Mean time the often Mentioned Ld: C[arlisle] will be a faithfull trustee to see this our last Will & Testament performed.*

*This with a Little Alteration may Serve for Westmorland.*[93]

The irony and invective of this document is sustained by implicit reference to the principles of country–Court opposition.[94] These principles may be reduced to three interrelated axioms: 1. The liberty of England depends on the free voice of the landowner in Parliament. 2. The source of all corruption is in the City and the Court, and any increase in government or the army is necessarily wrong. 3. Landowners are increasingly displaced and Parliament dominated by profiteers and placemen, Nonconformists and peers.

It will be evident that these beliefs do not belong to a particular election or, indeed, a single decade: they are in large measure a rationalization of rural prejudice and tradition. The idea that property confers citizenship was a common element of seventeenth-century political thought and stems in part from a Roman equation between honour, dignity and agriculture, in part from an Anglo-Saxon myth of the independent freeholder. Distrust of the City was a natural corollary of this attitude: as Sir Daniel Fleming, the Westmorland landowner, wrote warningly to his son, '*I know young men have often a great longing to see London, & if it be so with you, then perhaps a week or a Fourthnights stay there may do you good, and shew you ye vanity of your designes.*'[95] The feeling that the balance was shifting unfavourably towards the City and that bureaucracy was on the increase is a recurrent complaint of history. It is an attitude of mind kept alive in the backwoods and manor houses, at its best an honourable belief in independence, at its worst narrow-minded, provincial bigotry, which becomes politically significant during periods of high inflation, taxation and agricultural distress.

The language employed in the election manifesto of 1701 is closely akin to a literary and rhetorical tradition which employed the country house as an image of a particular type of society. This tradition viewed country houses as products of a stable society, a tendency which had its origins in a seventeenth-century myth of the country house as matrix of the community.[96]

This ideal of the country house as an image of patriarchy found its classic statement in Ben Jonson's 'To Penshurst':

> *Thou art not, Penshurst, built to envious show*
> *Of touch, or marble; nor can boast a row*
> *Of polish'd Pillars, or a Roof of Gold.*[97]

The house was seen as a model of order and usefulness, an emanation of locality and organic growth.

> *And though thy Walls be of the Countrey Stone,*
> *They're rear'd with no Man's ruin, no Man's groan;*
> *There's none, that dwell about them, wish them down;*
> *But all come in, the Farmer and the Clown.*[98]

This myth was powerfully articulated throughout the 1690s by moralists and architectural writers, that it was wrong to build on too lavish a scale, that building should be a demonstration of usefulness, sobriety and benefit to the public, and that the old days had seen more socially immovable forms of interior decoration. A good example comes from *Mundus Muliebris: Or, the Ladies Dressing Room Unlock'd, And her Toilette Spread*, published in 1690:

*They had Cupboards of Ancient, Useful Plate, whole Chests of Damask for the Table, and store of fine Holland Sheets (white as the driven Snow) and fragrant of Rose and Lavender for the Bed; and the sturdy Oaken Bedstead, and Furniture of the House, lasted one whole Century; the Shovel-Board, and other long Tables both in Hall and Parlour were as fixed as the Freehold; nothing was moveable save Joynt-Stools, the Black Jacks, Silver Tankards, and Bowls: And though many things fell out between the Cup and the Lip, when Nappy Ale, March Beer, Metheglin, Malmesey, and Old Sherry, got the Ascendant amongst the Blew-Coats, and Badges, they sung Old Symon, and Cheviot-Chase, and danc'd brave Arthur, and were able to draw a Bow, that made the Proud Monsieur Tremble at the Whizze of the Grey Goose-Feather: 'Twas then Ancient Hospitality was kept up in Town and Country, by which the Tenants were enabled to pay their Landlords at punctual day: The Poor were Relieved bountifully, and Charity was as warm as the Kitchin, where the Fire was perpetual.*[99]

Closely related to this attitude was the view, again described by both moralists and architectural writers, that the growth of luxury since the Restoration, the spread of precious objects into the households of trade, had blurred the lines of social hierarchy and made it less easy to differentiate the aristocrat from his servant.[100] Once again, this was nothing new, but an attitude of mind that had long animated the writings of books of etiquette and the decrees of sumptuary laws, the belief that the demarcation of rank was being undermined by the diffusion of wealth. It is the myth of the *nouveau riche*, the idea that opulent taste is a sign of social subversion.

During the 1690s luxury was viewed as a symptom and symbol of profiteering, of Court attachment and illicit wealth. While the bulk of the country could not afford any significant increase in expenditure and was suffering under the heavy burden of crippling taxation, a small minority could be observed indulging in increasingly ostentatious stylistic whim. As the author of *A Brief History of Trade* put it in 1702: '*It became popular Opinion, that never were greater Estates got, nor People live more Luxuriously in England, than during ten Years last past, when we had a heavy and destructive War upon us.*'[101] Or, as Charles Davenant wrote much more emotively in his *True Picture of a Modern Whig, Set Forth in a Dialogue between Mr. Whiglove and Mr. Double. Two Under-Spur-Leathers to the Late Ministry*, published in 1701:

*Now I am at my Ease, I have my Country-House where I keep my Whore as fine as an Empress: You know how I am lodg'd in Town, where I am serv'd all in*

*Plate. I have my French Cook, and Wax-Candles; no Butchers Meat comes upon
my Table; I drink nothing but Hermitage, Champagne and Burgundy: Cahors
Wine has hardly admittance to my side-board; my very Footmen scorn French
Claret. I keep my Coach and six, and out of my fine Chariot I loll and laugh to
see gallant Fellows, Colonels and Admirals, trudging a-foot in the Dirt. Poor silly
Rogues! their Honour forsooth led 'em to fight for England abroad, but I play'd
a much wiser Game, by joining with those who in the mean while were plundering
their Country at home.*[102]

These two attitudes of mind, the myth of ancient hospitality and the myth of
the *nouveau riche*, dominate the bulk of the writing and thinking about country
houses in the late 1690s. As Roger North, in his *Notes of Building* composed in
1698, wrote: '*Pomp and ornament are but fancy and chimera of the imagination,
and lean on pride, ambition, and envyous comparison. Ostentation draws
company and that vice; and the monster devours familys, by the enormous charges,
that are before, in, and after it.*'[103] John Pomfret in his poem *The Choice* described
an equally modest ideal:

> *Near some fair Town I'd have a private Seat,*
> *Built Uniform, not little, nor too great:*
> *Better, if on a rising Ground it stood,*
> *Fields on this side, on that a Neighb'ring Wood.*
> *It shou'd within no other Things contain,*
> *But what are Useful, Necessary, Plain:*
> *Methinks, 'tis Nauseous, and I'd ne'er endure*
> *The needless Pomp of gawdy Furniture.*[104]

In 1699 there were clear objections to building grandly. Country houses had
acquired offensive associations. In building Castle Howard, the third Earl of
Carlisle turned his back on the moral and economic objections to luxury. He
ignored the political associations of French taste and the flamboyant display of
wealth. He left the political community of Cumberland and his family's old border
castle at Naworth for the open hills overlooking the North York Moors. He
evicted the inhabitants of Henderskelfe and surrounded the park with massive
fortress walls. Everything was subordinated to the façades.

The years around 1700 were not years of peace and plenty, but of war,
corruption and instability, when new fortunes were made and old families felt
threatened. Seen through the eyes of a contemporary, the architecture of Castle

31

Howard looks superficial, dedicated to appearance, lacking the integrity of conception which would enable the mind to explore it with satisfaction. For the third Earl of Carlisle, building Castle Howard was a means of demonstrating the status of his family, his metropolitan connections and his position at Court, his knowledge of continental architecture, and his interests shared with fellow members of the peerage. From the point of view of a dispossessed tenant, it would have appeared bloated and overblown.

# CHAPTER TWO

# The Architect

## ARCHITECTURAL COMMISSION

In the middle of June 1699, the third Earl of Carlisle once again set out on the long road to Yorkshire, where it was said '*he intends to stay till after Michaelmas & to begin his new house*'.[1] His first action was to consult a neighbouring landowner, Thomas Worsley of Hovingham, about the probable costs of building work, including estimates for Norway oak for two staircases and for ashlar; Worsley claimed that '*the shortnesse of Time has only Produc'd Briefe Accts.*' and that '*Sash Windows I know nothing of.*'[2]

By 14 October 1699 another Yorkshire landowner, Sir Thomas Frankland of Thirkleby Park near Thirsk, was able to report to Thomas Worsley that he was '*glad to hear Lord Carlisle intends to build his house, for laying out so much money must needs be an advantage to the country*' – by which he meant, in the seventeenth-century idiom, the county.[3] Lord Carlisle returned to London at the beginning of November.[4] By Christmas Day 1699 the wooden model for the new house was already being built in order to be shown to the King and it was hoped to begin construction in the spring.[5] Yet the exact process whereby the plans were drawn up has always been a mystery.

Either during the summer of 1698 or, more probably, in March 1699, the gentleman architect William Talman had been invited to travel to Yorkshire to consider plans for building a new house, for which he was paid fifty guineas as well as his charges for travelling.[6] Talman was the obvious person to undertake this task. In 1689 he had been appointed both Comptroller of Works to William III and second-in-command to the Earl of Portland, who was superintendent of the King's gardens. During the intervening decade Talman had gained experience of the multiplicity of tasks involved in the supervision of the construction and embellishment of the royal palaces. During 1699 he was involved in the fitting-up of the State Apartments at Hampton Court and in major works of road-building and planting in Hampton Court Park.[7]

In addition to his work for the Crown, Talman had built up an extensive practice as a designer of country houses, unlike the Surveyor-General of the King's Works, Sir Christopher Wren. Of the houses which are likely to have influenced Lord Carlisle's decision to build Castle Howard, Talman had been involved with the plans for a substantial number. He had been responsible for the grand south and east façades at Chatsworth, before being dismissed from the service of the Duke of Devonshire in 1696. He had been consulted by Sir John Lowther about the designs for Lowther Castle in Westmorland. And he had drawn up a ground plan, which was not executed, for Kiveton in Yorkshire. As Talman said in a letter to William Blathwayt dated 12 September 1699, '*we have abundance of projects (if his Matie will like them) by severall noble Lords that wee here call the Critiques.*'[8]

For Lord Carlisle Talman drew a number of small sketches, which Vanbrugh was later to dismiss as nothing more than '*two or three little trifleing drawings as big as his hand*'.[9] Two of these outline ground plans survive in the drawings collection of the RIBA. The first shows a cubic block with a large entrance hall flanked by two sets of private apartments and leading to two staircases, the grander of which consisted of four separate flights. The second, which contains pencil additions and is inscribed '*Designed for ye Ld Carlisle*', is closely comparable, but has the addition of a large oval saloon likely to have been based on a French model.[10]

According to Vanbrugh, these outline sketches were '*of no use*' to Lord Carlisle and, following a second brief visit of four days, perhaps in late June or July 1699, Talman was dropped as architect. There are several possible reasons why this happened. First, he was so much occupied in the royal works that he was not able to give the time and effort to the designs which the third Earl required. Second, the designs he did prepare were too visually tame and too closely comparable to existing houses to satisfy the third Earl's grandiose expectations; Talman's houses always had an element of awkwardness in their planning and of mannerism in their detailing which produced a visual impact very different from the full-blown flamboyance which the third Earl may already have had in mind. Third, Talman was well known to be an extremely prickly character. On his second visit to Henderskelfe, he demanded a further payment of fifty guineas, when the third Earl was under the impression that he had only offered him thirty, so his dismissal may simply have been the result of a disagreement over costs.[11]

34

Whatever the reason for Talman's fall from favour, it placed Lord Carlisle in a quandary. He was committed to the idea of building a great country house; but he was not willing to employ the person who was best qualified to prepare designs. He solved this dilemma by asking Captain John Vanbrugh (*Plate 7*), an acquaintance from the Kit-cat Club, to draw up plans. Vanbrugh brought to the task the requisite degree of boldness and enthusiasm, even if he lacked Talman's experience and *gravitas*.

It obviously baffled contemporaries, and it has remained difficult to comprehend why a young soldier and playwright should have received such a wonderful commission when, so far as is known, he had absolutely no qualifications for the task.[12] Yet this account of the circumstances of the commission, however picturesque, is not altogether fair: Vanbrugh was almost certainly not as completely unprepared, nor Lord Carlisle so boldly enterprising, as has traditionally been represented.

Vanbrugh did have one qualification for architectural design which relatively few of his contemporaries possessed: he had spent a good deal of time in the early 1690s in Paris, the most exciting capital in Europe in terms of its current building programme. Admittedly, Vanbrugh had spent most of his time there in custody; but, from all accounts, the discipline of a diplomatic prisoner was fairly lax, and he would have had plenty of opportunity to walk the streets of Paris and admire the many newly constructed architectural projects.

Vanbrugh had been arrested in Calais in the summer of 1688 on the grounds of speaking in favour of William of Orange's proposed invasion of England. He was kept in prison there until April 1691, when his health began to deteriorate, so he was transferred to Vincennes. In July 1691 he attempted to obtain his release on the implausible grounds that he was an ardent Jacobite, writing to the exiled James II's Secretary of State, Henry Browne, that '*I am reduced either to Lye and Rott in prison or goe throw myselfe at the P[rince] of O[range]'s feete for protection and take the Oathes of Allegiance to him. This you may be sure I have noe mind to doe since I apply myselfe to you that I may avoid it.*'[13] The exiled King ordered his Vice-Chamberlain, James Porter, to try to obtain Vanbrugh's release; but this was unsuccessful, as was the attempt '*to let me have the liberty of the Castle upon du Liviers Bail for a Thousand Pistols, this Rogue has fail'd me saying 'tis true he promis'd me, but that men don't allwayes keep wt they promis*'.[14]

In November 1691, following endless complaints, the order was given that Vanbrugh was to be better treated and in February 1692 he was moved to the

Bastille. In August the same year William III began to take an interest in his fate, *'sorry to have so many of his subjects suffer'*, and on 22 November at eleven o'clock in the morning, he was given the liberty of Paris, on an assurance of a thousand pistoles in case of escape.[15] He did not return to England until April the following year, which meant he had at least four months of freedom in which to explore the streets of Paris.

This curious episode in Vanbrugh's career is important. Four years spent in France, even confined in a dungeon, and four months at liberty in Paris, must have left their mark. In 1692 he was able to see and admire such works as Louis Le Vau's Collège des Quatre Nations, with its prominent dome and grand entrance façade, flanked by projecting semi-circular wings; Jules Hardouin-Mansart's château at Marly with its great Corinthian pilasters running all the way along the two façades; and the same architect's domed church of Les Invalides, added to Libéral Bruant's court of round-headed arcades.[16] All these works left their mark in different ways on Vanbrugh's visual imagination and were echoed in the design of Castle Howard. Like Wren and Pepys before him, Vanbrugh may have spent time in the print shops, collecting *'the Draughts of their Palaces, Churches, and Gardens'*, which, as John Evelyn recommended to Pepys, *'will greatly refresh you in your Study, and by the fire side, when you are many years return'd'*.[17] It at least seems possible that Vanbrugh was able to impress Lord Carlisle with his up-to-date knowledge of French principles of planning and his recollection of the grandeur and plasticity of contemporary French architectural design.

The second special skill and expertise which Vanbrugh brought to the task of designing Castle Howard was his knowledge of the theatre. While serving in the army in the Earl of Huntingdon's foot regiment, Vanbrugh had borrowed money from Sir Thomas Skipwith, who owned the principal share in the United Company, which was responsible for the staging of plays at the Theatre Royal in Drury Lane. In 1696 all was not well at Drury Lane. The principal actor of the company, Betterton, had recently quarrelled with the theatre manager, Christopher Rich, and had departed in high dudgeon with all the best actors to establish a rival company in Lincoln's Inn Fields. The division was disastrous, for it meant that the two companies were competing for dwindling audiences and both were losing money. According to Colley Cibber, who is the source for this tale, Vanbrugh saw a performance of Cibber's own play, *Love's Last Shift*, at Drury Lane in January 1696 and thought that its ending was absurdly unrealistic and stupidly sententious. So, in order to repay his debt to Skipwith, he decided to write a better version, which he did in the space of three months. Vanbrugh's first play, *The Relapse: or*

PLATE 7

Sir John Vanbrugh painted by Sir Godfrey Kneller at the time that Castle Howard
was being built, c. 1705.

*Virtue in Danger*, opened at Drury Lane on 21 November 1696, with a drunkard, George Powell, who had been drinking brandy all day, in one of the lead roles. The play was colossally and deservedly successful.[18]

The importance of this episode in understanding Lord Carlisle's decision to commission Vanbrugh as the architect of Castle Howard is twofold. It brought Vanbrugh to the attention of fashionable London society, in particular Charles Montagu, Earl of Halifax, a worldly and talented Whig peer, who was to be first Lord of the Treasury, a prominent member of the Junto, and a political associate of Lord Carlisle. He commissioned Vanbrugh to write a second play, *The Provok'd Wife*, for performance at Lincoln's Inn Fields.[19] Thereafter, Vanbrugh was to move easily in aristocratic circles, known for his wit and immense joviality. Along with Lord Carlisle, Vanbrugh became a member of the Kit-cat Club, the group of thirty-nine Whig politicians and writers who met under the auspices of the publisher Jacob Tonson, *'for the Improvement of Learning, and keeping up good Humour and Mirth'*.[20]

More important, in terms of Vanbrugh's subsequent work as an architect, it needs to be remembered that theatre is an intensely visual medium, concerned with dramatic staging and the movement of figures through space in an appropriate setting. Accounts of late seventeenth-century theatre stress the extent to which it made its impact as much through the optical effect on spectators as through subtleties of dialogue and plot. Drury Lane Theatre was said to be the first public theatre in London to use elaborate scenery.[21] It had a deep stage across which painted flats were drawn in runnels lubricated with soap, creating dramatic illusory effects. Cibber remembered the visual impact of the Drury Lane stage fondly: *'All Objects were then drawn nearer to the Senses; every painted Scene was stronger; every Grand Scene and Dance more extended; every rich, or fine coloured Habit had a more lively Lustre.'*[22] By 1699 Vanbrugh must have been steeped in the language and consciousness of the theatre. It may well have given him the bravado to transfer his skills to architecture, a comparable artistic medium, which, like the theatre, is concerned with the manipulation of movement, of dialogue, and of human activity in artificial surroundings. Certainly the knowledge that Vanbrugh had been so exceptionally successful in the world of the theatre must have encouraged Lord Carlisle to entrust him with a new direction for his superabundant artistic energies.

Yet, while Vanbrugh's knowledge of French architecture and of the theatre may have prompted the third Earl's decision to ask him to undertake the design of Castle Howard, in the end it must have had as much to do with Vanbrugh's personality as anything else. At this stage in his career he seems to have been the sort of man who could undertake any task with enthusiasm. Everyone who knew him testifies to his colossal geniality, his great good humour, his easy-going temperament. According to Pope, who was never inclined to generosity, '*Garth, Vanbrugh, and Congreve were the three most honest hearted, real good men, of the poetical members of the kit-cat club.*'[23] Even Lord Chesterfield was prepared to say that '*he knew no man who united conversational pleasantry and perfect good humour in so eminent a degree.*'[24] In addition, the circumstances in which Vanbrugh wrote *The Relapse* suggest a degree of artistic arrogance. In 1699 the tide was running in Vanbrugh's favour, and Lord Carlisle's confidence in his potential abilities as an architect was more than justified by the result.

## VISUAL SOURCES

On Christmas Day 1699 Vanbrugh wrote a characteristically ebullient letter to Charles Montagu, Earl of Manchester, a fellow member of the Kit-cat Club, who was currently serving as ambassador in Paris. After recounting the hot news about parliamentary affairs, Vanbrugh described how

*I have been this Summer at my Ld Carlisle's, and Seen most of the great houses in the North, as Ld Nottings: Duke of Leeds Chattesworth &c. I stay'd at Chattesworth four or five days the Duke being there. I shew'd him all my Ld Carlisle's designs, which, he said was quite another thing, than what he imagin'd from the Character yr Ldship gave him on't; He absolutely approved the whole design, perticularly the low Wings, which he said wou'd have an admirable effect without doors as well as within, being adorn'd with those Ornaments of Pillasters and Urns, wch he never thought of, but concluded 'twas to be a plain low building like an orange house.*[25]

This letter supplies the only information available about the circumstances in which the plans for Castle Howard were drawn up. It indicates several things in the way that it is phrased: the great zest with which Vanbrugh undertook the task; the extent to which Lord Carlisle's proposals had been discussed by friends and associates from the Kit-cat Club; and the keen interest with which they were prepared to judge the designs. It suggests a creative milieu in which there was great enthusiasm for architecture, and a willingness to experiment and to listen to sympathetic criticism.

This letter also provides the clearest evidence of the sources which Vanbrugh investigated before making his own proposals for Castle Howard. It is likely that the plans had been discussed in London between April and early June 1699 – presumably, at that time, the ground plans which Talman had proposed. This, then, would have been when the idea of employing Vanbrugh was first mooted. Vanbrugh decided that he would need a better knowledge of current building projects, so spent the summer travelling round the north of England, inspecting work which was being undertaken.

The first house Vanbrugh mentions having visited was the Earl of Nottingham's at Burley-on-the-Hill. There were several features of Burley-on-the-Hill which Vanbrugh would have admired. The first was its situation on top of a high hill, with fine vistas down terraces to a lake in the valley below. As Sir John Perceval, subsequently first Lord Egmont, wrote at the time of his visit in the summer of 1701:

*The house stands in a Park about 4 miles round, well Stock'd with Deer & extraordinary well wooded in wch: are cut out Severall Visto's, & Severall Avenues leading to the House of above a mile long, wch: look very noble. The Gardins when finish'd will be very fine, being all upon a Declension, and at the foot of them, there is a Pond as broad as the Thames at Putney, & proportionably long. The House stands on a rising ground, & from the top of it wch: is leaded, may be Seen Severall Prospects, as to Lincoln wch: is 30 mile from it.*[26]

A second feature which may have influenced Vanbrugh's conception of the design for Castle Howard was the broad entrance courtyard flanked by pavilions, which accommodated '*brewhouses, bakehouses, kitchens & stables*', connected to the main house by a semicircular colonnade. This, too, deeply impressed contemporary visitors, like the Cambridge undergraduate who in 1725 described it as '*a Piaza supported by Dorick pillars widely extended, so that they and the house make a very large semicircle*'.[27]

The second house which Vanbrugh visited, Kiveton, was architecturally much more tame in appearance, although it may possibly have been more interesting internally since several well-known craftsmen had been employed (Jean Tijou had been responsible for the ironwork gates which led into the entrance courtyard).

The high spot of Vanbrugh's northern tour must have been Chatsworth, which made a tremendous visual impact on all contemporary visitors. What impressed them was not so much the architectural character of the main façades (although one visitor thought them superior to the Palazzo Farnese and Talman a better architect than Michelangelo), as the incredible lavishness and ornamental richness of everything about the house both indoors and outside. It had a sense of supreme, stupefying opulence.[28] As soon as visitors had left the rugged Derbyshire hills and entered the iron entry gates, on either side of which were palisades and pillars carved with military trophies, they were in a completely man-made dream landscape of display and artifice. The gardens were subdivided into different areas stretching up the hill to the east of the house: most of them consisted of a square of grass surrounded by gravel walks with elaborate statuary and a fountain in the middle.[29] Some of the fountains were enormous, with images of '*Sea Gods and Dolphins and Sea Horses*' and pipes which made the water froth like snow. Above these gardens was a so-called wilderness of close-planted hedges, which had a feature admired by every visitor: a realistic tree made of copper, which could be switched on, so that rain fell from leather leaves. Beyond this was a grove of cypress trees and a cascade, at the top of which were two sea nymphs, holding pitchers from which the water rumbled '*like what we may imagine of the Egyptian or Indian Cataracts*'.[30] As François Misson wrote, '*The Green-houses; the Voleries; the Park, and the Dog-Houses; the Avenues; the Gardens; the Parterres, and Terrasses; The Groves; the Statues; the Bowling-Greens; the Canals; the Ponds; the Arbours; the Cascades; the Fountains of running Water always Playing, surround, and adorn after a most charming manner that magnificent House.*'[31]

The interiors of Chatsworth were no less amazing. Here again it was not so much the quality of the architecture which was impressive, since the house had been built piecemeal, as the ornamental richness, the quality of the craftsmanship and the fittings. There were acres of ceiling paintings showing mythological and historical scenes by the continental artists Antonio Verrio and Louis Laguerre. There were huge looking-glasses, supplied by John Gumley, which created effects of perspective illusion. There were rooms made of lacquer or full of wood carving and marble and statuary. There was a bathing room with a tub, floor and a wainscot of imported Italian marble. There were fine tapestries and '*a very neat Chappell, pav'd with curious marble, and lin'd with Cedar*'.[32] As Sir John Perceval commented in 1701, '*The best Artificers of all Sorts have been employ'd upon this noble building where there is the best of carving, Architecture, painting, Tapistry &c.*'[33]

There were three features of Chatsworth which Vanbrugh is likely to have admired particularly and which may have fed his imaginative conception of what would be possible at Castle Howard: the first was the vivid contrast of the total environment of the house and the gardens with the roughness of the surrounding landscape; the second was the quality of surprise through the use of artifice, of the environment acting upon and deluding the spectator; the third was the extent to which the quality of the building was the product not just of the architect, but of a whole team of masons, painters, carvers, suppliers and decorators. These three qualities of Chatsworth may all have influenced the final design of Castle Howard; but, by the time Vanbrugh reached Chatsworth, probably in late September or October 1699, he had already made drawings of what he proposed.

## EARLY PROJECTS

Any attempt to reconstruct a chronology of designs for Castle Howard is necessarily hypothetical. What follows is an attempt to introduce a logical sequence into the various accounts of the plans.

On 26 June 1699, '*Mr London*' was paid £21 10s. by Lord Carlisle's London agent, Nevill Ridley, '*by Lordsp's order*'.[34] This refers to the gardener, George London, who was deputy superintendent of all the King's gardens at a salary of £200 p.a. and who was joint owner of a large nursery at Brompton Park, conveniently close to Kensington Palace.[35] According to Stephen Switzer, London was extremely energetic about travelling round the country advising owners on aspects of garden layout and planting, often riding fifty or sixty miles a day and covering a northern circuit in five or six weeks. This payment of £21 10s. in late June 1699, soon after Lord Carlisle had himself arrived at Henderskelfe, probably relates to a visit by George London to Yorkshire to draw up proposals for the garden.

Two plans by George London survive for Castle Howard.[36] It has always been assumed that one of these shows Talman's project and the other Vanbrugh's, on the basis of a rough sketch on the back of one of Talman's surviving ground plans. Whatever the authorship of the ground plans, London's drawings suggest an evolution in the design of the house from a rectangular main block facing west-south-west towards York, with wings projecting forwards round a large oval entrance courtyard, to a more open scheme of a house facing north, with two wings projecting north connected by straight corridors, and two side wings on the south front in the manner approved by the Duke of Devonshire.[37]

Several drawings survive which show Vanbrugh working on different ideas for the house, particularly for the north front, which he proposed should have coupled Corinthian columns, horizontally banded rustication, a vast entrance archway and a huge circular window punched into the façade above it (*Plate 8*).[38] In another drawing he can be observed experimenting with whether the windows should be round-headed or have a prominent keystone (*Plate 9*).[39] These drawings suggest Vanbrugh's active mind, testing out ideas, experimenting with different relationships of architectural form, exploring the general look of the façade.

The dominant architectural characteristic of Vanbrugh's designs during the autumn of 1699 was low wings, much admired by the Duke of Devonshire and described by him as resembling an orange-house. This description applies most accurately to one of the surviving drawings for Castle Howard in the Victoria and Albert Museum, which consists of a main block with arched windows and two-storey Corinthian columns and long, low, one-storey wings stretching out to either side, which do, indeed, resemble a late seventeenth-century orangery (*Plate 10*).[40]

If, at Christmas 1699, the proposals for Castle Howard had included a dome, Vanbrugh would surely have mentioned it. In fact, a surviving ground plan, which relates closely both to London's drawing and to the first proposal for the south elevation, shows only a conventional square entrance hall, leading through to a long corridor which lies behind the sequence of apartments lining the south front; and the two staircases likewise are completely standard forms, a grand one consisting of three flights at right angles to each other, and the other smaller and steeper of two flights doubling back.[41] Vanbrugh's early projects for Castle Howard, therefore, appear to have been unsophisticated. The Duke of Devonshire's comment that the wings '*wou'd have an admirable effect without doors as well as within*' suggests their origin: indoors, they were a way of accommodating an extended line of private apartments on either side of the public rooms in the main block; outdoors, they were a way of extending the length, and hence the architectural impact, of the garden façade with a minimum of expense.

At Christmas 1699 Vanbrugh was over-optimistic about the date of commencement of building. He told the Earl of Manchester that '*the Stone is raising, and the Foundations will be laid in the Spring*'. In fact, it was not until 20 June 1700 that the wooden model of Castle Howard was taken to Hampton Court for the King's approval.[42] On 26 July 1700 estimates were made for the cost of carpenters' and joiners' work; and it was only in spring 1701 that a contract was drawn up with the mason, William Smith, and that work on the foundations began in earnest.[43]

During this period of at least a year, the model for Castle Howard would have been displayed to members of the Court and the Kit-cat Club – those people whom Talman described as '*the Critiques*'[44] – for their comments and approval. According to Vanbrugh, when Blenheim was planned:

PLATE 8

Early proposal for the
north front, with
horizontally banded
rustication, a vast
entrance archway and a
huge circular window
punched into the façade
above it.

PLATE 9

Early proposal for the
north front, showing
whether the windows
should be round-headed
or have a prominent
keystone.

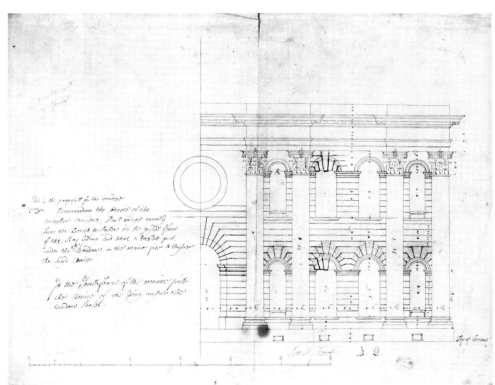

PLATE 10

Early proposal for the
garden front with low
wings 'like an orange
house'.

*The Duke of Marlborough your Grace [the Duchess of Marlborough] my late Lord Godolphin, the Duke of Shrewsbury, the late Duke of Montague, Sir Christopher Wren and several others were thoroughly consulted in the matter; and several meetings there were upon it, at Kensington, Montague House &c, when the Modells were inspected, and that of Sir Christopher Wren, Stuck full of pins.*[45]

This letter describes a milieu in which projects were subjected to detailed inspection. Presumably something comparable happened to the model of Castle Howard; and during the course of the year from Christmas 1699 to early spring 1701, ideas for the house were progressively modified and improved. A second, later ground plan shows the major changes which were made: by the refinement of the relationship of the main block to the two flanking wings; by clarification of the nature of the connecting colonnade; most of all, by the decision to build a dome (*Plate 11*).[46]

It is not clear where the idea for the dome came from. That it was an afterthought is evident from its lack of visual integration with the house as a whole – a grandiose, but conceptually superfluous, addition to an essentially rectilinear block. In some ways it is just an inflated version of the small wooden cupolas which had been a common feature of many late seventeenth-century houses, including Coleshill, Clarendon House and Belton. It is possible that Lord Carlisle recollected the powerful impact of the Roman domes he had seen in the early part of the 1690s; or that Vanbrugh remembered the dome of the Collège des Quatre Nations. Whatever its origin, the idea of the dome transformed the conception of the house at Castle Howard from a main block which was conventional, to a proposal of extreme visual excitement, quite unlike anything which had existed in a private house previously. As Joseph Addison was to write several years later in the *Spectator*:

*Among all the figures in architecture, there are none that have a greater air than the concave and the convex; and we find in all the ancient and modern architecture, as well as in the remote parts of China, as in countries nearer home, that round pillars and vaulted roofs make a great part of those buildings which are designed for pomp and magnificence.*[47]

It is clear that, although in the first few months of the project in the late summer and early autumn of 1699 Vanbrugh worked fanatically hard inspecting appropriate precedents, consulting the relevant authorities, and drawing up plans, his first projects were slightly crude and simplistic. These ideas were then allowed

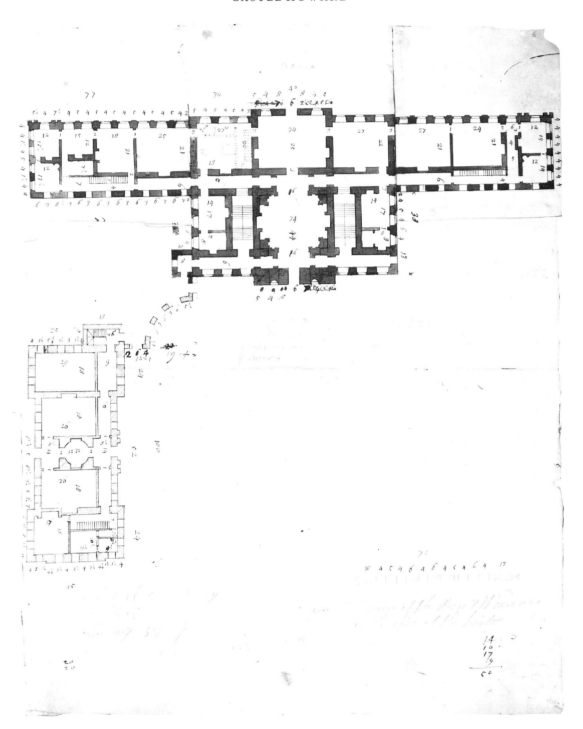

PLATE II

Revised ground plan, showing the introduction of the dome.

to develop through a process of discussion, with the help and criticism of contemporaries. From being a slightly jejune conception in the autumn of 1699, the fully fledged proposals for Castle Howard, as it was finally built, were unusually grandiose.

## VANBRUGH AND HAWKSMOOR

During much of this century it has been recurrently suggested that the design of Castle Howard is too complex and sophisticated to be the unaided work of Vanbrugh, because he had had no prior experience of building and because he was an incompetent architectural draughtsman; and that the reason Vanbrugh's first ideas for Castle Howard were transformed from a rough sketch to a mature architectural conception was the intervention of the architect Nicholas Hawksmoor. This argument was first proposed by H. S. Goodhart-Rendel in a short pioneering monograph, *Nicholas Hawksmoor*, published in 1924. In it he wrote of Castle Howard that 'Neither in the general conception nor in the details of Castle Howard is there any faltering; everywhere in it there is evidence of the great technical skill and experience of its author. It was built under the supervision of Hawksmoor.'[48] The inference was clear that Vanbrugh may have been responsible for sketching out the idea of Castle Howard, but that thereafter the execution of the project owed more to Hawksmoor. He concluded,

> Whether Hawksmoor was Vanbrugh's equal in imagination we are unlikely ever to know; that he was Vanbrugh's superior in the other essentials of architectural invention would seem undeniable. As to their respective roles in their collaboration many guesses may be made; all that can be said with certainty is that Hawksmoor could do without Vanbrugh a great deal more than Vanbrugh could do without Hawksmoor.[49]

Over the last three decades this advocacy of the superior architectural intelligence of Hawksmoor has been taken up by Professor Kerry Downes, the principal authority on the work of both Vanbrugh and Hawksmoor. In his first, excellent monograph on Nicholas Hawksmoor, published in 1959, the argument that the design of Castle Howard owed as much to Hawksmoor as to Vanbrugh was advanced tentatively on the basis of Hawksmoor's drawing style. His conclusion was that 'In the firm of Vanbrugh and Hawksmoor the latter was indispensable, but his role was to suggest, to confirm, not to command, and he would never be held the architect.'[50] In his second, shorter discussion of Hawksmoor's career,

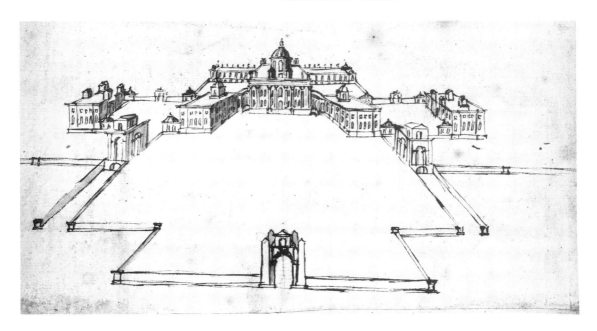

PLATE 12

This sketch, probably by Vanbrugh, shows the house as it was originally intended.

published in 1969, he withdrew slightly from this position, acknowledging that 'it is likely that the unusual or innovatory features of Castle Howard were due to Vanbrugh rather than to Hawksmoor, and that much of the detail – especially inside – was designed by the craftsmen who carried it out.'[51] In his first monograph on Vanbrugh, published in 1977, his position vis-à-vis Hawksmoor's role at Castle Howard significantly altered: 'it is likely that the private engagement of Hawksmoor was Vanbrugh's first practical step towards architecture. Indeed, their meeting was probably the decisive event leading Vanbrugh to that step.'[52] In Downes's most recent biography, *Sir John Vanbrugh*, his advocacy for Hawksmoor is more pronounced. The chapter on Castle Howard begins with a discussion of how Hawksmoor's widow put in a bill after his death for services rendered; and Downes suggests that Vanbrugh could not have contemplated the design of Castle Howard if he had not known that he could rely on the more professional expertise of Hawksmoor. 'What Hawksmoor showed [Vanbrugh] was that, as is claimed for certain postal correspondence courses today, he could start practising his new accomplishment while he was still learning it.'[53] The evidence for these claims needs to be reviewed.

The first documentation for Hawksmoor's involvement in the designs of Castle Howard comes in an undated letter, which Vanbrugh wrote to Lord Carlisle from Tadcaster near York:

*I am got no farther than Tadcaster yet, My Lord Burlington carrying me away with him to Lanesborough [Londesborough]. I wish't I cou'd possibly have stay'd there 'till tuesday, that I might have seen yr Ldship, and known whether you are come to an agreement with the Mason & Carpenter. I talk't a great deal to 'em both, the morning I came away; but found 'em very unwilling to come to any abatement. They made a world of protestations of its being impossible, without letting the work pay for't: they say'd they believ'd yr Ldship might expect some abatement from their proposall as a thing of course; but that Mr Hawksmoor had persuaded 'em to make no provision for that, but to make the lowest offer they cou'd possibly work for, and do it well. I ask't Mr Hawksmoor alone, what he really thought on't; He said they were indeed come as low, as he ever expected to bring 'em; and yet perhaps it was not impossible for 'em to work lower.*

The letter concludes:

*I spoak to Mr Hawksmoor about his perticular concern and found him as he us'd to be. so he intended to ask yr Ldship fourty pound a year Sallary & fifty each journey wch mounts to £100 clear. I hope he'll deserve it, and that all will go to yr Ldships sattisfaction.*[54]

The date of this letter is important. There is evidence that Lord Carlisle visited Castle Howard in March 1700; but during March and April Vanbrugh was occupied in rewriting Fletcher's play *The Pilgrim*, translating it from verse to prose, for performance at Drury Lane.[55] The first estimates for building work were made on 26 July 1700, when Robert Barker provided '*An Estimation of Carpentors & Joyners Work to be don for the Right Honble the Earle of Carlisle*'.[56] On 5 August Lord Carlisle's agent in London, Nevill Ridley, paid the boat-hire for sending goods to Henderskelfe, which suggests that the third Earl may have been there in August, spending September in Cumberland, returning to Henderskelfe in October, and to London in early November.[57] In future years Vanbrugh tended to visit Yorkshire in the late summer. So Vanbrugh's first letter concerning Hawksmoor's employment may have dated from the end of August or October 1700, at least a year after Vanbrugh had been first consulted about the plans for Castle Howard and several months after the model had been sent to Hampton Court for inspection. Yet the exact terms on which the masons were employed were only agreed at the end of March 1701, when the masons, William Smith and his partners, received their first payment. So Vanbrugh's letter about Hawksmoor might also date to March 1701, at the time when rates of payment

were most likely to have been contested; in which case, the first mention of
Hawksmoor would be a year and a half after Vanbrugh's first involvement with
projects for Castle Howard.

Vanbrugh's letter, written from Tadcaster, indicates that, when it came to the
question of drawing up contracts, his lack of experience in the practical world of
building became a handicap. He had approached someone who could make up
for this deficiency, namely Nicholas Hawksmoor. Hawksmoor, unlike Vanbrugh,
was uniquely well qualified to advise on contracts and rates of payment, having
worked as clerk to Sir Christopher Wren since around 1680, and been responsible
for many of the detailed decisions concerning the royal palaces, St Paul's and the
City churches: drawing up plans and elevations, visiting quarries, and supervising
workmen. In 1689 he had been appointed Clerk of Works at Kensington Palace,
and in 1698 at Greenwich Hospital. Vanbrugh invited him to take charge of the
executive part of building Castle Howard. However, the fact that Vanbrugh relied
on Hawksmoor's vastly superior expertise in the supervision of the workmen does
not mean that Hawksmoor was responsible for the plans and proposals, let alone
that Vanbrugh was dependent on his advice and his draughtsmanship from the
beginning.

Hawksmoor received his first formal payment of £150 for work at Castle
Howard on 25 May 1701.[58] The following day he wrote a long letter to Lord
Carlisle about the progress of work:

*I find the worke at Henderscelf to go on with vigour and grt industry altho there is not soe much done as I expected by this time but the impediment has been the backward season which has much obstructed us. I am come time enough to regulate some errours and difficultys the workmen were going into, and in generall the worke is firme and strongly performed; the situation yr Lp has chose is under the covert of ye Wood but it runs into some hardships about levelling & makeing our access to ye great façade and principall courts, I am takeing all the declivitys and disposition of ye ground at present, that yr Lp may consider your plantations which I wish were growing that they might not Loose time. the woods in the front of the house belonging to Sr Wm Strickland I heartily wish your Lp cou'd secure in your owne possession, and then I think the deal wou'd be without all objections I have severall instructions and memorandums to draw up for the workemen and I can see nothing to contradict the good execution of the worke: I desire the mason to sett on more hands that we may complete with expedition the two wings, and to do that will require another kil[n] for Lime. The coals come hard but now is the season to gett them in which I hope your Lp will order not to be wanting for now I shall wish the conclusion of the worke as earnestly as I was for opposing the beginning of it. I shall give your Lp a further acct the next post.*[59]

The tone of this letter indicates the difference between Vanbrugh's character and Hawksmoor's. Where Vanbrugh was ebullient and effusive, writing to Lord Carlisle on terms of amity, Hawksmoor was deferential. Where Vanbrugh was opinionated, Hawksmoor was quiet, conscientious and studiously professional. Where Vanbrugh took responsibility for everything that happened at Castle Howard, Hawksmoor occupied himself with practicalities, regulating the quality of workmanship, surveying the foundations, drawing up future instructions for the workmen.

The division of labour, therefore, between Vanbrugh and Hawksmoor in the design of Castle Howard seems to have been as follows. Vanbrugh was entirely and exclusively responsible for the first ideas for the house, as indicated in his letter of Christmas Day 1699. He took the project through to the stage of preparing the model in wood. At this point he realized that he would need the professional assistance of someone with more experience of the everyday practicalities of building. So he decided to employ Nicholas Hawksmoor in this capacity. It remains true that there is a considerable difference between the first faltering sketches for the façades at Castle Howard and subsequent, more fully worked-out drawings, which show signs of Hawksmoor's hand. It is probable that

Hawksmoor, with his much greater experience of the details of building and his responsibility for on-site supervision of masons and workmen, was able to render necessary advice on how to realize Vanbrugh's ideas, and so was deeply implicated in translating them into architectural reality.

Yet Hawksmoor's involvement should not be allowed to detract from Vanbrugh's overall sense of responsibility for, and involvement in, the project far beyond the initial plans. The exact nature of the division of labour between Vanbrugh and Hawksmoor is often the result of an intuitive assessment of the building as it was executed. For Goodhart-Rendel and for Professor Downes, it is the quality and complexity of the final building which makes it impossible to credit Vanbrugh with full responsibility for it. I am inclined to agree with Professor Geoffrey Webb, the editor of Vanbrugh's letters, that it is precisely the immaturity of the design of Castle Howard, the sense of ideas not fully integrated or worked out, of a certain raw vigour and visual excitement, of too much experiment and too little digestion, which marks the design of Castle Howard as the work of someone without previous architectural experience. As Webb wrote:

> It is upon this feeling that such a design as Castle Howard implies a practically experienced architect, that the 'Hawksmoor sous clef' hypothesis is based. But it is on precisely this point that the present Editor cannot agree with Mr Goodhart-Rendel; relative to Vanbrugh's whole architectural achievement it seems to him that Castle Howard is definitely an immature and tentative work, a work in which many of the later characteristic 'motifs' and qualities are indeed present, but only just – in embryo.[60]

In many ways, the question of who did what in late seventeenth-century architecture is an artificial one. Building is not like fifteenth-century painting, in which the work of different hands can be discerned by judicious connoisseurship. Building is essentially a collaborative activity, and was particularly so in the late seventeenth century, when there was not a fully developed conception of the professional function of the architect. It is likely that Lord Carlisle made many pertinent and helpful suggestions about the design of Castle Howard while plans were being made. It is equally clear that Hawksmoor was involved in the execution of the plans and made detailed drawings for many parts of the building, including the dome. Hawksmoor was a skilled architectural draughtsman, with an ability to convey the depth and character of a building with a cursory flick of the pen; Vanbrugh was never a good draughtsman, always working with simple outlines. Many other people will have contributed to the proposals for Castle Howard in discussion; many others contributed to its execution, especially the masons and craftsmen. Yet these facts should not be allowed to diminish Vanbrugh's achievements at Castle Howard. He undertook the tasks of design and of watching over the progress of building seriously, conscientiously, and with passion. If one single person is to be attributed with the quality of the building of Castle Howard, then it must be Vanbrugh, working within a matrix which was essentially collaborative.

## DESIGN ANALYSIS

Critical assessment of the design of Castle Howard needs to be divided into three parts: an examination of the way the ground plan was conceived and how it works; of the various elevations and their visual effect; and of the quality of the building as a whole and how the different parts interrelate.

It is clear from the surviving George London drawing that Vanbrugh worked out the essential features of the ground plan at an early stage, and left the detailed working-out of the elevations to later. This suggests that he regarded the layout of the various parts of the building and how it operated internally as the first requirement of any design. Taking the ground plan of the house as it was submitted to Colen Campbell for publication in volume one of *Vitruvius Britannicus* as signifying Vanbrugh's final intentions for the interior layout, there are several major features (*Plate 14*).[61]

It was planned that the visitor should approach the house axially through a grand entrance gate, leading to a courtyard, described on the Campbell plan as '*The Great Court*'. On either side of the entrance courtyard were two flanking wings, containing on the left-hand side the kitchen and offices, and on the right-hand side a projected chapel, which was never built. These two flanking wings were built quite close to one another, and to the main block, partly as a matter of internal convenience, so that it was a short walk from the kitchen to the so-called '*private eating parlour*' on the left of the great hall, partly in order to ensure that the wings were seen as part of an architectural whole, surrounding the arriving visitor with an impression of magnificence on three sides.

Immediately on entering by the main door, the visitor was confronted with the vertiginous experience of entering '*The Great Hall*', which must have been deliberately contrived to provide an immediate visual impact, a single *coup d'œil* replacing the possibility of a slow visual exploration of the interior (*Plate 26*). Two long flights of stairs were wrapped round on either side of the great hall,

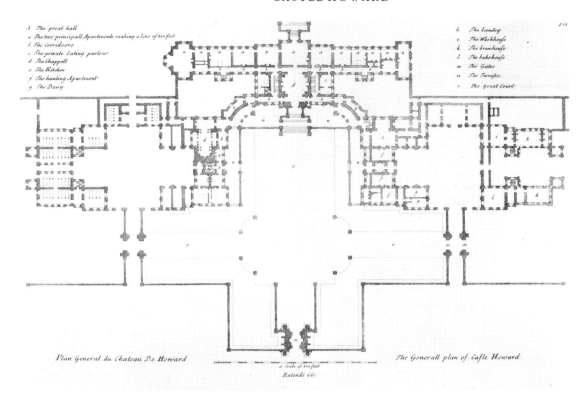

PLATE 14

The plan of Castle
Howard, as published in
volume one of Colen
Campbell's *Vitruvius
Britannicus* (London,
1715) shows the layout
of the house and
outbuildings as intended
by Vanbrugh.

allowing vistas through to them, making the interior of the hall architecturally
more complex and preventing too great a feeling of claustrophobia.

Beyond the great hall, stretching out on either side, were two long corridors.
Although short corridors had been used previously in this way, the word 'corridor'
itself was still enough of a novelty in 1716 to need explaining by Vanbrugh in a
letter to the Duchess of Marlborough: *'The word Corridore Madam is foreign,
and signifys in plain English, no more than a Passage, it is now however generally
us'd as an English Word.'*[62] Vanbrugh used the corridors to great effect: they
permitted independent access to the two cabinets at either end of the façade and,
perhaps more importantly, of the servants to the close-stool rooms which lay off
the corridors; and, they created an extended and architecturally impressive vista.

Beyond the corridor lay the three major state rooms of the ground floor: a
saloon in the centre (*Plate 25*), flanked by a dining-room on the left and an ante-
room on the right. Ephraim Chambers wrote of saloons in his *Cyclopedia* that
*'The Salon is a State Room. 'Tis much used in the Palaces in Italy; and from thence
the Mode came to us. Embassadors, and other Great Visitors, are usually received*

*in the Salon.*'[63]. The most unusual feature of Castle Howard, as has already been described, was the way the two sets of principal apartments were added on either side of the main block, making, as was proudly announced on the ground plan in *Vitruvius Britannicus*, '*a line of 300 feet*'. These two sets of apartments were arranged in the way that had become standard in the late seventeenth century, consisting of a sequence of ante-room, withdrawing room, bedchamber, closets and, at the end of the line, a cabinet.[64]

What was ingenious about Vanbrugh's ground plan at Castle Howard was the way that it contrived to create the maximum visual effects of architectural scale and magnificence out of the minimum number of rooms. Both externally and internally it looked and felt like a much larger house than it actually was, if calculated in terms of floor space. Instead of there being a single main block on its own, as was usual in late seventeenth-century country houses, the main block was drawn outwards in two different directions, like the claws of a crab. This meant that, whether viewed from the north or the south, the house appears enormous, extending into the distance; the blank space behind the projecting wings on either side of the main block does not register on the spectator. And viewed diagonally, the house appeared as a mass of domes and statuary, difficult to read in terms of the ground plan, and so, once again, exaggeratedly impressive.

It seems that Vanbrugh had an intuitive understanding of how a ground plan might work internally. He was able to understand space in terms of movement through it, of the internal experience and visual exploration of a building. He thought of the use of the house not just, as the Duchess of Marlborough would have liked, in terms of straightforward convenience, but more in terms of the relationship of the plan to the dignity of the owner: as Palladio had written, '*we Commonly call a House convenient, when it is suitable to ye quality of its Master*';[65] or, as John Evelyn described Diathesis, '*where all the parts and Members of a Building are assign'd their just and proper Places, according to their Quality, Nature, Office Rank and Genuine Collocation*'.[66] The interior of Castle Howard gives an appearance of being carefully, cleverly, indeed brilliantly planned to create the appropriate effect of controlled, ceremonial magnificence.

The quality of the façades at Castle Howard is less successful. The most exciting is undoubtedly the garden front, particularly when viewed at a sharp angle from the side. Its great length and the rhythmic succession of round-headed windows (which were, as Hawksmoor wrote, '*divided into a perpetuall Arcade*'[67]) provide a strong counterpoint between the distant horizontal perspective and the tendency of the eye to lift upwards into the visual splendour of the dome and

PLATE 15

The earliest known view of the garden front drawn by P. Lathbury and subsequently engraved by the book illustrator, Anthony Walker, in 1758.

surrounding statuary. Also, the so-called main block protrudes slightly from the flanking wings, and the central section of the main block protrudes further. This creates the visual effect of the main block thrusting forwards, as if a huge body of stone were escaping its shackles. But it is also in the garden front that the main weaknesses of the overall composition are most visible, particularly if it is viewed head on. Then the three primary elements – the dome, the main block and the flanking wings – are inclined to appear dislocated, as if they do not properly belong to one another. This feature of the external architecture to produce grand, but essentially simplistic, effects of instant *éclat* at the expense of integration between the various parts is evidence of Vanbrugh's immaturity in architectural composition.

Like the garden front, the north, or entrance, front is intended to be taken in at a glance and not subjected to detailed inspection (*Plate 16*). Its principal features are four sets of massive, flat, coupled Doric pilasters which provide the requisite stability for the façade. In between them the windows are squeezed as if they need space to expand, and there is a strongly horizontal effect provided by banded rustication. According to Hawksmoor writing to Lord Carlisle in 1734, '*I humbly observe to yr Lordship touching the North front that it was intended, much in the*

*same Style as Mr Inigo Jones, and Mr Webb intended the Kings pallace at Greenwich (now Turned into an hospitall).*'[68] There is no reason to dispute this as a source for some of the ideas; but there is a feeling about the north front that Vanbrugh was using too many features of an architectural palette simultaneously, that it is too profuse, and lacking the quality of sustained and systematic invention.

The fundamental weakness in the design of Castle Howard is the lack of relationship between its different parts: each part viewed separately is successful, but they do not fit harmoniously together. Every visitor to the house must have experienced disillusionment at the conflict between the excessive grandiosity of the exterior and the disappointing smallness of the rooms inside. The exterior establishes expectations which are not fulfilled indoors. Although both the elevations and the ground plan are, by themselves, magnificently conceived, there is a curious lack of relationship between the two, a feeling of physical incongruity and architectural disjunction. There is only one set of quite small rooms behind much of the great length of the south façade. There is no organic relationship between the layout of the interior and the architectural forms outside. Too much is gratuitous. As Sir John Clerk of Penicuik, a Scottish landowner who had travelled extensively on the continent and was himself an amateur architect, commented on the occasion of a visit on his way to London in 1727, *'there is not one good apartment in the whole house, at least not one which is in any way suitable to the grandure and expense of the outside.'*[69] This is fair criticism.

A second major defect in the design of Castle Howard was also noted by Sir John Clerk. As he wrote, *'The ornaments on one side is of the Ionick order and of the Corinthian on the other side.'* This, too, is fair criticism, that the two façades do not relate architecturally, which produces a sense of unease at their conjunction in a single building. Vanbrugh was himself sensitive to this criticism that he did not use the classical orders in a correct or orthodox way. As he wrote to the Earl of Manchester about proposals for Kimbolton, *'I hope your Ldship won't be discourag'd, if any Italians you may Shew it to, shou'd find fault that 'tis not Roman, for to have built a Front with Pillasters, and what the Orders require cou'd never have been born with the Rest of the Castle: I'm sure this will make a very Noble and masculine Shew.'*[70]

Hawksmoor specifically defended Vanbrugh from the accusation that the north and south fronts of Castle Howard were of a different architectural order on the grounds that *'The South side, and North front of your Ldships house cannot be seen together at the same Time, nor at any time upon the Diagonall (or angular view).'*[71] Yet it must be admitted that Sir John Clerk has a point, that the fact that the two sides of the building do not relate to one another, even if they cannot be seen together, means that the mind cannot dwell on the building as a whole with any sense of satisfaction, that it is conceived too much in terms of two separate façades and not enough in terms of what the eighteenth century would have called *conformity*. There is no doubt that it looks extremely well and makes a very noble show; but when the eye comes to explore the individual details, it finds them too superabundant and perhaps slightly coarse; and when the mind begins to consider the structure, it discovers that there are areas which are not fully worked out, that the internal courtyards are left rough-hewn, that the illusion breaks down.

Yet these criticisms of Vanbrugh's design should not be allowed to detract from his overall achievement in the design of Castle Howard. They are precisely the types of defect which are to be expected from an inexperienced designer, from someone who still tended to think in two dimensions. What Vanbrugh did manage to provide at Castle Howard was a raw vigour, a richness of invention, an immensely dynamic vitality. It conveys the feeling of someone with enormous fertility of imagination who has been unleashed to experiment with architectural form. The qualities as well as the defects of Castle Howard would appear to derive precisely from the fact that Vanbrugh was relatively untutored as an architect and was able to make up in *brio* what he lacked in previous experience or in architectural qualifications.

# CHAPTER THREE

# The House

## BUILDING CONSTRUCTION

Although the first ideas for building Castle Howard probably dated back to 1698, it was not until 1701 that construction began. There were delays in finding suitable workmen, delays, too, while the plans were adjusted and arrangements made for the supply of materials. Lord Carlisle travelled to Yorkshire in early January 1701 for some hunting, and on 13 January 1701 a memorandum was drawn up *'concerning deals fetch'd from Norway and deliver'd at Scarborow'*. Including customs charges, they cost a total of £368.[1] On 21 February 1701 the first payment of £8 was paid to *'Mr Etty Survayor'*. This refers to William Etty, the local master carpenter from York, who was recruited to act as clerk of works at a rate of 5s per day. His father, John Etty, was the most prominent local architect, with extensive experience of the supervision of building works in the neighbourhood. William Etty was admitted a freeman of York in 1694, described as a carpenter, and had been married in York Minster in 1700.[2] He must have taken on many of the day-to-day responsibilities of recruiting and supervising workmen. According to Hawksmoor, writing after Etty's death in 1734, when he *'first began, along with me in Your Lordships service he was but young, tho' he soon improved, and so would any man of common capacity in so Noble a Building'*.[3]

The first payment to the masons was made on 31 March 1701.[4] The principal mason was William Smith in partnership with John Elsworth and a Major Smith, presumably William Smith's brother. On 9 April the carpenter, John Milburn, received his first payment *'upon acct. of work wch he hath obliged himselfe to doe'* and, during April, barrows were made for the masons and more deals were supplied by Mr Harrison of Malton *'for artching ye Sellers'*.[5] Hawksmoor received his first payment of £150 on 25 May, and on 26 May he was able to report to Lord Carlisle on the progress of work and the fact that it was *'firm and strongly performed'*.[6]

Work proceeded in distinct stages; indeed, one of the great benefits of the sectionalized ground plan was that this was possible (*Fig. 1*). The first part to be completed was the east wing on the entrance front, the so-called kitchen wing, which contained one set of small private apartments as well as the kitchen. This wing was described by the Earl of Oxford in 1725 as *'the useful part where the family live'*[7] and presumably was built first in order to provide Lord Carlisle with somewhere to stay while the rest of the house was built. In 1702 sufficient progress was made on this wing for the carpenters to be paid for work done *'In the Office Wing'* on 24 August, and on 23 September boards were bought for wainscoting.[8] This would suggest that most of the masons' work on the kitchen wing was already complete by 29 September 1702, by which time they had been paid a total of £1,233, although there was still work to be done in *'Altering ye Cupelo'* and *'pulling up and Altering ye Intabelment of ye Kitchen Wing Acording to ye plumers Directions for there Lead lying'* the following year.[9]

On 8 March 1703 William Etty was paid *'for freight of Glass from London'*.[10] The best quality glass was still shipped from France: according to William Leyburn in his *Architectonice: Or, a Compendium of the Art of Building* (London, 1700), it was *'much thinner, clearer, and more transparent than English Glass'*, as well as being *'much dearer, as quantity for quantity, there are but Twenty five Tables in a Case'*,[11] but perfectly acceptable crown glass was made in London, both at the Bear Garden, Southwark and at Lambeth. In July 1703 the smith was paid *'for 120 Brass pulleys for ye Sashes'*; in September, so was *'ye Roper for Ropes for ye Sashes'*, and in November Lawrence Dickinson was paid *'in full of Glaising, done att ye Kitchen Wing'*.[12] (Plate 17)

More or less simultaneously with work on the kitchen wing, the east wing on the garden front was being built. This was to contain Lord Carlisle's private apartments, including, in sequence, a withdrawing room, a bed chamber, two dressing rooms and, at the end, the room which was known as *'My Lord's Cabinet'*. The essential masonry work of this part was done during the summers of 1702 and 1703, but it was not until the summer of 1704 that the masons were paid for clearing the basement *'of my Ld Apartment'*.[13] During 1705 *'My Lord's Apartments'* were fitted out internally by specialist craftsmen and joiners, who were brought from London. As in the kitchen wing, John Milburn did the basic carpentry in the cellars, but a Mr Sabin or Sabyn was responsible for more sophisticated work upstairs, which included *'Chasses Sent from London In Number 13'*, *'Circular Suffitas of Wainscott in the Windowe heads'*, *'Large Italian Molding'* and *'Architraves above ye Doors'* in the drawing room, and *'Two deal*

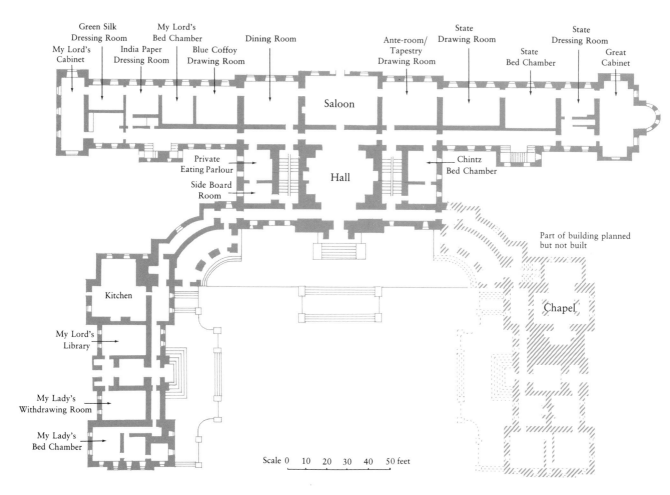

Green Silk
Dressing Room
My Lord's
Bed Chamber
Dining Room
State
Drawing Room
State
Dressing Room
My Lord's
Cabinet
India Paper
Dressing Room
Blue Coffoy
Drawing Room
Ante-room/
Tapestry
Drawing Room
State
Bed Chamber
Great
Cabinet

Saloon

Private
Eating Parlour
Side Board
Room
Chintz
Bed Chamber

Hall

Part of building planned
but not built

Kitchen

My Lord's
Library

Chapel

My Lady's
Withdrawing Room

My Lady's
Bed Chamber

Scale 0   10   20   30   40   50 feet

FIG. 1
Ground plan adapted
from Colen Campbell's
*Vitruvius Britannicus*, I,
London, 1715, p. 63.

pilasters fluted' in 'My Lords Grand Cabinet'.[14] This work was examined and measured by Hawksmoor on 1 October 1705 and Mr Sabyn was paid £99 19s. 8d. Other specialist wood carving was done by Samuel Carpenter, a skilled local craftsman who also worked in stone and who had previously worked with Hawksmoor and William Etty on the obelisk at Ripon.[15] He produced cartouches for the drawing room, a cornice for one of the closets and Corinthian capitals 'In My Lords Dressing Room'.[16] This wing was glazed by August 1705.[17] In 1706 'Mr Harvey Carver' was paid for a 'frame for my Lds bed Chamber', 'Lords Cabinett Chimney peece', 'Glasse frames for ye Cabinett', and 'frames for pictures above ye Glasses in ye Cabinett'.[18] This refers to Daniel Hervé, a Huguenot carver, who anglicized his name to Harvey and subsequently settled in York.[19] In October 1706 the masons received a further payment 'for Wheeling Rubish out of My Lords Appartment'.[20]

Once the work on the two east wings was well under way, the construction of the central block, the so-called main pile, could begin. Labourers were paid *'for Diging ye foundations of ye grtt. pile'* on 16 April 1703.[21] On 15 September 1703 the masons were paid *'for all the mason Worke In the Office Wing and Likewise all ye Mason Worke in My Lords Appartment & Circuler Coridoore and the Maine Pile Measurd up as to ye Setting on of the Great Bases'*.[22] This work included *'Leighing foundations in ye Main Pile'*, *'Making a triall ffor Stone in ye botom of ye old quarrie'* and *'Leighing Earth for pillars to stand in ye Main Pile'*.[23] In his letter to the Duke of Newcastle, dated 15 June 1703, Vanbrugh was able to boast that *'My Lord Carlisle has been Now three Years at work, and has neither had vexation nor disappointment yet; no not even the vexation of having paid a halfpenny too dear for any thing, nor being drawn into two pence of expence more than he propos'd.'*[24] The following month, he was due to set out on a Northern Progress, and on 13 July 1703 he reported to Jacob Tonson that Lord Carlisle had already been in Yorkshire for three weeks *'and writes me word he has near 200 men at Work; there's a new Quarry found, much better than the Old one, so all go's on smooth'*.[25] On 31 October 1705 the masons were paid £217 1s. 6d. for work on the north front and £247 2s. 7d. on the south front, with further payments for work on the *'Hall inside'*, the galleries, the staircase and the *'Buffett'*.[26]

By the summer of 1706 work on the central block was nearing completion. On 2 July 1706 Hawksmoor was able to report to Lord Carlisle:

*I have Recd. a letter from Mr. Etty giving an Account that we goe on wth vigour at Hinderskelf and are turning the window arches of ye Cupola, John Milburn has Layd on all the Roofs and I begg your Lordship will hasten ye Laying on the Lead. We intend to bring downe the Rain Water at each end of ye house in stacks of pip[e]s on the outside if your Lp. object not.*[27]

On 22 October 1706 the masons were paid *'for Cuting holes for the Sallown floore'*, *'for Cuting and Puling Peeces in the Capitals of the Hall'* and *'for Raiseing 3 Statues upon the South Pediment'*; and Hawksmoor was able to check and measure up their work *'at ye Cupola, and coving of ye great pile'*.[28]

As in Lord Carlisle's private apartments, once the basic structure was complete, specialist craftsmen were brought in to do the detailed stonework carving. The most important of these specialists was a French Huguenot stonecarver, Mr Nadauld, otherwise known as Nedos, who received his first payment of £75 *'upon Acctt. of Carved work'* on 29 September 1705.[29]

Nadauld is an obscure and interesting figure, responsible for the quality of

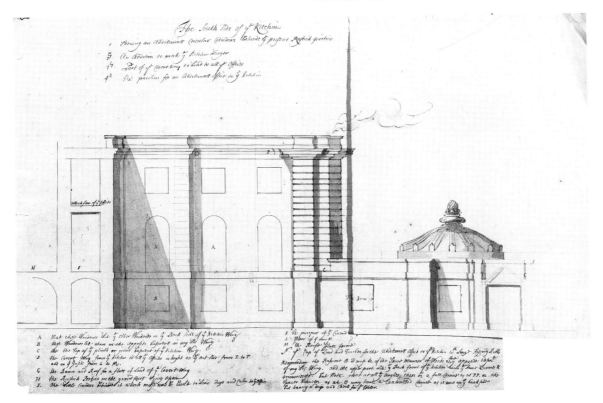

PLATE 17

Elevation of the south
side of the kitchen at
Castle Howard by
Nicholas Hawksmoor,
showing 'an additional
office' in the form of a
domed pavilion.

much of the carved decoration both outside and within Castle Howard, for its
luxuriance and liveliness and rumbustious character. He has been identified as the
'*Mr Nedoe*' who was paid £50 for plasterwork in the Queen's Closet in the Water
Gallery at Hampton Court between July 1689 and March 1692.[30] He was
subsequently employed at Chatsworth, where the first recorded payment to him
is dated 28 April 1700 and where his work included '*Carving 2 Busto Heads set
in the Neeches upon the Staircase before ye West front*' and '*41 foot superficiall
of Frost worke about the Grotto in the West Court*'. In July 1701 3s. was spent
on '*thatching a shed for Mr. Nadauld the carver*'.[31] At Castle Howard, his work
'*Done for the Rait honorable the Earle of Carlile at Henderskelfe since the 21 of
june 1705 til the 15 Dessember 1709*' included:

> *Foure Little figures called the foure Sezons made at Chattsworth*
> *a freeses in the South front with Sey boy ent Sey horses*
> *a freeses the boy en festons*
> *freeses with Lyon*

*trophees in the South front in the Returning angles*
*in the north front – metopes – trophees*
  *wood worck*
*in the fust closset*
*in the great closit*
*the freeses over the Cappitels in the great hall*
*troppheees in the north front*
*freeses in the Rond the coppullo*
*13 Rosses under the wouttes*
*4 great Rosses under the first dore*
*4 Cey-Setones in the great hall*
*2 great hurne adornet with 4 head Set upon the Corniche in the South Front*
*2 figures Called Seres en flora*
*a figure Called pallas upon the pediment*
*4 figure Called vestalles*
*The Cote of armes in the pediment*
*8 head or bust Set upon the Corniche the Coppullo*
*a fleuron for finisching the top the coppullo*
*4 Rosses under the Little dore in the gred hall*
*9 Rosses under the Corniche in the north front*
*in the west front the figure Called Diana*
*4 hurne upon the south front*
*a freese in woode for the closset chimly*
*a Cappitell the Corintien order*
*a figure called Seneco*
*a figure called Socrato*
*the Carved Corniche in the South front*
*Portique Corniche north front*
*Couronet an Shefers in the cey setone*
*festons upon the Rond the window*
*for the bois en festons in bos side the window*
*a Leven hurnes – 4 with head an piramides and flames*
*4 oders*
*for to have mendet 11 gread Cappitels corintien order*
*for the figure called Sicero*
*for the figure called plato*
*for 3 cey setone in the gread hall*
*for to have mendet hal the cappitels in the grd hall.*

For all this work, and more, Nadauld put in a bill for £863 13s. Lord Carlisle reduced it by £19.[32]

Most of Nadauld's work can be readily identified. On the north front can be clearly seen the various forms of martial trophy – flags, breastplate and cannon – between the metopes, the coronet and ciphers on the keystone, and the fat boys perched on the central window surround, holding festoons (*Plate 18*). On the south front appear the seahorses flowing through the frieze in company with seaboys blowing trumpets, the coat of arms in the pediment, and the various forms of urn enlivening the skyline (*Plate 19*). Diana the huntress, goddess of woods, of mountains and of huntsmen, has been moved from her place on the west front to the east end of 'My Lords Apartment', where she survives with a bow in her hand and a quiver full of arrows hanging about her shoulders (*Plate 21*). Pallas presides, as she ought to, over the pediment of the south front, since the art of building, especially of castles, was thought to be of her invention. She is flanked by the two figures called Ceres and Flora, Ceres with a sheaf of corn, Flora with a cornucopia of flowers.

From Nadauld's work, which has been identified, it is clear that he was able to produce carving that was exceptionally vigorous – goddesses that are full of movement, fat, flowing and robust, as well as highly sophisticated floral ornament, straight out of contemporary French pattern books. He, at least as much as Vanbrugh, was responsible for the liveliness and surface animation of the two main façades.

Indoors, Nadauld's work included the frieze of scrolled ornament over the huge Composite capitals in the hall, the floral bosses under the four main arches supporting the vaults and their equally fine keystones, and the frieze round the kerb of the cupola (*Plate 26*).[33] He was assisted in the carving of the Composite order by another Huguenot, Gideon du Chesne, who had previously been employed at Boughton and whose name appears in the Castle Howard accounts as '*Mr Tushaine*'.[34] He was responsible for the '*Impost Mould in ye StareCases Arches*' and the '*Roases in ye Great Arches*'.[35] The account for their work in the hall was settled in October 1706. On 3 March 1707 Mr Jackson, the plumber, was paid '*in full for finishing ye Maine pile*'; and on 1 October 1707 a sum of £6 19s. 6d. was '*pd. for Gold for Guilding ye Top of ye grt Cupola*'.[36]

Once the work on the main block was more or less complete, the masons moved on to the construction of the west wing on the garden front, which was known as '*ye Grand Appartment In ye West Wing*' and was to contain, in sequence, the state drawing room, the state bedchamber, a state dressing room, and, at the west

PLATE 18

The north front, showing the '4 *Statues for the neeches in the north front*' by the
Huguenot carver, Nadauld, and the sumptuous decorative detailing.

PLATES 19 & 20

The pediment of the south front showing the sea horses and the sea boys blowing
trumpets in the frieze and the statue of Pallas. (*Below*) A detail of the carving on the
garden front, demonstrating the complexity of surface effect.

PLATES 21 & 22

The carving of Diana the huntress, goddess of woods, of mountains and of huntsmen,
by Nadauld. (*Below*) A detail of the masonry in the stable courtyard, which gives
some idea of the massiveness of the stonework.

end of the garden façade, the great cabinet, subsequently demolished to make way for Sir Thomas Robinson's west wing. On 18 April 1707 labourers were paid '*for removeing ye Earth out of ye grtt. Sellers in ye Maine Pile*'.[37] By 27 July 1708 Vanbrugh could write to the Earl of Manchester, who was himself involved in building at Kimbolton in Huntingdonshire, that '*My Ld Carlisle has got his whole Garden Front up And is fonder of his Work every day than Other*.'[38] The leadwork of the west wing was paid for on 22 January 1709; and the gilding of '*ye 4 Caps upon ye East & West Wings*' was done during the summer.[39] So by the summer of 1709 the bulk of the exterior structure of the house was complete. The masons should have gone on to build the proposed west wing on the entrance front, which, according to the ground plan published in *Vitruvius Britannicus*, was intended to contain a chapel; but instead they began work on the offices and courtyard to the east of the kitchen wing.

70

PLATE 24

A pre-war *Country Life* photograph of the north front.

## SOURCES OF INCOME

One aspect of the building process which has not been much studied is how it was actually paid for. Apart from a pioneering article by Professor H. J. Habbakuk published in 1955, which examined the process of financing Burley-on-the-Hill, it has been too easily assumed that country houses are a natural part of the landscape and not the result of conscious decisions and deliberate investment.[40] Architecture is often represented as if it consisted solely of work by a single autonomous individual, sitting in front of a drawing board with an encyclopedic knowledge of the past and an unlimited supply of pattern books. Yet it is a highly physical process, requiring great skills of organization and management, and an adequate supply of materials and capital, alongside large numbers of craftsmen and labourers, each with a specialized knowledge of a particular technology. Architecture is not just a cerebral statement, but the manipulation of capital and the more substantial properties of glass, timber and stone.

Fortunately, but perhaps not coincidentally, the third Earl of Carlisle was meticulous in keeping his accounts, so that it is possible to work out in considerable detail how he actually raised the money to pay for Castle Howard. He kept in close touch with his various agents in London and Cumberland and enough of this correspondence survives to give an idea of the extent to which he expected to be informed of any matters relating to the management of his estates. For example, his steward at Naworth, James Maxwell, would write to him about the weather and the quality of the harvest and the seeds that the gardener wanted.[41] In January 1695 Maxwell reported that he intended '*to plow up the Cloases att Colthouse & Sowe oates on them. for theye growe litle Grass & now theye are full of Moalhils*';[42] in March, '*we had the greatest storme of ffrost & snow & the Bitterest winde that ever was Knowne att this time of ye yeare . . . the Catle standing Belly Deep in the snowe Readye to starve & I much Doubt of saveing them alive*'.[43] On 22 April 1696 Lord Carlisle was informed that '*it will bee a very hard time with ye poor people for all mannor of provision is a full third part Deerer than theye were when yr. honr. was here*';[44] by 29 April there was:

*now a greater Confusion about moneyes than ever was yet; for here is noe New moneyes att all. & poore people is Like to starve for what moneyes they have will not pass to gitt soe much as a peck of Corne, & the Kings Receivors has appointed the 12 of Maye for to Receive the Rents yt was due at Ladye Day. and they saye yt theye will not receive any Clipt or Coarse Moneyes after the fourth of Maye neither for taxes or Rents; soe yt the Countrye is and will bee in a miserable condicion.*[45]

Alongside this constant flow of communication about local matters, Lord Carlisle would twice annually examine detailed accounts which he required to be sent to him and which he would approve only subject to comments and corrections. If there was any mistake, he would spot it. In 1695, for example, in a page of forty-six entries for fines received from the manor of Irthington, he notices the miscalculation of a single shilling and writes, *'this leaf is cast up too much by a shilling'*; against a payment of £20 in wages, he notes alongside it, *'I suppose it is meant for ye whole year which I allow & not for ye half year'*; and having allowed the accounts, he adds as a postscript, *'Thomas Smiths fathers fine is charged to me pay'd at London by his son (as it was) but I do not find it charged in your receipts as it ought to be.'*[46]

In 1699 there is evidence, as might be expected, that Lord Carlisle was watching with particular care his sources of landed income. On 7 September 1699 he noticed that his fishing rights had not been let at Ainstable in Cumberland, so ordered that *'I would have ye fishing let for what can be got for it.'* He examined the rental of both his Cumberland and Northumberland estates and calculated exactly how much he had received, how much was still due, and how much he could expect to receive during the coming year. In 1700 the flyleaf of his household book is covered with annotations: they record *'Debts due to My Lord May 1 1700'*, a number of long lets, and the first instance of timber being sold to raise capital, *'Aprill 19 1700 Sold to Mr. Patrickson Mr. Russell Mr. Fawcett & Mr. Dodshon 500 trees at Castlecaroke for one Thousand Pound, to be paid for 3 yeares'*. On 22 July 1700 a sum of £385 1s. was *'pd. yt. is sent to my Lord at Henderskelfe'*.[47] He needed it.

Any money that Lord Carlisle received from his agents was recorded by him against the date, in his unchangingly neat, slightly spidery handwriting, with its distinctive backward loops. Twice a year, usually at midsummer and Christmas, he would work out how much he had received *in toto*, how much money he had given to Elstob, his Yorkshire steward, *'for ye use of ye Building'*,[48] how much had been *'Disbursed as it appears by my book of private expenses in ye same time'*, how much had been spent by his stewards in both ordinary and extraordinary expenditure, thereby providing himself and us with global figures for both income and expenditure.[49] Fig. 2 provides a breakdown of figures for those years for

FIG. 2    Sources of the third Earl of Carlisle's income 1700–8

|  | 1700 | 1701 | 1703/4 | 1705/6 | 1707/8 | Total | % |
|---|---|---|---|---|---|---|---|
| Rents | 2432 | 3410 | 4805 | 4823 | 7457 | 22927 | 59 |
| Family | 572 | 265 | 622 | 0 | 9 | 1468 | 4 |
| Office | 0 | 537 | 167 | 593 | 167 | 1464 | 4 |
| Sales | 10 | 33 | 115 | 1643 | 524 | 2325 | 6 |
| Savings loans | 546 | 1294 | 152 | 3369 | 745 | 6106 | 16 |
| Play | 175 | 204 | 876 | 0 | 1428 | 2683 | 7 |
| Other | 587 | 595 | 419 | 112 | 149 | 1862 | 4 |
| Total | 4322 | 6338 | 7156 | 10540 | 10479 | 38835 | |

which a complete set of records survives. From this it is possible to see, in some detail, how Castle Howard was paid for.

From Fig. 2 it can be seen that an average of 59 per cent of Lord Carlisle's income came via his agents from his landed estates; also, that the sums increased quite dramatically between 1700 and 1708. Unfortunately a rental for all his landholdings only survives for the year 1717. From this it is clear that the largest section, approximately two-fifths of the rental, lay in Yorkshire, in two main areas: first, scattered round Castle Howard itself, including the mill at Henderskelfe and 'A Close belonging to ye 4 Poor People' at Welburn; second, on the far side of the River Derwent round Pocklington, including land at Fangfoss, Meltonby and Millington. A second area of Lord Carlisle's landholdings was round Morpeth in Northumberland: individually, these were much more diffuse and less lucrative; however, included with them was the income from a number of collieries, at Heddon-on-the-Wall, Newbiggin, Hepscott and Stannington, as well as tolls, a fulling mill, a valuable corn mill, a bakehouse and a smith's shop. In total, the Northumberland estates provided a potential gross income of £3,740 out of £10,234, not much less than Yorkshire. Ironically, the least valuable assets are the best documented: those in Cumberland, round Carlisle and Naworth, including shops, tithes and tolls in Brampton, lime kilns in Farlam and socage in Carlisle.[50]

Comparison of these rentals for 1717 with two earlier rentals for 1699 reveals that the increase in Lord Carlisle's income was not reflected in a corresponding increase in rents. In Northumberland, rents had apparently risen quite slowly in the intervening eighteen years, with certain conspicuous exceptions, such as Longbenton, close to Newcastle, where the rent had more than doubled. The overall increase was just over 25 per cent, representing an annual increase of only about 1 per cent; leaving out Longbenton, Heddon and Newbiggin, all of which had industrial assets, the figure would look rather different; and in some cases the income had actually dropped.[51] In Cumberland, the rental for 1699 was only £1,777, which presumably omits all fines, since the total received between 1687 and 1717 was always more than that, fluctuating between a high point of £4,623 in 1694 and an all-time low of £2,066 in 1702, remaining fairly constantly below £2,500 throughout the period 1695–1712.[52] So the apparent increase in Lord Carlisle's income from land during the first decade of the eighteenth century does not seem to derive from a change in the value of land or from more efficient administration of his estates.

In 1700, the first year that Lord Carlisle had to find funds for building, the income available from his landed estates was only £2,432. It was supplemented from a variety of sources. The income from his family includes payments from his mother-in-law, Lady Essex, which may have been the residue of his wife's marriage settlement, and from Lady Mary Fenwick, his great-aunt, whom he may have helped financially at the time of the trial of her husband in 1696 and the early part of 1697. Sales did not amount to much: £5 received on 1 August 'for a hors sold' and a few things sold by Elstob. The remainder came from savings and loans, apart from £175 which was 'won at play', the first indication that gambling was to form a surprisingly large and reliable source of income, amounting to an average of 7 per cent over the years for which there are records.

This pattern repeated itself over succeeding years. The bulk of his income, on average up to 60 per cent, came from land. It was then supplemented quite substantially from the sale of horses, jewellery, a ring, diamonds and a diamond buckle, and, in one case, land, when Lord Carlisle received £335 from 'Sr William Blacket for lands sold at Stanhope'; from savings, principally 'taken out of my grandmother's strong box'; from loans, for example £1,000 'receiv'd from Mr Walters' – that is, Peter Walter, the scrivener, described by Swift in the lines 'That rogue of genuine ministerial kind, Can half the peerage by his arts bewitch, Starve twenty lords to make one scoundrel rich';[53] and from gambling, which, in 1707, provided considerable sums. On 18 July 1707 Vanbrugh wrote to the Earl of Manchester that 'My Lord Carlisle has been a good while in Towne, won Two thousand pounds of the Sharpers, and is gone downe again to lay it Out in his Building; but they are following him to Henderskelf to have their Revenge, And ten to One they get it.'[54] They may have, but in the year as a whole, the third Earl made a total profit of £2,683 from gambling, including, on 3 December 1707,

£1,000 'From Mr Dunch mony won at play', Edmund Dunch being a fellow member of the Kit-cat Club and, according to Hearne, 'a very great gamester'.[55] On average, Lord Carlisle made more from gambling than he did from his various offices, which included his long overdue salary as Gentleman of the Bedchamber, his pay as Governor of Carlisle, and occasional fees due to him as Earl Marshal, for example £60 'Receiv'd of Mr Shales in lieu of ye gold state my fee at ye Coronation'.[56]

With an average annual income of £7,767 during the first decade of the eighteenth century, Lord Carlisle was, by almost any standards, enormously wealthy; but this needs to be set into perspective. In 1641, Lawrence Stone has estimated, there were at least five families with an annual gross rental of over £13,000, which included the two family fortunes from which Chatsworth and Petworth were built. A rental of between £6,600 and £8,699 was, in 1641, not unusual among the peerage.[57] From 1670 to 1688, annual net receipts at Chatsworth consistently averaged £8,000.[58] The Duke of Somerset's annual net receipts survive for most years between 1689 and 1701 and average over £15,000 p.a., far more than Lord Carlisle could ever hope to receive.[59] Between 22 May 1702 and 22 April 1704, the Earl of Nottingham, who built Burley-on-the-Hill, received £16,279 14s. 8d. as the profits of office.[60] The personal estate of Thomas Osborne, Duke of Leeds, who built Kiveton in Yorkshire, was valued in 1699 at £41,436 9s. 10d. 'besides leases and grants, Household Goods and Furniture'.[61]

In 1696 the herald and pioneer historical demographer, Gregory King, reckoned that the average annual gross income of members of the peerage in 1688 was £2,800.[62] This has been subjected to savage criticism by Professor Geoffrey Holmes:

> King's £2,800 for the peers' gross income in 1688 is as ludicrous as the somewhat earlier figure in his notebook of £2,000 for their annual rental income. No doubt the peerage was a wealthier body a generation after 1688 than at the time of the Revolution: by 1710 three giants were topping £30,000 a year, at least four other peers were amassing between £20,000 and £30,000; over £10,000 had become perfectly commonplace. But the change inside a mere twenty years can hardly have been a massive one.[63]

Judged by these standards, the third Earl of Carlisle was not colossally rich. Compared to the other peers who were building great houses during the 1690s, he appears, if anything, slightly poorer.

The conclusion to be drawn tentatively from this survey of Lord Carlisle's sources of income is that, when he embarked on building Castle Howard in 1700, he cannot have thought that building on such a scale was going to be easy financially. He must have expected to stretch his assets to their utmost and he may have hoped to supplement his regular landed income with the profits of office. If so, Castle Howard was a high stake in the gamble for power. It was a gamble which did not pay off, because, in March 1702, when the kitchen wing was only half complete and the foundations laid of the main pile, William III fell off his horse and died. Soon afterwards, Lord Carlisle was dismissed from his post as first Lord of the Treasury. On 13 March 1703 Francis Atterbury wrote to Bishop Trelawny that 'My Lord Carlisle is, it is said, out of all.'[64] It may not have been just the loss of office that he resented, but the loss of necessary income as well.

## FINANCIAL DIFFICULTIES

Building in the early eighteenth century was a notoriously unpredictable activity in terms of cost. For example, in a letter written to his brothers in case he died before completing Burley-on-the-Hill, Lord Nottingham wrote that it 'may cost £15,000'.[65] In the event, he spent a total of about £80,000, including the colonnade, court, stables, gate and ironwork, dog-kennels, gardens, wooden rails and gates. In 1701 he wrote sourly to his neighbour, Lord Normanby, that he was engaged in building 'which is a pleasure your lordship will not envy me when once you have tried it.'[66] Viscount Lonsdale, following the experience of building Lowther Castle, wrote to his son to say:

In Buildings it is advisable to perform them by contract since the charge would be Endlesse if you should trust to the consciences off Artificers in performing their Days Work. But ffor the same reason you must be carefull never to trust to them the Providing certain Materialls as Lime Lead Timber or Iron, for they will so slenderlie Provide these Principall Parts off Building, that you may perhaps see your Buildings ruinous as soon as raised if trusted to them.[67]

At Chatsworth, Wren advised the Duke of Devonshire that the local workmen were 'scarce to be trusted',[68] and at Dyrham, where a new east front was constructed in 1700 to a design by Talman, William Blathwayt wrote that 'These People want stirring up roundly and not to be overfed with money'.[69]

At Castle Howard, as the scale of the building operation increased, so too did the cost. In the half year between Lady Day and Michaelmas 1703 Lord Carlisle spent a total of £1,759 0s. 1d. on building, which included sums of £590 paid to the masons, £109 to John Milburn the carpenter, £87 for ironwork and £86 for lead, £124 for coal and £117 for quarrying and carting the stone.[70] In the following half year, from Michaelmas to Lady Day, the figure dropped to £1,182 19s., since, in the winter months, there was inevitably less activity, when the stone had to be covered against frost and rain. Even so, if this figure is compared to the nearest half year for which the figure for income exists, from Midsummer to Christmas 1703, Lord Carlisle spent £1,182 19s. out of a net income of £3,506 18s. 11d., or 33.7 per cent. Fig. 3 gives figures for succeeding years, which demonstrate that Lord Carlisle generally spent a third of his income on building, and that in 1704 the proportion rose to nearly half. If these figures are then set alongside a comparable set which survive for the Duke of Somerset's expenditure on building Petworth, it will be seen that Lord Carlisle was spending more than he was likely to be able, at least easily, to afford.

The cost of building Castle Howard should not be seen in isolation from Lord Carlisle's other expenditure. Just as he had grandiose ideas about building, he was extravagant in his other requirements. In January 1704 his purchases in London included two pairs of boots, five quarts of brandy, half a hogshead of Canary, a pair of buckskin breeches for the postilion, six neckcloths, six pounds of chocolate, two pounds of tea, thirty-one and a half yards of stuff for window curtains, more buckskin breeches for the coachman and silver dishes costing £47 from Mr Morgan. In February he acquired two teapots, three china cups, two fine basins, a hogshead of wine, and ninety-seven yards of damask. In March he bought two gallons of brandy, damask table linen, maps and gloves; in April three pictures from Mr Hassell, a suit, two beds, more damask for napkins, besides seeds and plants from Mr London; in May, a set of china, livery lace, gloves and stockings, pearls for his buttonholes, two picture frames, twelve dozen oranges and lemons, two bells sent to Henderskelfe, and glasses bought from Mr Lewin for £15.[71] In the early part of 1705, when the cost of building must have been alarming, he spent money on different types of tea, both bohea and Imperial, on shagreen and silk buttons, on asses' milk, grapes, and both white and blue figs, on twelve quires of gilt paper, so-called '*Vermagelly*', two bottles of orange-flower water, and more silver from Mr Morgan.[72]

A further idea of Lord Carlisle's general wants and needs is provided by the letters he wrote from Yorkshire to Nevill Ridley, who, during the first decade of the eighteenth century, acted as his steward in London. Although the year is not given in any of these letters, they can be dated from internal evidence to 1704–9, that is, when expenditure on building was at its peak. These letters include the

FIG. 3   A) The third Earl of Carlisle's income and building expenditure 1703–9 (calculated half yearly)

| Year | Income | Expenditure | % |
|---|---|---|---|
| 1703 Midsummer | – | 1759 | – |
| Christmas | 3506 | 1182 | 33.7 |
| 1704 Midsummer | 3650 | 1657 | 45.4 |
| Christmas | – | 1171 | – |
| 1705 Midsummer | – | 1880 | – |
| Christmas | 4990 | 1788 | 35.8 |
| 1706 Midsummer | 5550 | 1527 | 27.5 |
| Christmas | 4758 | 1734 | 36.4 |
| 1707 Midsummer | – | 1855 | – |
| Christmas | 5017 | 1264 | 25.2 |
| 1708 Midsummer | 5462 | 1954 | 35.8 |
| Christmas | 4594 | 1322 | 28.8 |
| 1709 Midsummer | 4648 | 1146 | 24.6 |
| Christmas | – | 1354 | – |

Total building expenditure 1703–9 £21593
Average annual building expenditure 1703–9 £3084
Average % income 32.2

B) The seventh Duke of Somerset's income and building expenditure 1689–97

| Year | Income | Expenditure | % |
|---|---|---|---|
| 1689 | 21534 | 1536 | 11.5 |
| 1690 | – | 949 | – |
| 1691 | 11830 | 873 | 7.4 |
| 1692 | 13913 | 1933 | 13.9 |
| 1693 | 15196 | 1564 | 10.3 |
| 1694 | 15433 | 1338 | 8.7 |
| 1695 | 16201 | 679 | 4.2 |
| 1696 | 13670 | 570 | 4.2 |
| 1697 | 16746 | 797 | 4.8 |

Total building expenditure 1689–97 £10239
Average annual building expenditure 1689–97 £1137
Average % of income 8.2

Sources: C.H.J8/3/1; P.H.A.243

order to '*Mr Morgan to make me two silver dishes*', for '*good pickled herrings & smoaked salmon*' to be sent from Holland and a note of appreciation for '*ye Indian Pictures & ye pistols*' which had been sent, as well as oysters. In one letter he wrote,

*I would have you send me down some choice figs, if any be come over. There used to be good ones at ye Italians in Suffolk Street & I would have 4 or 5 pounds of ye french raisins, which are dryed grapes, sent me, not green ones, as you sent down before, but such as I used to have for desert.*

In another letter he wanted '*a handsome summer druget for a coat, & a pritty fashionable dammask silk for waistcoat & britches*'. He needed a new cook and would have liked the one '*yt served my Ld. Jersey in ye late King's time*'. He could not find a good baker in Yorkshire, so proposed that one should be sent down along with '*ye cidrato*'. He asked for Mr Ellis, the periwig-maker, to be paid for two bob periwigs, and for Mrs Robinson to bring '*more figs, & a little quantyty of Parmasen cheese, if any good is to be had*'. He ordered a handsome walking cane and large quantities of tea and wine, including '*six dozen of pints of ye best canary*' and '*some extraordinary good rich Florence, or some very good Burgundy, of ye strongest or any other rich good wine*'. He particularly commended the '*chocolate from Mr. Bull's in Ludgate Hill*' and the '*green tea from Mr. Contarelle's*'.[73]

It was hardly surprising that, when great expenditure on building was allied to an undiminishing appetite for trifles only obtainable in particular shops in London, Lord Carlisle began to find that his expenditure exceeded his income. From Midsummer 1704 he was in debt, to begin with for only £188, but increasing in the next half year to £489, reaching, in the first half of 1705, a sizeable discrepancy between an income of £1,866 3s. 11d. and expenditure of £3,206 5s. 6d.[74] Clearly this state of affairs could not continue.

Although Lord Carlisle's letters to Nevill Ridley have been quoted to give an impression of extravagance, this did not mean that he was altogether improvident. In fact, he was rather the opposite. The impression of expensive personal tastes is exactly counterbalanced by tight fiscal administration and control, qualities which are not as incompatible as they might at first appear. The desire for ostentation required brinkmanship in the exploitation of funds.

As has already been seen, the years between 1704 and 1706 saw the greatest number of sales and loans. The fact is reflected in the correspondence to Ridley. Lord Carlisle writes to remind Lord Hartingdon, *of ye summ he owes me, I have told him at Christmas I shall have occasion for it, & do then expect it, & you are then to attend him for it. I wou'd have you take ye mony I have directed of Mr. Walters, & let Coll. Seymour know, yt my occasions do require it, therefore I hope he will let me have £500 at Christmas. when you have received this mony, you will regulate ye old bills (as you think fit,) & clear them off.*[75]

In another letter he writes,

*I will not enter into any other engagements to Mr. Thornhill, nor lay down ye mony due from Mr. Lovel, unless I have his security assigned over to me. I do not see what Mr. May can doe, unless what I adviced by my last. You will find in my library a little black box with writings relateing to ye purchase of Ramscope Tyth, I think it is in one of ye low places, yt opens with ye pannel next ye window on ye left hand. I would have you give it to Mr. Ward to bring down to me. You will send down by Mr. Simpson his bills, corrected by Mr. Walters.*[76]

He asks for a valuation of his jewels and, when he hears that there is difficulty in settling Mr Armeger's account for wine, he recommends that Ridley should '*dispose of ye great buckle, & ye other loose stones*'.[77] He leases out the colliery at Netherton and acknowledges '*ye inconveniences I put you to supply my occasions with mony, & as it is but reasonable I will allow you interest for all ye money you advance*'.[78] He reports that

*my Tenants failing me in Northumberland, has put me to some inconvenience & under ye necessity of being supply'd with £500 which I desire Mr. Walters will let me have upon my bond, for which I will allow him six per cent. I think I shall repay him at Mich. or otherwise I may have occasion for more to perfect this new Purchase I am about, & then it shall be put upon a land security.*[79]

Lord Carlisle was evidently manipulating his assets and using them to their utmost capacity.

At one point it looked as if Lord Carlisle would have to adopt the rather more desperate expedient of leasing his house in Soho Square and retreating to Yorkshire; this did not prevent him attempting, as with the masons, to drive a hard bargain. He first mentions the matter to Ridley as follows:

*I have thoughts of staying in ye Country for three or four years, therefore should be willing to let my hous in Town for three, or five years if I could meet with a good chapman. £300 per. ann. is what I shall hold it at, & you may make enquiry,*

FIG. 4   The third Earl of Carlisle's building expenditure 1703–10

☐ Building   ▨ Masons   ■ Craftsmen

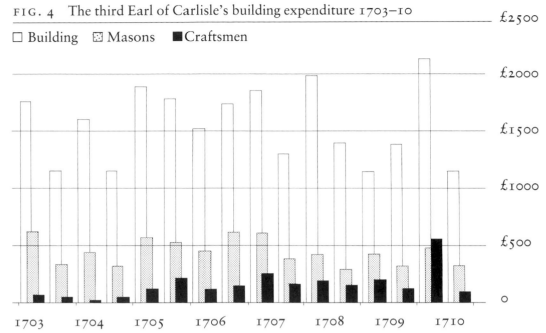

*Charge, and Expence*.[85] Although Vanbrugh is generally believed, from the appearance of his buildings, to have been a grossly wasteful architect, sparing no thought for cost in the aggregation of stone, his letters to the Duke and Duchess of Marlborough concerning the building of Blenheim suggest that he was much more interested in making the most of available resources than anyone, including the Duke and Duchess, has thought. In a letter to the Duke of Marlborough dated 8 July 1708 Vanbrugh gives a clear definition of his duties as an architect:

*Tis most certain the good Husbandry of the Money in the Most Essential and Significant part, lys as entirely upon the Surveyor, as the Designing of the Building: All that comes in the Way of a Comptroller, or a Clark of the Works is to See, That the Prices are right, And that there is no more work allowd for than is done: And with the first of these, the Surveyor is chiefly intrusted, the Comptroller being only an Assistant to him writ So that in this part of the good Husbandry I am at least of Equall Service with those joind with me, But in the great Article of Management, they have no sort of Concern Which is in so casting things in the Execution of the Building, And disposing the Materialls that nothing may be Superfluous, or Improperly Apply'd; But that the Appearance of every thing may exceed the Cost: Tis upon this that a Surveyor is to be reckond frugall or Lavish.[86]*

However, although there is evidence that Vanbrugh continued to travel to Yorkshire in order to inspect the progress of work, although he accepted responsibility, as well as taking the credit, for what was being built, he was not there often enough to 'haunt the Building like a Ghost, from the Time the Workmen leave off at Six a Clock, till tis quite Dark'.[87] Instead, there is no reason to doubt Vanbrugh's own statement that it was Lord Carlisle himself who 'has during the whole Course of his Building managed all that part himself, with the greatest care'.[88] It was Lord Carlisle himself who entered into his notebooks the exact sums he had 'Disbursed upon account of ye building', who calculated exactly how much had been spent every half year and, throughout his life, kept a running total of the cost.[89] It was Lord Carlisle who inspected all the bills and annotated them where necessary. More than Vanbrugh, it is Lord Carlisle himself who is likely to have haunted the building while it was dusk and watched over the annual progress of the shell, making sure that the workmen were following instructions and everything was proceeding according to plan.

Once it is acknowledged that both Vanbrugh and Lord Carlisle were extremely anxious about the cost of materials and how to extend and capitalize finite resources – how, in Vanbrugh's own words, to ensure 'that the Appearance of every thing may exceed the Cost' – it becomes quite possible to adjust one's perception of the building as it was being completed. The ground plan, instead of being regarded just as a way of organizing space and contriving a visual experience, can be seen as a way of allowing the building to progress by stages, so that each part, or unit, could be completed before moving on to the next (Fig. 1). The rough surfaces of the stone in the servants' quarters suggest, not so much a taste for Palladian plainness, as a way of using 'a great Quantity of Stone, which neither for the Size nor Quality is capable of being used in the Principle parts of the House'.[90] The way that the outbuildings were brought into the architectural effect of the whole was justified by Vanbrugh at Blenheim on the grounds that they 'Form a Court, which by this means Adds to the Magnificence of the Dwelling, but not to the Quantity of it'.[91] In the light of knowledge of Lord Carlisle's financial circumstances, the extent to which the main pile of Castle Howard is a surface skin, in which all the sculptural effect is concentrated only on those parts which are immediately visible, and the way that the ground plan is arranged to create an immediate dramatic impression upon the arriving spectator, begin to be seen in terms of a taste for extravagance and display financed by an income which could not easily afford it.

## ECONOMIC IMPLICATIONS

Economic historians have not, on the whole, been interested in country-house building because it involves a restricted clientele, is a highly specific activity without implications for broader consumer demands, and consists of a relatively unchanging, traditional technology. They have concentrated their minds instead on the more obviously productive and supposedly progressive aspects of the eighteenth century – the second half of the century rather than the first, statistics of growth rather than patterns of behaviour, the metalwork and textile industries rather than the luxury and building trades, the origins of a mass market rather than changes in the habits of consumption of a restricted social elite.

One of the few economic historians who did consider the implications of country-house building was the late M. W. Flinn, who wrote in a short text, *Origins of the Industrial Revolution*, as follows:

> Since so much of the surplus income above normal consumption was concentrated in the landed class, changes in the habits of consumption of this class would have a significant effect on their savings. It was a characteristic of this class to spend a high proportion of its income above what was required for current consumption on building stately homes . . . The chronology of trends in investment in stately homes may therefore have some relevance for the freeing of capital for more productive uses.[92]

Flinn speculated that country houses tied up capital which might have been devoted more profitably to other forms of investment.

This tendency to regard country houses as an uneconomic form of investment, a way of buying status in the countryside and thereby removing merchants and capitalists from the more active sector of the economy, has been reinforced by the publication of Lawrence and Jeanne Fawtier Stone's massive study of the pattern of country-house building, *An Open Élite? England 1540–1880*.[93] The Stones argue for a polarity in the upper echelons of English society with a rural elite of patricians, secure in their country houses, commanding access to political power and patronage, and continuously replicating themselves through three centuries, while the industrial entrepreneurs were excluded. They examine the mobility of English society (or rather the lack of it) on the basis of changes in the ownership of country houses in three counties, Hertfordshire, Northamptonshire and Northumberland. Even if merchants did penetrate this elite, then it is assumed that it was an unproductive way of using capital, buying social status instead of reinvesting.

There are several reasons for wishing to adjust this view of country-house building as a massively unproductive way of sinking capital. It is important to acknowledge that, by comparison, say, with the organization of the early eighteenth-century textile or metalwork trades, the building of Castle Howard was a very large-scale activity, involving a complex organization of labour and the supply of materials from distant markets. Vanbrugh's letter to Tonson in the summer of 1703 in which he records that nearly 200 men were at work gives some idea of the scale of the operation.[94]

The people who are remembered in connection with the building of Castle Howard are the architects, the aristocrats of the building process, commanding the operation, drawing up contracts, watching over the quality of workmanship and specifying in detail how the house was to be built; yet many others were involved as well. Underneath the architects was William Etty, who was more continuously available for consultation and inspection of the progress of work. In March 1703, for example, he travelled to London, presumably to consult with Vanbrugh and Hawksmoor.[95] Next in the hierarchy were the skilled specialists, like the French Huguenots who travelled from country house to country house practising a particular trade. Then there were the masons. But there were numerous other workmen as well, who needed to be recruited. There was the carpenter, John Milburn, the glazier, Lawrence Dickinson, the unnamed smith and the roper. There were the lime burners, who operated the lime kilns, like Simon Bradley from the local village of Ganthorpe, paid in 1706 *'for making a New Lime Kiln'*.[96] There were the woodcutters and quarrymen. There were the carters who were responsible for transporting supplies, stone from the quarries, wood from Bridlington and lead from York. There were the wheelwrights who made the barrows to carry the stone. There were the three men of Bulmer, who, in June 1703, were paid £5 for bringing 100,000 bricks from Bulmer.[97] There was *'ye Naile man for nailes'*, Mr Wood who supplied a gavelock and hammer, and Roger Bradley who was paid for cramps. There were the innumerable labourers, named and unnamed, who were required for the more mundane task of digging and moving earth. All these had to be organized, supervised, disciplined and paid. A great building was, compared to other industrial operations in the early eighteenth century, an exceptionally complicated activity, requiring considerable specialization of skills and an abundant supply of labour.

Two recent trends in historiography make it possible to view the country house as an active factor in the economy, rather than just a vast drain on productive investment. The first of these trends is the movement away from a teleological description of the process of industrialization, the realization of the continuing vitality and importance of craft industries in the nineteenth century, the recognition of the relatively minor role of mechanization in the late eighteenth century, and the rediscovery of the multiple roots of industrialization in defining what, for better or worse, has become known as proto-industrialization.[98] The second of these trends is a shift from a concentration on the mechanism of production towards an examination of patterns of consumption.[99]

By now it should be clear that the building of Castle Howard was not a static, conventional or straightforward operation. It made heavy demands on skilled labour. It required the frequent movement of goods by coastal shipping, so that, for example, Ridley in London had to pay *'boat hire to ye Custom house, Sufferance, Wharfinger, porters and Cart for ye goods going to Henderskelfe'*.[100] Glass might come from Newcastle or London, deal planks from Bridlington, shipped from Norway; locks were supplied by Mr Bayly of Malton or, by an agreement dated 12 January 1710, by the King's Blacksmith, Josiah Kay.[101] The whole network of skilled craftsmen who were such a feature of the early eighteenth century, particularly in London, the coachmakers, glovemakers, silkweavers, tailors, clockmakers and jewellers, all required clients to survive, clients who would appreciate and could afford the display of skill in luxury goods.

Once it is acknowledged that units of small-scale production linked by national markets are of great interest and importance in the eighteenth century, then the patterns of expenditure established by the aristocracy and the role of fashion and social emulation in causing these patterns to be replicated becomes a subject of considerable historical significance. Sufficient evidence has been presented concerning the building of Castle Howard to indicate the part that fashion played in it, the recognition of the different skills that were available locally and in London, and the movement of luxury tastes into the countryside. This was the feature of the building of Castle Howard which Thomas Frankland recognized when he wrote to Thomas Worsley that he was *'glad to hear Lord Carlisle intends to build his house, for laying out so much money must needs be an advantage to the country'*.[102]

Certainly, building Castle Howard had dynamic repercussions on the spending habits of the local aristocracy and gentry, many of whom made substantial improvements to old houses or constructed new ones in the years between 1710 and 1730, thereby establishing York as a Mecca of luxury trades and metropolitan culture in the north. For example, at Bramham, the other side of York, Robert Benson, the son of a prosperous attorney, and MP for York until raised to the peerage as Lord Bingley in 1713, was building a large house in the first decade of the eighteenth century, possibly to his own designs.[103] At Duncombe, near to Castle Howard, Charles Duncombe, a former city scrivener, built a house which was described in 1741 as '*quite a Palace, it was design'd by Sr. John Vanbrugh. The outside is in very grand Doric taste, rather heavy. The Hall is prodigious Grand, and in my opinion unexceptionably the finest Room that ever I saw.*'[104] At Beningborough, John Bourchier employed William Thornton to supervise the construction of a new house completed by 1716. At Ebberston, William Thompson, MP for Scarborough, built a small seat to a design by Colen Campbell, reputedly using craftsmen from Castle Howard. Round Beverley in the East Riding, there was a whole circle of literati and connoisseurs, many of whom were involved in building: Sir Charles Hotham, MP for Beverley and known as a classical scholar, Hugh Bethel, friend of Pope, Colonel James Moyser, who himself practised as an amateur architect, and, not least, Lord Burlington, whose main country seat was on the edge of the Wolds at Londesborough.[105] Many of this circle of gentry and peers would meet each summer at the York races; most, including Lord Carlisle, were involved in the subscription for the York Assembly Rooms; some had grand town houses for the winter season in York. Thus a pattern of competitive emulation was transferred to a more local level; or, as Vanbrugh wrote in a letter to Lord Manchester, dated 27 July 1708, '*All the World are running Mad after Building, as far as they can reach.*'[106]

This point does not need to be laboured further: competition fostered demand, while demand, in turn, created the conditions for the production of a huge range of manufactured goods. Castle Howard was not a symbol of a completely static social order, but one small cog in the vast engine of changing tastes and economic growth. Every capital and every pilaster was not just the product of a simple aesthetic decision, but of a huge, complex machinery of labour and craft skills, of national and international markets, of landholding and saving and investment, of innumerable men, besides the architect and patron, stretching out into the local and national economy.

# CHAPTER FOUR

# The Interior

## TEXTILE FURNISHINGS

The first indication of the third Earl of Carlisle's plans for the interior decoration of Castle Howard occurred on 6 May 1706 when John Vanderbank was paid a sum of £40.[1] Vanderbank was a prosperous and successful tapestry weaver who ran a large workshop in freehold premises in Great Queen Street, Covent Garden.[2] Not only was he '*His Majesty's Chief Arras Maker*' from 1689 until the time of his death in 1717, but he also supplied many of the great country houses of the period, including Boughton, where he was paid £237 10s. '*for making 2 great pieces of Elements*' in 1699, and Burghley House, Northamptonshire.

On 2 July 1706, Hawksmoor wrote to Lord Carlisle from Greenwich as follows:

*I have consider'd ye hangings in the App of State as followeth.*
*1st. That there be a Basment of Wainscot 2 foot 6 Inches or Three foot from the floor. haveing a proper molding to keep the hangings from Injury.*
*2ly. That there may be a Coveing and Small Entablement next ye Ceiling above*
*3 That ye Compartments be very considerable about ye Dores and Chimny.*

Hawksmoor then listed the proposed dimensions of the tapestries and concluded:

*These are ye Neat measures between Wood and wood, what Mr. Vanderbanc will allow on all sides for nailing, he can best judge.*
*I am able now to give you ye Measures for ye Little Roomes and the Drawing Roome by your Lps. Bedchamber if requir'd, but your Lp seemd resolved to Respite the furnishing 'em for som: time.*[3]

In 1706 the only rooms which were ready to be furnished were the third Earl of Carlisle's private apartments, so Hawksmoor must be referring to the bedchamber, the second room in the sequence along the south front, between the drawing room and the so-called little rooms. This room was described in the probate inventory of the fourth Earl of Carlisle as the second state bedchamber and, at that time, contained, as well as '*A 4 post Bedstead with Crimson Flowers & silver Tissue Ground*', '*4 pieces of fine Tapestry Hangings Tartary & Chinese Figures*'.[4] These were the tapestries which were so much admired by John Tracy Atkyns on the occasion of his visit in 1732, when he described it as having '*a very beautiful mixture of colours, Chinese men & women in variety of postures all sorts of birds, beasts & fish, more I believe than the voluminous Ogilby has collected together in his travels*';[5] and the Countess of Oxford, who visited Castle Howard in April 1745, described the room as being furnished with '*Green Damask and Tapestry of Chinese figures which is extreemly pritty*'.[6] The specialist carpenter, Mr Sabyn, was paid '*ffor Plaine deale Worke behind ye hangings*';[7] and Vanderbank received a further payment of £30 on 12 June 1707.[8]

The centre rooms on the garden façade began to be fitted out in 1708. On 26 November 1708 an agreement was made '*betwixt the Right Hoble my Lord Carlisle on the one part and Will. Thornton on the other that the Said Will Thornton shall Wainscott the Rooms Calld Sallown dining roome and Anty Roome*'.[9] William Thornton was a successful local carpenter and joiner, who, like William Etty, was subsequently to turn his hand to architecture. The rooms referred to were the three central rooms on the garden façade, the great state rooms (*Fig. 1*). The work was completed by 14 August 1711 when it was measured up.[10]

Three other rooms on the ground floor, according to the later inventory, also contained tapestry hangings.[11] The room immediately west of the saloon, called the ante-room in the accounts, was described in the inventory as the Tapestry Drawing Room. According to John Tracy Atkyns:

*in the next Room to [the Hall] are some of the most beautiful hangings that I ever saw done by Vanderbank. The imagination of the artist in tapestry, is equal to the imagination of the poet, for Thompson in his Seasons, has not more lively descriptions than are express'd in the rural landscapes here.*[12]

This refers to the Vanderbank tapestries of the Seasons, which were subsequently moved (as is clear from the way that they were altered) to the room to the west, described in the inventory as the state bedchamber. Confusingly the state bedchamber was subsequently also known, when it ceased to be a bedchamber, as the tapestry drawing room. At the time of the inventory it contained '*5 Pieces of Brussels Tapestry Hanging & 5 red Canvas case curtains*'. Beyond the state bedchamber, the state dressing room also contained '*4 Pieces of Tapestry Hangings a Roman Story with 4 red Canvas case Curtains & Rods*'. Vanderbank was paid

£144 17s 6d. on 6 May 1709, £20 on 6 February 1710, £20 on 5 April 1710, £20 on 12 May 1710, £60 on 13 March 1712, and £12 2s. 8d. *'to Mr. Vanderbang for ye Ladys'* on 2 May 1712.[13]

Other textile furnishings were obtained either direct from the London mercers, who specialized in the supply of silks, velvets and brocades and had shops in Cheapside, Covent Garden and, most of all, on Ludgate Hill; or in made-up form from an upholsterer. The upholsterers were the most significant figures in the London furniture trade, responsible for the fitting up of interiors. In the middle of the eighteenth century, it was said that the upholsterer *'makes up most of the furniture of a dwelling-house, and puts it up, especially the beds, hangings and curtains, and employs a great many tradesmen, as the cabinet-maker, skreen-maker, chair-carver, glass-grinder, and frame-maker'*.[14] On 28 April 1709 a payment of £20 was made to '*Mr Hebbert uppolsterer in full p acq:*'. This is likely to have been John Hibbert, a successful upholsterer who traded in Bartholomew Close, Little Britain, behind St Bartholomew's Hospital, and who at his death in 1717 was said to be worth £100,000.[15] But the principal supplier of the rich silk damasks and velvets which lent surface richness to the interiors of Castle Howard was a Huguenot, Remy George, also based in Bartholomew Close, who had supplied fabrics to Boughton.[16] On 3 April 1710 he was paid £150; on 15 February 1711 he was paid £100 for '*160 yards of Damaske*'; on 17 May 1711 he received £50 12s. 6d. for worsted damask; and on 19 October 1711 a further £100.[17]

The materials sent from London by Remy George gave the various rooms on the garden front their predominant character. The first room in Lord Carlisle's private apartments was known in a later inventory as the '*blue drawing room*' on account of the '*4 Pieces of blue Coffoy Hangings*' the '*10 Chairs Cushion Backs & Seats cover'd with blue Coffoy*' and the '*2 blue Lutestring festoon Window Curtains and Cornishes*'.[18] Caffoy, or coffoy, was a woollen velvet, akin to what in the nineteenth century became known as plush; it was cheaper than silk velvet and was often made with bolder patterns in the pile.[19] Lady Oxford described the furniture in this drawing room as of '*blue flower'd velvet*'.[20]

Beyond the drawing room was '*My Lord's Bedchamber*', with the Vanderbank tapestries and, according to Lady Oxford, green damask hangings; but she is likely to have confused this in her memory with one of the dressing rooms beyond, because, in the fourth Earl's probate inventory, the bedroom is described as having '*2 Crimson Silk Damask festoon Window Curtains & Cornishes*' to match the bed which likewise had '*Crimson Flowers & silver Tissue Ground*'.[21] Silk damask was the richest and most expensive of all possible hangings, often imported from

Genoa or Lyons, and so appropriate for the bedchamber, which was the most important, because the most intimate, room of the set; the silver tissue ground of the fabric on the bed is an added sign of luxury. It is not known who supplied the bed, but it is likely to have been of the colossally ostentatious mode favoured at the time, covered in cascades of material and the Cadillac of the early eighteenth-century interior.[22]

Beyond the bedchamber were two dressing rooms. The first was described in the inventory as the '*India paper Dressing Room*', on account of the India paper hangings, long rolls of imported wallpaper which were first pasted on canvas-lined wooden stretchers, then fixed to the wall;[23] but it also contained '*2 Crimson Lutestring festoon Window Curtains*', '*a Wainscot dressing Table with a Crimson Lutestring Cover laced*', and '*4 Mahogany French Chairs cover'd with Crimson flower'd & Silver Tissue Ground Velvet & Crimson Serge cases*'.[24] Lutestring, or lustring, was a light crisp silk with a bright, glossy sheen, obtained by stretching the material over a brazier and smearing it with gum. It was supplied by the Royal Lustring Company, which was incorporated by Act of Parliament in 1698 and had a monopoly on its manufacture. The other dressing room was furnished with '*Green silk damask Hangings compleat*' and '*2 Elbow dressing Chairs cover'd with Green Velvet*'.

The room at the end of this sequence, described in the building accounts as '*My Lord's Grand Cabinet*' and in the inventory as the '*East End Room or Gallery*', was said to have '*8 pieces of Old Green Mohair Hangings very bad*'.[25] Mohair was a fine worsted material made from the wool of the Angora goat, which was imported at vast expense by the Turkey Company.

By examining the materials used in this set of apartments, it is possible to reconstruct something of the way the room sequence was articulated by different types and richness of fabric. Given the smallness of the rooms and the quantity of furniture they were to contain, they must have been oppressive in their immensely ornate *haut luxe*, with great swathes of shiny fabric and highly coloured silk covering every surface.

In the matching set of state apartments at the other end of the garden façade, the first room of the sequence was a state drawing room. This had '*4 pieces of blue Velvet Hangings with 4 blue Canvas Case Curtains & Rods*', '*3 blue Lutestring festoon Window Curtains*', and '*11 Chairs Gilt Frames stuft Backs & Seats cover'd with blue velvet & blue Serge cases*'.[26] John Tracy Atkyns described it as *a room hung with blew velvet, in it are 14 very large silver sconces, the whole furniture of the chimney of plate: the chimney of Italian Marble after the model of Inigo Jones, festoons of Flowers, very prettily carv'd of each side.*[27]

The dominant feature of the State Bedchamber was, not surprisingly, the State Bed, which was described as being '*A 4 Post Bedstead with Crimson Velvet Furniture Gold laced and fringed with plumes of red & white Ostrich Feathers all compleat*'. The ostrich feathers at the corner were a feature of the great state beds of the period; and the fact that the velvet was gold laced rather than silver indicates its greater expense than the bed in the third Earl of Carlisle's private apartments. The fabric of the bed was matched by a counterpane of the same crimson velvet embroidered with lace, and even by the bedside carpet. There were also '*10 Mahogany French Chairs stuft Backs & Seats cover'd with Crimson flower'd Velvet trimm'd with Gold Lace & Crimson Serge Cases to all*', and the Vanderbank tapestries of the Seasons. The State Dressing Room beyond was also furnished with tapestry hangings and crimson silk damask curtains. This was the style of textile decoration which led Sir Harbottle Grimston to describe it in 1768 as '*of an old date, but exceedingly superb*'.[28]

The room at the west end of the ground floor was the Grand Cabinet, approached either through the State Dressing Room or, along the corridor, through a Waiting Room with an adjacent close-stool room in which to answer the calls of nature. The Grand Cabinet was universally admired, described by John Loveday in 1732 as '*very elegant, partly wainscotted with ye Derbysh: Marble, ye large Chimney-piece & Doorcase of ye same*'.[29] According to John Tracy Atkyns, also writing in 1732:

*The last room is what they call the Grand Cabinet, and is indeed a very elegant room, there are two domes in it, one at each end, the butler told me the painting upon the cieling was the story of Aminadal & Dina, I puzzl'd my brain for a considerable time, and upon a narrow inspection discover'd it to be Endimion & Diana, all the doors and windows are of Derbyshire marble, there are my Lord's three daughters in one picture my Lady Irwin my Lady Lechmere and Lady Mary Howard. The furniture is crimson velvet.*[30]

The ceilings were, according to Lord Oxford,[31] painted by Mr Harvey, that is, Jean Hervé, elder brother of Daniel Hervé, who had continued to do a considerable amount of gilding and ornamental carving. The picture of the three Howard sisters was a *jeu d'esprit* by Pellegrini.

The Grand Cabinet completed the sequence of main rooms all of which lay in a line alone the south front. It should by now be evident that they were indeed as Sir Harbottle Grimston called them, exceedingly superb. Compared to the rooms that survive from the period of William III's reign at Dyrham or Chatsworth, for example, the rooms at Castle Howard appear to have been, if possible, more brazenly ostentatious, combining the richness of texture provided by tapestry and damask with the more architectural feel of gilt furniture and Derbyshire marble, in rooms which were not sufficiently spacious to contain them completely effectively.

## PAINTED DECORATION

Several members of the late seventeenth-century peerage were genuinely interested in and knowledgeable about paintings, haunting the auctions of Covent Garden and assiduously accumulating works of art while abroad on the Grand Tour or as ambassadors in foreign capitals.[32] Thus, for example, Robert Spencer, second Earl of Sunderland, added a number of pictures of exceptional interest, including Holbein's *Henry VIII*, now in the Thyssen collection, Rubens's *David Sacrificing before the Ark*, now in the National Gallery at Washington DC, Bourdon's *Deposition* and Lebrun's *The Martyrdom of St Andrew*, to the collection of paintings which he had inherited at Althorp.[33] John Cecil, fifth Earl of Exeter, spent much of his life abroad collecting paintings, particularly in the 1690s, when he was out of favour politically. As Sir John Perceval wrote of Burghley House,

*Without it is finely addorn'd wth. towers & Statues, but within it is much finer, being furnish'd wth. multitudes of pictures & Statues done by the finest hands in Italy & brought over at Severall times by the Late Ld. Exeter, who was extream curious this way, & at a great charge in procuring them.*[34]

Thomas Herbert, eighth Earl of Pembroke, assembled a remarkable collection of coins, medals and statuary at Wilton House, and pictures, which he deliberately purchased on grounds of historical interest.[35] Even the Duke of Marlborough seems to have been genuinely interested in paintings and in the way that Blenheim was furnished. By November 1706 the Duke had begun to acquire paintings for the proposed gallery at Blenheim, including Van Dyck's King Charles I on horseback. In May 1708 he wrote to the Duchess that he had been to see the Brussels hangings that he had commissioned and that '*you would direct Vanbrook*

94

*to finish the breaks between the windows in the great cabinett with looking glasses, for I am resolved to furnish that roome with the finest pictures I can gett'.*[36]

The third Earl of Carlisle, by contrast, appears to have lacked much interest in, or appreciation of, works of art. Lord Carlisle's principal commissions in the first decade of the eighteenth century were to Michael Dahl, the conventional and unremarkable Swedish artist, who on 25 May 1700 was paid £10 15s. *'for my Lady's picture'*, and on 26 June 1703 £5 7s. 6d.[37] He also employed William Hassel, an extremely obscure landscape painter, to *'make a picture for over ye chimney in my withdrawing room in ye room of ye flower peice'*.[38] On 21 May 1705 Hassel was paid £5, on 13 June £3 12s. *'the Remd. for the 4 piktures'*, and in May 1707 a further £1 1s. 6d.[39] The nearest Lord Carlisle comes to expressing an interest in pictures is in one of his letters to his agent, Nevill Ridley, concerning the possible letting of his London house, in which he writes,

*I will leave all ye Pictures over ye doors, & chimneys except ye Pictures, which my wife desires, which must be sent to her, & ye Picture over my withdrawing room chimney below I mean ye flower Peice, as also ye Pictures over ye dining room chimneys above, & below stairs, these are peices I value, & would have sent down with ye rest of my pictures into ye Country.*[40]

Yet in 1709 Lord Carlisle was responsible for two great acts of artistic patronage: he employed Gianantonio Pellegrini to paint the staircase walls, pendentives and dome of the great hall at Castle Howard, and Pellegrini's friend and fellow countryman, Marco Ricci, to paint a series of genre scenes for the overdoors. It was agreed that Pellegrini should receive a total of £800 for his services and he received his first payment of a bill for £100 and an extra ten guineas *'when he went from Castle Howard ye first time Nov: ye 6th. 1709'*.[41] Marco Ricci, or 'Sigr. Marco' as he is described in the accounts, received his first payment of £20 from Nevill Ridley in London on 15 November 1709 and another £20 on 21 November.[42] On 20 October 1710 Lord Carlisle recorded in his own handwriting that he paid 'Sigr. Marco' *'when he went from Castle H ten guineas & a bill for fifty pounds'*.[43]

It is not, unfortunately, recorded how these two Italians had come into Lord Carlisle's orbit. The most likely way would have been through a recommendation from Vanbrugh. Since 1705 Vanbrugh had been involved in the frustrating task of attempting to introduce Italian opera to England. The foundation stone of his new theatre in the Haymarket had been laid on 18 April 1704 by the Duke of Somerset and had been built with the help of subscriptions from many members of the nobility, including Lord Carlisle who made four payments of 25 guineas *'to Mr Vanbrook . . . for his Playhous'*.[44] The theatre, which was completely unlike any previous example in England, with three tiers of seats arranged in a semicircle round an apron stage and subdivided, according to the Italian fashion, into boxes, opened on 9 April 1705 with a catastrophic performance of Giacomo Greber's pastoral opera *The Loves of Ergasto*.[45] The group of visiting Italian singers was apparently appalling, according to Downes's *Roscius Anglicanus 'the worst that e'er came from thence, for it lasted but 5 Days, and they being lik'd but indifferently by the Gentry; they in little time marcht back to their own Country'*;[46] and the acoustics of the great dome *'occasioned such an Undulation, from the Voice of many Actors, that generally what they said sounded like the Gabbling of so many People, in the lofty Isles of a Cathedral'*.[47] Vanbrugh, however, was undeterred, and, following the establishment of his monopoly over the performance of opera in January 1708, he wrote to Lord Manchester, then ambassador in Venice, to say that *'people are now eager to See Operas carry'd to a greater perfection. And in order to it the Towne crys out for A Man and Woman of the First Rate to be got against Next Winter from Italy.'*[48] Along with the great Italian singer, Nicolini, who arrived in Lord Manchester's entourage in autumn 1708 and whose first performance was in *Pyrrhus and Demetrius* on 14 December 1708,[49] came Pellegrini and Ricci. On 17 August 1708 Vanbrugh wrote to Lord Manchester, *'If the Painter yr Ldship brings over be a good one, he may find work enough.'*[50] He was right. On 30 March 1709 the *Daily Courant* announced *'an Opera call'd Pyrrhus and Demetrius. With an entire Set of new Scenes, Painted by two famous Italian Painters, (lately arriv'd from Venice)'*.[51] Among Pellegrini's first commissions were the hall and staircase of Lord Manchester's house in Arlington Street; and in 1710 he was employed at Kimbolton, Lord Manchester's country house, extensively rebuilt by Vanbrugh.[52]

Lord Carlisle's employment of Pellegrini and Ricci does not appear, therefore, as an isolated act of artistic whim, but as part of a more general vogue for things Italian – opera, scenery, art, damask and decoration – which had become a cult amongst the nobility in the first decade of the eighteenth century, and of which Vanbrugh was one of the principal instigators. Nor is this altogether surprising when Pellegrini's work in the Great Hall at Castle Howard is examined (*Plate 27*).

The dome of the hall was painted with the Fall of Phaeton and showed Phaeton dropping through the air from his chariot amidst a great swirling mass of clouds and horses' hooves, a brilliant and sophisticated *trompe l'œil* scene, painted with

PLATE 25

The overmantel in the Great Hall, probably the work of the *stuccadore*, Giovanni
Bagutti, and, beyond, Apollo and the Muses by Pellegrini.

PLATE 26

The Great Hall, demonstrating the quality of visual excitement
obtained by the immense height of the hall combined with vistas
through to the staircases.

PLATE 27

Pellegrini's Fall of
Phaeton in the dome
of the great hall,
photographed before the
fire of 1940.

great vigour and producing a strongly dynamic visual effect. It meant that the
already complicated architectural spaces of the interior of the hall, with vistas
between the great corner columns to the anterior staircase walls, were further
complicated by the sensation of air and light and movement disappearing into the
vortex of the dome.

On the pendentives immediately beneath the dome were representations of the
four elements, air, fire, earth and water (*Plate 27*). These followed the conventional
formulae, as established by Cesare Ripa, a version of whose *Iconologia: or, Moral
Emblems*, was published in 1709.[53] Air is shown as a handsome Juno clutching a
peacock and straddling a cloud, with, beneath, a cluster of appropriate emblems,
including a star and trumpet. Earth is shown as a big-busted female with, in one
hand, a cornucopia of fruit and flowers and, in the other, a globe. Fire is shown
clutching a flaming vase. And Water is resting against a large upturned urn from
which her element flows.

On the staircase walls there were subsidiary scenes depicting Apollo and the
Muses on one side (*Plate 25*) and Apollo and Midas on the other. In lunettes on

the staircase walls there were further, smaller illustrations of the continents and river gods. Together these works represented, until they were burned during a disastrous fire in 1940, a remarkable *tour de force* of vivid and fluent mural decoration, full of visual excitement and entertainment. As Tancred Borenius wrote in 1931, they were 'extraordinarily well suited to the architectural setting, and forming with it a most effective, unforgettable ensemble'.[54]

Pellegrini seems to have worked at Castle Howard during the summers of 1709, 1710, 1711 and 1712. On 30 April 1710, Nevill Ridley paid £4 for '*taking 4 places in the York Coach for the painters*' and then, on 17 May, a further £5 '*pd. in full for senior Peligrinies place in the York Coach (4 formerly pd)*'.[55] On 6 November Lord Carlisle gave him a further '*ten guineas & a bill for £300 when he went from Castle H*'.[56] By 25 September 1711 he had received a total of £852 5s. Then on 21 June 1712 he was back on the York coach and received a final payment from Ridley of £40 on 25 December 1712.[57] As a result of Pellegrini's great success in painting the dome, he received two further commissions from the Earl of Carlisle. The first was to paint the ceiling of the ground floor saloon which led out from the hall. This, too, was destroyed in the fire, but originally depicted Aurora, the goddess of dawn (*Plate 28*). More importantly, Pellegrini was invited to paint the room which lay immediately above the ground-floor saloon and which was known as the High Saloon (*Plate 29*).

The decoration of the High Saloon was completely lost in the fire of 1940. It was an important part of the interior and, since it has been suggested by Alastair Laing that some of it might have been a nineteenth-century fake, it is worth trying to reconstruct it carefully from literary sources.[58] The first visitor to describe it was Edward Harley, second Earl of Oxford, who kept notes describing his visit during his tour of the north in May 1725. He wrote that it was

*painted by pelegrini, and with ornaments of stucco work with gilding this room seems very gawdy, the sides of the room as well as [the] ceiling being gilt, but the painting has in this faired better than in the other rooms because this has some sun upon it, it being to the south. The doors out of this room are of stucco work in imitation of coloured marble the door cases are four feet deep.*[59]

Then, in July 1732, John Tracy Atkyns described it in his Iter Boreale, an unpublished manuscript now in the Yale Center for British Art:

*The dining room is the only grand room above stairs, the height is about 27 foot, Pallas & Venus conferring together are painted upon the cieling, in seven*

*compartiments round the room are represented the story of the Trojan War, the 1st: is the Rape of Helen, the 2d: the discovery of Achilles by his making choice of a sword in the school of the girls, ye: 3d: the contention between Ajax & Ulisses for the armour of Achilles, the 4th: the sacrifice of Iphigenia the 5th: the town on fire. The 6th: Aeneas conveying off Anchises and leading Ascanius. The seventh the sailing of Aeneas for Italy.[60]*

Surviving photographs confirm the truth of these descriptions. On the walls were painted scenes from the life of Aeneas, including the Rape of Helen, the Sacrifice of Iphigenia, Achilles with the daughters of Lycomedes, Ajax and Ulysses contending for the armour of Achilles, the Burning of Troy, and Aeneas bearing Anchises on his back (*Plate 29*). On the ceiling were Minerva and Venus, a lively curved composition, in which amorini led the eye into the clouds where Venus perched in a scene of appropriate lightness and energy (*Plate 30*). As Tancred Borenius wrote, recording his recollections of this room immediately after the fire:

PLATE 29

The High Saloon, showing Pellegrini's Rape of Helen to the left of the door and the
flamboyant stucco overdoor by Giovanni Bagutti.

PLATE 30

Minerva and Venus by Pellegrini on the ceiling of the High Saloon.

This date – 1710 – struck one as almost incredibly early for that most remarkable series of subjects from the Trojan War, with which he decorated the walls of the room upstairs known as the High Saloon. In their brilliant luminosity of colour, these compositions gave the clearest possible anticipation of the style of Giambattista Tiepolo, Pellegrini's junior by more than twenty years; and they were throughout of the most charming happiness of invention. At times, indeed, the artist hit upon devices of truly astonishing originality; as when a very narrow strip of wall had to be decorated, and he painted on it a vista of the sea, with nothing to enliven it but a sail in the far distance.[61]

Although Pellegrini was the most significant decorative artist to be employed at Castle Howard, he was not the only one. At least on his first visit to Castle Howard, he was accompanied by his compatriot, Marco Ricci, who, like Pellegrini, was an extremely accomplished Venetian artist, but who specialized in smaller genre scenes. He was responsible for two surviving paintings, *The Rehearsal of an Opera* and *The Mall, St. James's Park*.[62] The ceiling of the Grand Cabinet was, as mentioned above, painted by the Frenchman Jean Hervé, who, according to the antiquarian George Vertue, was *'much admired for his facetious conversation, light loose & prophane'*.[63] And in 1709 an obscure Dutch artist, Jacob Campo Weyerman, who was known to be a free-thinker and subsequently became a freemason, arrived at Castle Howard in search of work. A passage of his autobiography gives a clear idea of the spirit with which these painters travelled round Europe looking for lucrative commissions:

*He travelled to York, a town provided with 28 churches and chapels and the capital of the county of the same name. However it was not the number of places of worship that brought him there but the new building of the earl of Carlisle, one of the most beautiful palaces in England. He offered his brush to the earl and was accepted at once, because he showed the earl a painted panel for a cabinet, being the last piece he had painted in Oxford. For this 'Mylord' he painted five big flower and fruit paintings, of which the biggest is still to be found over a chimney in the dining room of that palace. Besides that he painted several 'cabinet pieces', as well as some animals, birds as well as quadrupeds, all pictures being extremely well painted.*[64]

## ICONOGRAPHIC INTERPRETATION

In his first biography of Vanbrugh Professor Kerry Downes suggested that the image of Phaeton on the dome of Castle Howard might refer back to the Queen's Staircase at Windsor, where Antonio Verrio had depicted Apollo giving Phaeton permission to drive the chariot of the sun.[65] The argument was as follows.

Having worked in France and been associated with the Academy, Verrio must have been aware of the extent to which Louis XIV had, from early in his reign, identified himself with Apollo; and that this motif formed the subject of innumerable sycophantic odes and was the basis for the decoration of Versailles.[66] As a contemporary guidebook described Versailles:

*It is worth saying straight away that since the sun is the device of the king and the poets equate the sun with Apollo, there is nothing in this amazing house which is not associated with the divinity; every single figure and every ornament that you see there is not placed by accident, but has some relationship either to the Sun or to the position in which they are found.*[67]

At Versailles, sunbursts appear on doorways. Apollo is seen riding his chariot at the end of the *tapis vert*. Each of the King's Apartments was dedicated to a planet, culminating in the Throne Room, which was devoted to Apollo. The consequence of all this conscious symbolism was that any image of Apollo would necessarily have been associated with Louis XIV, the Sun King.

When, therefore, Verrio chose as subject for the Queen's Staircase at Windsor the scene of Apollo giving Phaeton permission to drive the chariot of the sun, he must have known that it would have been identified in the minds of contemporaries with autocratic monarchy and the divine right of kings. When, thirty years later, Pellegrini was invited to paint the Fall of Phaeton on the dome of Castle Howard, it could be concluded that contemporaries would have seen it as an image of the collapse of such ambitions, of the detestation of the English for French forms of government and a celebration of the individual liberty established by the Glorious Revolution. As Professor Downes has suggested,

At Windsor the corners of the ceiling were painted with figures representing the Four Elements and the roof of the lantern with Phaeton taking the chariot of the sun; at Castle Howard the Elements would be painted in the pendentives and the dome would show the scene of Phaeton's subsequent fall from heaven. Thus an architectural borrowing is turned into a political comment on the presumption of the absolutist monarchy of Charles II and James II.[68]

I am sceptical of this interpretation.[69] It is true that there was a well-established tendency to read the legend of Phaeton in terms of hubris. George Sandys, in the most commonly available seventeenth-century translation of Ovid's *Metamorphoses*, commented that, '*This fable to the life presents a rash and ambitious Prince, inflamed with desire of glory and dominion: who in that too powerfull, attempts what so ever is above his power; and gives no limits to his ruining ambition.*'[70] During the Civil War a translation of the second book only, described as *Phaeton's Folly, or, the Downfal of Pride*, was used as a vehicle for a political tract.

*This fable sets forth to the life, the Nature of rash, ambitious, inconsiderate Rulers, who being inflamed with a desire of Government, aim at things above their reach, to their own ruin and downfall. Many rash, young Phaetons who want experience, take upon them the ruin of Commonwealths, yet cannot rule themselves; will teach others when they themselves had need to be taught; and will needs be Governours of others, when yet they cannot govern themselves: Let these Phaetons remember Phaeton.*[71]

By 1699 the legend of Phaeton was being used as a metaphor for the Civil War. Denzil Lord Holles, in his *Memoirs* published in that year, described how it was '*altogether impossible ever to obtain a Peace, whilst there were Rulers, who Phaeton like, were able to set the whole World on fire*'.[72] The problem with this form of interpretation is that what applies to Pellegrini must apply to Verrio. It is highly unlikely that Verrio did not know that, after being given permission to drive the chariot of the sun, Phaeton fell to earth. If the legend of Phaeton was associated with the brief and catastrophic reign of a juvenile and overreaching prince, it is curious that Verrio represented it on the staircase at Windsor.

There is a further problem. Ralph Montagu, first Duke of Montagu, known as Montagu the Magnificent, an ardent francophile and former ambassador extraordinary to Paris, commissioned Charles de La Fosse, who had painted Apollo in his chariot in the King's Apartments at Versailles, to decorate Montagu House in Bloomsbury. In the saloon he showed Phaeton driving the chariot of the sun, preceded by Aurora; in the ante-room, he depicted Phaeton's Fall.[73] It is improbable that, in his saloon, Ralph Montagu should have demonstrated himself to be an adherent of autocratic monarchy and, in his ante-room, celebrated the collapse of James II. The Earl of Devonshire rented Montagu House while Ralph Montagu was travelling on the continent, and one of Devonshire's servants set the house on fire. There was a lawsuit. Soon after, Devonshire began to decorate *if you can meet with a Chapman for it. if it is required, it shall be ready for them at Christmas next.*[80]

Yet when he hears that the Duke of Newcastle might like it, he revises his price:

*Mr. Walter has writ to me to know, whether I would dispose of my Hous in Town, he says ye Duke of Newcastle would treat me for it. I am resolv'd not to sell it, nor am I very desirous to let it, you may let him know, yt I shall expect £400 per. an. for it unfurnish'd & ye Tenant to pay all ye taxes.*[81]

It subsequently appeared as if a foreign ambassador might take it, at which point the terms are once again adjusted:

*I am very indifferent whither I let my Hous or no, especially to a Forrainer therefore I will not take one shilling less than £500 per ann. for it, which I think, (considering ye furniture I shall leave in it, & ye Person yt is to take it), is a very reasonable demand, but whither it shall be thought so or no, yt is my price, with this ye Tenent is to pay all Parish dutys, & taxes saveing ye Parliament tax, & to keep ye Hous, & garden in sufficient, & good repayre.*[82]

Lord Carlisle managed to combine aristocratic hauteur with a total command of financial detail.

The complexity of Lord Carlisle's financial affairs and the fact that he was over-stretching his resources necessarily affected the way that Castle Howard was built. At the most obvious level, it meant that certain items of expenditure had to be deferred until funds were available. For example, Lord Carlisle wrote to Ridley that '*If Mr Vanderbank has not begun ye hangings, I would have him let them alone till I come to Town,*'[83] and on another occasion, '*Acquaint Mr. Nost ye Statuary yt I would have him defer makeing ye Statues I writ to him for till I came to Town.*'[84] More generally, financial constraints meant that the building operation as a whole had to be spaced out over a number of years. Once the building costs had reached the high point of £1,759 between Lady Day and Michaelmas 1703, they remained remarkably constant right up until 1714, twice rising over £2,000, to £2,180 in the summer of 1710 and £2,078 in the summer of 1712, and usually dipping below £1,500 in the winter, but generally fluctuating around the mean of £1,500 every half year over a period of twelve years (*Fig. 4*).

This suggests that the level of expenditure was being very carefully planned and regulated. Ultimately, it was the responsibility of the architect '*whose Business it is to consider of the whole Manner, and Method of the Building, and also the*

Chatsworth. He commissioned Louis Laguerre, who had been trained as a Jesuit and was godson to Louis XIV, to paint the Music Room ceiling. The subject was Apollo granting Phaeton leave to drive the chariot of the sun.[74] Some years later Thornhill went to Chatsworth to paint the West Front Staircase. The subject was the Fall of Phaeton.[75] So the image of Phaeton is not peculiar to Castle Howard, and any interpretation of its iconography must take account of its appearance elsewhere.

The source for the story of Phaeton was presumably Ovid's *Metamorphoses*, Book 2. Lord Carlisle possessed more editions and translations of Ovid than of any other book.[76] Sandys's translation went through innumerable editions, its muddled illustrations were repeatedly pirated, and there were various attempts to improve the text. Ovid ranked high in school curricula and poets translated individual books of the *Metamorphoses* as a literary exercise. When William Kent drew the Palace of the Sun, he wrote on the back '1st Book of Ovide';[77] by a happy coincidence, Kent's own copy of the *Metamorphoses* survives in the Cambridge University Library.[78] It is the second enlarged edition of the 1717 Garth translation. In the preface is the following passage.

*As to that Part of Description which is peculiar to this Book of Ovid's, that relates the gradual Progress, or different Manner of the Changes and Transformations of Persons, every Story in his Book is a convincing Instance of the Exactness of his Judgement. The Masters of Painting know this so well, that hardly any of them attempt a Story of his, without consulting the Poet; and some of their best pieces of this Kind, are only so far beautiful and natural, as they come near the Descriptions of Ovid. I remember that I took a great Pleasure, when I was very young, in comparing many of his Stories done by the late famous Verrio, with the Originals in the Metamorphoses.[79]*

Ovid, then, was the natural, almost inevitable, source to turn to. At the beginning of Book 2 Phaeton, wishing to prove his paternity, visits Apollo in the Palace of the Sun. It is one of the great set pieces of literary description, elaborate, imaginative, expansive; it is easy to comprehend why it might have appealed to the builder of a palace. According to the translation by Sandys:

*Sol's loftie Palace on high Pillars rais'd,*
*Shone all with gold, and stones that flamelike blaz'd.*
*The roofe of Ivory, divinely deckt:*
*The two-leav'd silver-doores bright raies project*

*The workmanship more admiration crav'd:*
*For, curious Mulciber had there ingrav'd*
*The Land-imbracing Sea, the orbed Ground,*
*The arched Heavens, Blew Gods the billowes crown'd.*[80]

Apollo was thus surrounded by continents, seasons, signs of the zodiac and elements. Phaeton was speechless with amazement. And while he stands there, *'Aurora's splendor re-inthrones the Day'.*[81] It is a brief glimpse of the splendour of cosmology, both visual and evocative, but short-lived. Phaeton asks that he should be granted a single wish, which, once allowed, is that he should drive the chariot of the sun. Apollo cannot revoke his permission and Phaeton plunges headlong to the earth. This combination of a vision of the empyrean with the dramatic failure of human endeavour is sufficient explanation of the story's appeal, without recourse to secondary meaning. All aspects of the story are present in the Hall at Castle Howard: in the pendentives are the Elements; on the staircase are the continents; on the side walls are two scenes featuring Apollo; and, in the saloon next door, Aurora spreads the dawn. The Great Hall at Castle Howard appears as an attempt to reconstruct the Palace of the Sun, with its lofty pillars, elaborate workmanship, marble-decked, surrounded by continents and elements, presided over by Phaeton and Apollo.

Upstairs in the High Saloon, or Grand Painted Anti-Chamber as it was described in the fourth Earl of Carlisle's inventory, were scenes from the Trojan War, also from Ovid, and in the Grand Cabinet at the west end of the garden front appeared Diana and Endymion – Aminadal and Dina as the butler called them. This, too, was the natural counterpart of the great hall. Endymion lies asleep on Mount Latmos and Diana, the moon goddess, falls in love with him; she enjoys his company for a night and Jupiter condemns him to sleep forever. Just as Phaeton was able to view the heavens, so Endymion was traditionally supposed to be an astrologer who had fallen asleep through excessive contemplation of the course of the moon.[82] Just as the associations of Phaeton are with day, light and sun, so Endymion represents night, sleep and the moon.

## FURNITURE AND FITTINGS

Pellegrini's final payment of £40 was on 25 December 1712. By this time the interior decoration of Castle Howard must have been nearing completion.

In 1711 Lord Carlisle had employed two other specialist Italian craftsmen. On

10 February 1711 a payment of £25 was made to 'Mr. Bargotee Italien' and he received further equivalent sums throughout the course of the year. He was assisted by another Italian described as 'Mr. Plewra', who was given £10 15s. when he went to London in March 1712. In August 1712 they were both paid 'in full of all work done to this day', £156. Together they were paid a total of £371 17s.[83] These payments refer to the great Italian *stuccadore*, Giovanni Bagutti, and an otherwise unidentified assistant.[84]

The most important surviving work of these Italians is likely to be the brilliant overmantel in the Great Hall (*Plate 25*). This consists of two winged herms flanking one of Pellegrini's representations of a river god. The herms support two baskets of *trompe-l'œil* flowers and their tails terminate in scrolled conches and cascades of flowers, a remarkably sophisticated example of decorative plasterwork for this early date.

At the same time, it is inconceivable that the great amount of money they were paid was only for a single decorative overmantel, fine though it is. It is likely that they were also responsible for the remarkable plasterwork formerly in the high saloon and now destroyed. This consisted of fantastically elaborate ornamental door surrounds. The doorway out on to the hall gallery was draped in long swags of flowers and had unexpectedly playful scrollwork corners, which were pushed outwards to enclose military trophies, cannon and flags, which, in turn, supported a shield with the letters CC intertwined, standing for Carolus Carleolensis (*Plate 31*). On another door there was an equally, if not more, festive construction of a shield surrounded by sheaves of corn (*Plate 29*). And Pellegrini's ceiling painting of Venus and Minerva was incorporated in further plasterwork decoration, including great shells at the sides and flowers at the corners. It is disastrous that this work has been lost. According to H. Avray Tipping and Christopher Hussey who saw the work before it was destroyed:

> The stucco decorations that frame the painted panel of the ceiling will, surely, have been by the same hand as the hall chimneypiece: and that may also be said of the curiously composed and extravagantly enriched compositions that surmount the doorways and windows. They show a different decorative conception and handling to anything else at Castle Howard, and sit curiously upon the simple and massive bolection mouldings of William III type that form the door architraves.[85]

The marble door surrounds, a feature of several rooms, were the work of a Derbyshire man, John Thorpe, who came from Bakewell. He received his first

PLATE 31

The doorway leading from the High Saloon onto the balcony of the Great Hall with
decorative surrounds attributable to Giovanni Bagutti.

payment of £220 on 11 August 1711 '*upon Acct. of Marble*';[86] and he was also responsible for '*The Marble Chymney Piece in the Salloone*', which cost £23 and was measured and paid for on 9 August 1712.[87]

It remained to supply the rooms with furniture. Of all the interior decoration of Castle Howard, least is known about the furniture – what it was like and how it was supplied. The best evidence is supplied by the undated probate inventory which was prepared following the death of the fourth Earl of Carlisle.

Upstairs there were four bedrooms besides the so-called '*Grand Painted Anti-Chamber*'. They had beds of varying degrees of expense. One had '*A 4 Post Bed stead with Crimson Silk Damask Furniture fring'd & furbelow'd with Feathers at the Corners, compleat*'. Another was covered with serge, a much lighter and cheaper material, woven in Yorkshire. Adjacent to the bedchambers were closets, which in one case contained '*A Square Walnuttree Dressing Table, A Walnuttree Writing Desk, and Paper Hangings*', while another had '*A Walnut tree Beauroe & BookCase*'. The most interesting feature upstairs was that the High Saloon contained '*A Billiard Table cover'd with Green Cloth & a Leather Cover lin'd with Green Baize*', as well as '*4 Ivory Balls 12 Masks 2 Kews & a long Stick*'.

Downstairs, on the principal floor, the rooms contained a variety of furniture. In the saloon there were '*2 Sconce Glasses in Carved & Gilt Frames*', '*2 Large foreign Marble Sideboard Tables on Iron Frames with Green Baze Covers*', and two more '*Derbyshire Marble Side Board Tables on Iron Brackets*'. In the Tapestry Drawing Room next door to it there were '*2 large Pier Glasses in carv'd & Gilt Frames*', '*2 Fine Marble Tables*', '*A large Porphyry Side board Table on a carv'd & Gilt Frame with a Green Baze Cover*', as well as '*8 Mahogany French Elbow Chairs*' and '*A large India Furniture Chest on a Gilt Frame*'. In the State Drawing Room there were '*A Pair of Dogs for Wood Fires with bronz'd Metal Figur'd Fronts*', '*2 Easy Chairs*' and '*A fine Persian carpet*'. In the State Bedchamber there were two more '*large Pier Glasses in carv'd & Gilt fframes*' and '*A large Walnuttree Cloaths Chest with Drawers*'.

The other set of rooms on the garden front likewise contained richly elaborate mirrors, tables and upholstered chairs. In the dining room adjacent to the saloon were '*A scallop'd India Close Table*', '*2 Pier Glasses in carv'd & Gilt Frames*', '*2 Foreign Marble Tables on Iron Brackets*', '*2 Foreign Marble Tables on Iron Brackets*', '*A Derbyshire Marble Sideboard Table on a Walnuttree Frame*', '*2 small Wainscott Side board Tables*', '*A small Wainscott 2 Leav'd Table*', '*A small 2 Leav'd Canvas Fireskreen*', '*A Mahogany Barometer*' and '*A Month Clock ornamented with Brass Figures & Gilding on a Mahogany Bracket*', as well as

'*10 Mahogany Chairs stuff'd Seats cover'd with Red Morocco Leather & brass nail'd*'. In the blue coffoy drawing room there was a further profusion of chairs and pier glasses and marble tables, a tea table and a fire screen and a '*Muscall Carpet*'. In the end room, '*My Lord's Cabinet*', a small and narrow room, there were '*2 Walnuttree Beauroes*', '*A Walnuttree Chest of drawers*', '*4 Pier Glasses*', '*A Chimney Glass*', '*An Iron Chest*', as well as '*73 small Pieces of Painting of different Sizes & subjects all in Frames*', '*A Duck in Cast Metal*' and '*The Head & Claw of a Tyger in Allabaster which appears to have been the Leg of a Table*'.

It has become fashionable to regard eighteenth-century interior decoration as austere, as if every room were as formal and as empty as those in which the provincial artist Arthur Devis depicted his sitters. But it should be evident from the sheer physical quantity of furniture listed in this inventory that the rooms, far from being empty, with a few chairs stuck against the wall, were, on the contrary, full of different types and styles of furniture, some of it gilt, some of it walnut, and some mahogany.

Of course, it is arguable that some of this clutter was acquired by the fourth Earl of Carlisle, subsequent to the original furnishing of the house; and certainly he added the many pieces of antique statuary which are listed and some of the antique marble tables. But, even so, it is evident that the rooms cannot have been in any sense bare, when they were first furnished and occupied by the third Earl. He was surrounded by a profusion of chairs and tables and mirrors, as well as festive textiles. There is no evidence of completely unified schemes of interior decoration and, on the contrary, the furniture seems to have matched the textiles, in being full of rich surface effects and ornament. As Werner Sombart wrote in his classic monograph on *Luxury and Capitalism*:

Reading the descriptions of the city and country homes of the well-to-do in France or England, for example, as they are handed down to us by the writers of the close of the seventeenth and the beginning of the eighteenth century, we are at first inclined to believe that they exaggerate. But, eventually, by discovering an ever-increasing number of identical writings, we become aware that the luxury display in the residences of that time must, indeed, have been tremendous, even from the point of view of our own sumptuous time. We think of the remnants of splendid furniture in quaint and rococo style as we see them on sale today in antique shops; we think of individual pieces of furniture of that time as we find them in art history books, and we remember that what we now see as individual pieces, pictorial or real, once stood assembled in the halls of the marquis and of the financial baron of the ancien régime.[88]

## LIFE STYLE

On 23 October 1713 Vanbrugh was staying at Castle Howard and wrote with glee to Edward Southwell, who had succeeded his father as Secretary of State for Ireland and who was employing Vanbrugh to build a new house at King's Weston outside Bristol:

*I hope, however, at last, I shall see you as well pleased as the Lord of this place is; who has now within this week had a fair tryall of his dwelling, in what he most apprehended, which was cold. For, tho' we have now had as bitter storms as rain and wind can well compose, every room in the house is like an oven, and in corridors of 200ft. long there is not air enough in motion to stir the flame of a candle.*[89]

The letter is interesting in that it demonstrates the extent to which Vanbrugh was anxious about the domestic comfort of the houses he planned. Presumably he had grown sensitive to the criticisms of Blenheim, particularly those of the Duchess of Marlborough, that it was all very well as a palace for the purposes of ceremony and display, but not as a house for living in. He was pleased and reassured that the small rooms of the grand apartments at Castle Howard were, if not cosy, at least perfectly habitable, and that draughts were excluded by the quality of the internal fittings and the wealth of drapery.

The following week he supplemented this account in a letter to an unidentified correspondent:

*I am but lately got to Lord Carlisle's, which is now so agreeable a being, from the nature of the Place, the Works he has done, and the manner of his Living, that I shall have much ado to leave it . . . I am much pleased here (amongst other things) to find Lord Carlisle so thoroughly convinced of the Conveniencys of his new house, now he has had a years tryall of it: And I am the more pleas'd with it, because I have now a proof, that the Dutchess of Marlborough must find the same conveniency in Blenheim, if ever She comes to try it (as I still believe she will in spite of all these black Clouds). For my Lord Carlisle was pretty much under the same Apprehensions with her, about long Passages, High Rooms &c. But he finds what I told him to be true. That those Passages woud be so far from gathering &*

*drawing wind as he feared, that a Candle wou'd not flare in them of this he has lately had the proof, by bitter stormy nights in which not one Candle wanted to be put into a Lanthorn, not even in the Hall, which is as high (tho not indeed so big) as that at Blenheim. He likwise finds, that all his Rooms, with moderate fires Are Ovens, And that this Great House, do's not require above One pound of wax, and two of Tallow Candles a Night to light it, more than his house at London did Nor in Short, is he at any expence more, whatsoever than he was in the Remnant of an Old House, but three housemaids and one Man, to keep the whole house and Offices in perfect cleanliness, which is done to such a degree, that the Kitchen, and all the Offices and Passages under the Principall floor are as dry as the Drawing room: And yet there is a great deal of Company, and very good housekeeping. So that upon the whole (except the keeping of the New Gardens) the expence of living in this Great fine house, do's not amount to above a hundred pounds a year, more than was Spent in the Old one.*[90]

This idea of Vanbrugh's that the interiors of Castle Howard were planned with frugality in mind may strike the visitor as peculiar and the last thing which might be expected from an architect who is so much associated with visual effect rather than economy of means. Yet the sentiment appears genuine and not just a matter of special pleading. Vanbrugh was proud that the interiors of Castle Howard worked well, were dry, and could easily be kept clean.

In fact, the more one studies the interior of Castle Howard and the way the rooms were set out, the more it becomes possible to acknowledge the justice of Vanbrugh's claims. Although the hall and state rooms were, in some ways, incredibly grandiose, they do not appear as mere vehicles of formal display. And the life that the third Earl of Carlisle was to lead in them was comparatively modest, not dedicated to the rituals of lavish entertainment.

On Monday, 2 August 1714, Lord Carlisle was present at the York races when he heard of the death of Queen Anne:

*During the time of running this day, an express arrived with advice of the death of her MAJESTY QUEEN ANN; upon which the Nobility and Gentry immediately left the field, and attended the Lord Mayor, (William Redman Esq.) and Archbishop Dawes, who proclaimed his Majesty KING GEORGE I after which most of the Nobility set off for London.*[91]

The next day, Lady Mary Wortley Montagu supplemented this account as follows:

*This morning all the principal men of any figure took post for London, and we*

*are alarm'd with the fear of attempts from Scotland, tho all Protestants here seem*
*unanimous for the Hanoverian Succession. The poor young Ladys at Castle*
*Howard are as much afraid as I am, being left all alone, without any hope of*
*seeing their father again (tho things should prove well) this 8 or 9 months. They*
*have sent to desire me very earnestly to come to them and bring my Boy. Tis the*
*same thing as pensioning in a Nunnery, for no mortal man ever enters the doors*
*in the absence of their father, who is gone post.*[92]

Lord Carlisle was appointed one of the Lords Justice in the absence of the King,
but he appears to have lost his appetite for power, since he compained to Bothmer
that Lord Wharton could have performed the task much better.[93] Owing to an
attack of the gout, he was unable to greet the King on the occasion of his arrival
from Hanover and it was hardly surprising, although he bitterly resented it, that
he was not again made a Gentleman of the Bedchamber.[94] In May 1715 he did
briefly become first Lord of the Treasury, but the appointment was short-lived,
since, by 27 August 1715 it was reported by James Lowther to William Gilpin
that '*Ld Carl: resolves to leave the Treasury & retire into the Country, it is said*
*he wil have some Office of little attendance.*'[95]

What appears to have happened is that, during the long years which it had
taken to build Castle Howard, years of necessary financial retrenchment and
compulsory political exile, Lord Carlisle had become disillusioned by the faction-
fighting of the Court and attached to his life of proud isolation in Yorkshire.
Instead of Castle Howard being used for the purposes for which it was originally
intended, as an instrument of power and self-aggrandizement, a demonstration
of personal and political prestige, it became an expensive retirement home and,
as Lady Mary Wortley Montagu described it, a nunnery for Lord Carlisle's
unmarried daughters. The life that the third Earl led in the house, as suggested by
his personal accounts, appears to have been circumscribed, devoted to a small
amount of hunting, when his health permitted it, an occasional evening of cards
with the domestic chaplain, annual visits to York for the races, and visits to
London only when it was absolutely necessary. One senses a curious irony in
comparing the great lavishness of the Castle Howard interiors with the third Earl's
life of modest domesticity, of gossip and conversation, and long winter evenings
without company, as he grew old and lame.

CHAPTER FIVE

# The Garden

## EARLY PLANTING

In order to understand the slow stages in the evolution of the Castle Howard gardens, it is necessary to return to the summer of 1699, the time at which the first plans for the house were made. As has been mentioned in connection with Vanbrugh's designs, the nurseryman, George London, was employed to draw up plans for the garden at that time.

George London was the most prominent and influential garden designer in the reign of William and Mary.[1] According to Stephen Switzer, the greatest contemporary authority on the gardens of this period, London had been trained under Charles II's principal gardener, John Rose, and had been sent to learn the art of formal planting in France.[2] After his return, he worked for several years for Henry Compton, Bishop of London, who was well known to be a knowledgeable botanist and plantsman, interested not only in the cultivation of exotics, but also in different species of vegetables. Benefiting from this experience, George London was able to establish his great nursery in Brompton. In 1684 he travelled to Holland to gather plant specimens; and in 1689 he was appointed deputy superintendent of His Majesty's gardens, with an income of £200 p.a.. Working as a nurseryman, George London supplied the nobility and gentry with fruit trees, evergreens, plants and shrubs, and also worked as a designer and surveyor, drawing up plans for gardens, and supervising the planting. As John Evelyn wrote, in the advertisement to *The Compleat Gard'ner: Or Directions for Cultivating and Right Ordering of Fruit Gardens* (London, 1699), which George London wrote with his partner Henry Wise:

*They have a numerous Collection of the best Designs, and I perceive are able of themselves to Draw, and contrive others, applicable to the places, where busie Works, and Parterres of Imbroidery for the Coronary and Flower Gardens*

116

*are proper or desired. And where Fountains, Statues, Vasas, Dials, and other decorations of Magnificence are to be plac'd with most advantage.*[3]

George London's proposals for the gardens at Castle Howard, which survive in the Department of Designs, Prints and Drawings at the Victoria and Albert Museum, were for a radical transformation of the existing landscape. All vestiges of the old village to the south of the proposed house were swept away. A new model village, conceived as a miniature *ville radieuse*, was to be set out at a convenient distance to the south-west of the house. The contours of the surrounding landscape were ignored in favour of long avenues running axially away from the house. The ideas demonstrate, in full measure, the currently fashionable ideas of garden planning, with avenues bisected by rond-points, and formal canals.[4] London had recently visited France in company with the Duke of Portland and these projects suggest the full-blown magnificence of contemporary French gardens. Yet the third Earl of Carlisle rejected them.

The principal concern was an area of woodland, immediately to the east of where the house was planned, known as Raywood. This consisted of mature beech trees, described by Timothy Thomas, Lord Oxford's chaplain, in 1725, as *'the noblest Beach trees, which I believe are to be met with in England, both for ye fine Shade which they cast, and for ye largeness of ye Stock of 'em'*.[5] According to Switzer, writing in *Ichnographia Rustica*: *'Mr London design'd a Star, which would have spoil'd the Wood; but that his Lordship's superlative Genius prevented it, and to the great Advancement of the Design, has given it that Labyrinth diverting Model we now see it.'*[6]

There is no reason to doubt Switzer's account of events. Mature woodland was a valuable asset and Lord Carlisle may have been reluctant to cut down trees simply in order to replant them. He may well have felt that, while spending so much money on the house, he did not want to be as ambitious in planning the surrounding landscape. Also, George London was almost certainly too closely associated with William Talman, and so followed Talman's fall from favour.[7] Whatever the reason, Raywood survived.

On 25 January 1700, Nevill Ridley's accounts show that £2 was *'given ye gardner yt went to Hindersk:'* and on 27 February 1700 a further £95 16s. (a considerable sum) was *'payd ye Dutch gardner for Seeds trees, and plants Sent to Hinderskelfe'*.[8] The Dutch gardener is identified elsewhere in the accounts as being a Mr Frederick, who was responsible *'for keeping ye gardens at London'*, but the gardener who travelled to Yorkshire is unnamed. Two other gardeners are

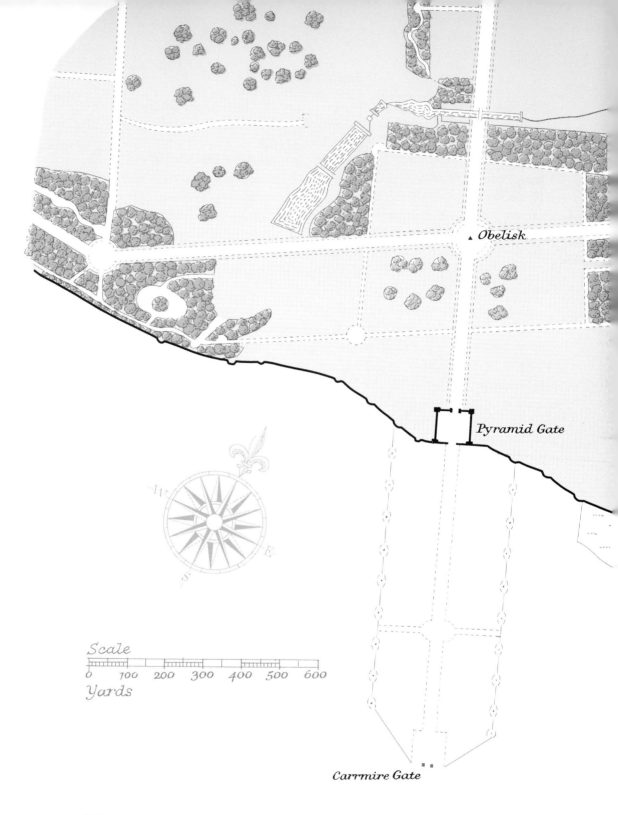

Obelisk

Pyramid Gate

Scale

0     100    200    300    400    500    600

Yards

Carrmire Gate

FIG. 5

Plan of garden adapted
from Ralph Fowler's
estate map of 1727.

Fish Ponds

Ray Wood

Temple of Venus

Obelisks

Parterre

Lake

Temple of
Four Winds

Wilderness

Pyramid

Mausoleum

mentioned, but were probably only employed in Soho Square. The first was '*Mr Carylls gardiner*', who was paid fifteen shillings on 17 December 1700. This is likely to have been the gardener at Ladyholt, the house at West Harting in Sussex, belonging to John Caryll, subsequently Pope's correspondent. The second was Richard Griffin, the gardener at Gorhambury, the Grimston estate outside St Albans, who, on 7 August 1701, was paid £8 10d. for '*6 weekes work in ye gardens and things bought*'.

In his letter to Lord Carlisle dated 26 May 1701, Nicholas Hawksmoor had described how important it was to acquire the neighbouring woods belonging to Sir William Strickland, in order to ensure that it would be possible to provide suitable planting in full view of the house.[9] It suggests that, right at the beginning of building, the quality of the outlook was considered, and the relationship of the house to the surrounding garden.

In fact, given that Vanbrugh was so much concerned with the look of a house and its scenic effect, it would be most surprising if he had not been anxious to ensure that the surroundings were organized and planned appropriately. From his letter to the Duke of Newcastle dated 15 June 1703 he is known to have supplied '*the plan of the Garden*' at Welbeck;[10] and on 17 June 1703 Sir Godfrey Copley, a fellow of the Royal Society and owner of Sprotborough in Yorkshire, wrote to Thomas Kirke, a local Yorkshire antiquarian, '*I pray give my Service to All att Arthington & Mr Dyneley, I am glad the Canalls & Ponds go on so Well, but I am told great Lakes are now ye mode, Vanbrook set out one for ye Dk: of Newcastle to front his new house of 40 acres.*'[11] This is an interesting comment, demonstrating that, at the beginning of his career as an architect, Vanbrugh was associated with a sense of scale in the organization of landscape, and that he was considered to be a garden designer as well as an architect.

In his correspondence with both the Earl of Manchester about Kimbolton and with the Duke of Marlborough about Blenheim, Vanbrugh refers to the relationship of particular rooms to the external physical setting. For example, he wrote that the saloon at Kimbolton

*looks mighty pleasantly Up the Middle of the Garden and Canall, wch is now brim full of Water, and looks mighty well: The Espalier Hedges will be in greater perfection this Year, and the Fruit Trees are now Strong enough to produce abundance.*[12]

To the Duke of Marlborough he suggested

*That Part of the Park which is Seen from the North Front of the New Building, has Little Variety of Objects Nor does the Country beyond it Afford any of Vallue, It therefore Stands in Need of all the helps that can be given.*[13]

The same sort of considerations about vistas and the planting of espalier hedges must equally have entered Vanbrugh's mind at Castle Howard, although no record survives.

On 11 June 1703 William and John Blathwayt, the two young sons of the owner of Dyrham Park, wrote on the occasion of their visit to Castle Howard that '*as for the gardens they are yet such a jumble that one makes nothing out of them*'.[14] However, on 9 October 1703 two local labourers, Matthew Nettleton and Philip Clarke, were paid £20 18s '*for ye foundation walls in ye Garding*';[15] on 10 December 1703 the mason, William Smith, was paid for '*Worke Don Att ye Garding House*';[16] and on 14 January 1704 Matthew Nettleton received a further £24 7s. '*for ye Garding walls & Masons work Done att ye Garding House*'.[17] These were the walls of the gardener's house and of the kitchen garden, south-west of the house.

Later in 1704 Matthew Nettleton was paid for '*Coopeing of the ffountain*', '*Paveing the Bodam of the ffountaine*', '*Worke don att the Brest Wall or Low South Tarrass*', '*Worke don att Coopeing the Said Tarrass Wall, the dementions taken When Mr. Hawksmoore was present*', '*A Note of alterations att the Said Tarrass Wall By My Lords Order*', '*ffor making a Peece of wall ffor a Pattern his Lordship not approveing of the Same orderd itt to be puld down*', '*Worke don att the Great Peers In the Garding and Measurd up by Mr Hawksmore and Will Etty*'.[18] Progress was being made on the architectural features of the garden, as always under the keen critical glare of Lord Carlisle.

Throughout 1704 there are signs of a certain amount of activity in planting. George London continued to supply seeds and trees, for which he was paid £25 18s. on 4 April 1704.[19] In a letter to Ridley, Lord Carlisle wrote that '*Mr. London must send us down a note of ye parcels of trees put on board*';[20] and on another occasion, perhaps in 1704, he instructed him as follows:

*I want a pritty large quantity of forest trees, I would have you look out amongst ye Nurserymen, & see where you can have them cheapest, & best. I would have 600 limes, 300 chestnuts & 60 English Elms they must be about eight foot high, good fresh trees, I shall be ready for them about six weeks hence, you must agree for ye freight, I think they would come best by a Scarborough, or a Burlington*

*[Bridlington] Vessell, I desire you will take care, yt they may be here against ye time I name.*[21]

This letter indicates the scale of planting at Castle Howard and the way trees were sent by boat from London. Apparently, it was common practice for nurserymen to send plants long distances either up the coast or by carriers' waggon, wrapped in sacking or placed in wicker baskets.[22] In January 1704 labourers were paid for '*Seting Trees in ye park*', for '*Planting Trees in ye Park & Garding*', while in June men from Bulmer were '*Leeding Manure to ye Trees in ye Park*'.[23]

Up until November 1705, when Samuel Carpenter was paid for carving the highly unusual '*Saytyr Heads*' on the side of the Satyr Gate into the kitchen garden, as well as baskets of ornamental stone flowers above (*Plate 32*),[24] work on the garden was generally conventional and what might be expected in the vicinity of a great house: the first priority was growing vegetables and the second planting trees.

Unfortunately, not much further evidence survives concerning the horticultural side of the kitchen garden, but it needs to be remembered as a constant background to the more architectural and scenic parts of the rest of the garden. Artichokes and broccoli were appreciated alongside obelisks and statuary. Certainly, much later in the eighteenth century, the kitchen garden at Castle Howard was greatly admired. In 1771 Sir John Cullum, a horticultural enthusiast from Suffolk, wrote in his *Journal of a Tour to Yorkshire*:

*The Kitchen Garden is a remarkably good one. it is an Area of twelve Acres, inclosed and Intersected with lofty Walls. the Gardener's House stands in the middle of it: here live two young Men, who are studying Botany, and have brought into the Garden a considerable Number of curious Plants, which grow wild in these Parts, and are rarely to be met with elsewhere. Scarcely any where perhaps in the whole Kingdom is Horticulture carried on with greater Spirit. the Hot houses, Hot Walls &c. are without Number. no less than 26 Fires were last Winter burning here at the same Time. in this, and the Pleasure Grounds 33 Persons are employed. the Pine Apples are cultivated to a Degree of Luxuriance almost beyond Belief. some of their Leaves were much above 6 Feet high; and the Fruit, I was told, frequently weighed between 4 and 5 pounds. thus much Art may do, but the Climate is very unfriendly.*[25]

In 1795, the Rev. W. MacRitchie was likewise impressed:

*Here is the first pinery I ever saw, and upon the whole the best kept hot-houses.*

PLATE 32

The remarkable Satyr Gate, by the York carver, Samuel Carpenter.

*The vines most luxuriant; and here is what I never saw before, almond-trees, peaches, nectarines, etc., trained upon spars placed not as usual in a perpendicular but in a horizontal position, about two feet from the ground, and bearing abundance of rich fruit.*[26]

Some, although not all, of this activity may date back to earlier in the century.[27] By 1705 there was a convenient walled kitchen garden to the south-west of the main house, complete with a small house for the head gardener.

## RAYWOOD *REDIVIVA*

In 1705 there is the first indication of what was being done to Raywood, instead of the radical plan proposed by George London. On 31 November 1705 the masons were paid for '*8 Pedastalls in Ray Wood*'.[28] The abstract for the masons' work between October 1706 and December 1710 includes the following entries for the so-called '*New Gardin in Wray Wood*':

*Building of Wray wood wall, Seats in wray wood wall, More Seats, Fountaine att ye Summerhouse, The Pedestall of Flora Backus and Steps and Seat att ye Rock, Pedestall of ye Saytir and Venus, Pedestall of ye Shepard Diana Venus and ffoott of ye Term and Steps in Seaverall Places, Pedestall of Appollo flags att Wraywood Gate, Steps and Draines in Seaverall places.*[29]

On 28 June 1706 labourers were paid £12 3s. '*for making ye Ditch Round Wraywood*';[30] on 17 May 1708 three men from Bulmer were paid '*for Leeding Gravell to Raywood*';[31] on 24 June 1708 labourers were '*pd for Makeing ye Ditch round ye North Side of Raywood*',[32] and on 25 October 1709 8 shillings was '*given Mr. Etty wch he gave for paveing ye Bridge into Raywood*'.[33]

These entries in the building accounts give some idea of the type of work which was going on in Raywood. Unfortunately, they do not give any indication of the sensibility that informed it. The essential features were as follows: a heavy wall around the wood; a number of gravel paths; stone seats on which to sit; and a profusion of statuary. Some of the many pedestals made by the masons for Raywood may have been graced by lead statues bought at John Nost's yard in the Haymarket and then sent to Yorkshire in packing cases. Nost was a Flemish sculptor who had come to England as a young man and subsequently established a profitable business supplying the aristocracy with lead copies of classical antiques.[34] According to Ridley's accounts, Nost was paid £12 19s. 6d. on 18

September 1708, £8 on 10 December 1709, £40 on 28 June 1710 and £15 on 15 February 1711.[35] None of the subject-matter of this statuary is identified. Meanwhile, between 21 June 1705 and 15 December 1709, Mr Nadauld, as well as carving figures to adorn the parapets of the house, is also known to have carved *'a figure called foune in the Raywood'* (presumably a faun), *'an hurne in the Raywood'*, *'for the termes with 3 fase in the Ray wood'*, *'for the figure called apollo'*, *'for the Rocher under apollo'*, *'for the see horsses and see boy in the bassain'* and *'for the figure called baccus'*.[36]

The point at which Lord Carlisle turned away from George London with his ideas of formal, axial planning and decided instead to leave Raywood as it was, with paths instead of avenues, and a certain degree of asymmetry instead of long, straight, boring vistas, has always been regarded as a key moment in the evolution of English landscape gardening. This belief in the significance of Raywood in the transition from French formality to the English picturesque dates back to Stephen Switzer, who gave Raywood and the third Earl of Carlisle prominent places in his early history of English gardening, *Ichnographia Rustica: Or, the Nobleman, Gentleman, and Gardener's Recreation*, first published in 1715. As Switzer wrote,

*I shall conclude this History with that truly Ingenious Lover of Architecture and Gard'ning, the Right Honourable the Earl of* Carlisle, *in his Wood at* Castle-howard, *the highest pitch that Natural and Polite Gard'ning can possibly arrive to: 'Tis There that Nature is truly imitated, if not excell'd, and from which the Ingenious may draw the best of their Schemes in Natural and Rural Gardening: 'Tis There that she is by a kind of fortuitous Conduct pursued through all her most intricate Mazes, and taught ever to exceed her own self in the* Natura-Linear, *and much more Natural and Promiscuous Disposition of all her Beauties.*[37]

This belief that there was something peculiar and highly original about the layout of Raywood has been followed by later authorities on the subject. As Christopher Hussey wrote in his *English Gardens and Landscape 1700–1750*, 'Landscape design can be said to have originated at Stowe and Castle Howard simultaneously, in the second decade of the 18th century. Indeed landscape in the sense of scenic values was appreciated earlier at Castle Howard and shaped subsequent developments more consistently.'[38]

Yet careful examination of contemporary descriptions of Raywood reveals that, except by Switzer, its design was not regarded as particularly unusual. Instead, its principal feature appears to have been a large amount of ornament, especially fountains and statuary, which were placed along the gravel paths, in order to provide enjoyment and an element of surprise as the visitor wandered round. As the accounts indicate, Raywood was a very elaborate, semi-architectural garden, with gravel paths which subsequently needed weeding, a fountain and a summerhouse, innumerable works of appropriately mythological statuary – including Diana, Bacchus and Venus, a satyr and faun – and a surrounding ditch and wall.

Raywood was the feature of Castle Howard most admired by visitors in the 1720s. In 1724 it was written that *the Wilderness of 40 acres is cut out into most beautifull walks & Stars, with a pretty Cascade thro' Rockwork, & a Small Waterfall*.[39] In May 1725 the second Earl of Oxford's chaplain was less impressed by the water-works, declaring that *there seems too great a poverty of that Element to make any thing fine of that kind*. On the other hand, he thought that *the close walks, when it is dryer and warmer weather than it was at our passing through them, must be very Pleasant & Delightfull*.[40] In the same year, 1725, a Cambridge undergraduate on a tour of England was much more enthusiastic about the artificial features, recording, rather breathlessly, that on the side of the house was:

*the wood, the beauty of this place, which for fine walks A fountain of a rock dropping water having a swan on it's top, Statues, Urns but especially Diana's statue with a stag, Gardens enclosed by a wall with sumerhouse, Cascade from a heap of stones, and other things agreable and very surprizing in a wood, may well be prefered to the finest Gardens.*[41]

Even the critical Sir John Clerk admired it, declaring that *the finest thing here is the wood which is cut into a great variety of walks and cabinets*.[42]

The fullest account of the original appearance of Raywood was provided, as for the interior of the house, by John Tracy Atkyns, whose *Iter Boreale* permits a rudimentary reconstruction of its layout. Atkyns set out along the terrace which ran parallel to the garden front of the house. At the end was a large gilt urn which led to a walk,

*where there's a statue of an Apollo, one of the prettiest things I ever saw, the basis at a distance seems a rude heap of stone but when you come nearer you may see in it, all the variety of prospects that the country can afford, villages, rocks, mountains, cataracts of water rolling down, and ev'ry thing that can be beautiful in a landscape, carv'd on each side of it.*

Passing Diana in one of the openings to the wood, Atkyns reached *a temple of the Ionic order* with *at the corners the 4 Sybills upon Ionic pedestals* – that is, what is now known as the Temple of the Four Winds, with the four Sibyls still *in situ*. From here, he records,

*Another part of wood opens, and shews you a piece of ground laid out in the manner of parterre slopes one below another yews and other trees planted round 'em in the middle a large bason with a piece of rock work in it, and on the top the figure of a swan spouting water, the several cavities trickling at the same time. There are two summer houses that are just finish'd the painting in 'em very pretty, in one ships represented in various attitudes, some in full sail others at anchor, unlading their goods, some in an engagement others burning. Upon the cieling the skie with birds of all kinds. The other has a variety of landscapes upon the cieling an Aurora drawn by Cupids the pavement in each of the Bremen stone, that has an equal cast of the purple and red. There are several openings in this part that as Mr Pope expresses it,*

*Calls in the country catches opening glades.*

*In the most agreable manner that can be imagin'd, from hence you are carry'd through a winding walk which brings you to a piece of ground laid out in the form of an amphitheatre opposite to the alcove here, is a rude heap of stone with several hollows in it, from whence issue very large streams of water which fall down 50 or 60 steps and roll in a winding manner quite out of sight, there is a large reservoir of water that will supply it with the proper quantity for six hours together, on each hand of you a mount, with a flower pot on one, and a seat upon the other.*

From this amphitheatre, Atkyns walked along the boundary wall on the north side of the wood '*built in the fortification way with several bastions*', turned up a steep ascent back to the statue of Apollo,

*which I mention'd before, it's cover'd with trees of various kinds, but not dispos'd in any set form: at the foot of it, is an octagonal fountain, in the middle the figure of a Neptune mounted upon a sea horse that throws up water above 30 foot high, which makes a pretty murmuring as it trickles down the leaves of some old beaches, a small summer house stands just by it that is furnish'd in a very elegant manner, a grass plot before the house, in the shape of a diamond, gilt Cupids and vases plac'd so as to humour the laying out of the grounds, from hence you have a gravel walk that brings you directly to the house.*[43]

John Tracy Atkyns's remarkably detailed description of Raywood as it was in the summer of 1732 makes it possible to conjure in the mind's eye its original extent and elaboration: the maze of walks with vistas out into the countryside; the two fountains spouting jets of water from a swan on a rock or a seahorse ridden by Neptune; the various summerhouses, elegantly decorated with landscape or seascape; the central amphitheatre with rills of water running down a stepped descent; and the statuary situated in glades on elaborately carved bases. These contemporary visitors' descriptions help to make sense of exactly what Stephen Switzer meant when he wrote that, *''Tis There that Nature is truly imitated, if not excell'd, and from which the Ingenious may draw the best of their Schemes in Natural and Rural Gardening.'*[44]

In order to understand the originality of Raywood and why it appeared ostensibly so natural to Stephen Switzer, it should be compared to other gardens of the period. For the essential elements of Raywood were no different from what might be seen in any other garden at the time. The use of ornamental statuary was a common feature. The fountains, although impressive, were nothing compared to those at Chatsworth, where there were said to be fifty in all, including '*a Basin with a Groupe, being Neptune in the midst of four sea horses, wonderfully fine, with water spouting out of their mouths and Nostrills, and between the leggs of each a Jet deaux playing*'.[45] At Chatsworth could be found, likewise, '*summer-houses, walks, wildernesses, orangerys, with all the furniture of statues, urns, greens &c. with canals, basons and waterworks of various forms and contrivances, seahorses, drakes, dolphins, and other fountains that throw up the water*', as well as '*a wonderful cascade, where from a neat house of stone like a temple, out of the mouths of beasts, pipes, urns &c. a whole river descends the slope of a hill a quarter of a mile in length over steps, with a teribl noise and broken appearance*'.[46] In terms of its mechanical effects, Raywood was in no way unusual.

Three things appear to have been unique about Raywood for its period. The first was, as already remarked, that it made use of existing mature trees, instead of, as at Hampton Court and Chatsworth, planting a so-called wilderness with a geometrical maze of new yew trees. The second was its scale, that it was adapted to the pace of walking and that it acknowledged that there could and should be some differentiation between a garden in the immediate vicinity of the house, where diversity was desirable, and the avenues of the park beyond. The third and most significant feature of Raywood was its necessary asymmetry, that it contained all the familiar features of a formal garden, but disposed comparatively informally.

It is the asymmetry of Raywood which gives a possible clue to its derivation. There is no reason to think that Lord Carlisle was not himself, as acknowledged by Switzer, entirely responsible for its form. It is worth, then, pointing out that in

December 1697 Lord Carlisle had visited the old philosopher-statesman, Sir William Temple, in his house of retirement at Moor Park in Surrey.[47] Temple's views on gardening, as expressed in his essay *Upon the Gardens of Epicurus*, were in some ways old-fashioned. He praised the fact that there had been a great increase in recent years '*in the number of our plants*' and was proud to have introduced four varieties of grape;[48] he gave his name to a nectarine;[49] he reserved his greatest praise for the pre-civil war gardens of the Countess of Bedford at Moor Park in Hertfordshire.[50] Where Temple gives instructions, he is dubious of novelty:

*The part of your Garden next your House, (besides the Walks that go round it) should be a Parterre for Flowers, or Grass-plots bordered with Flowers; or if, according to the newest mode, it be cast all into Grass-plots and Gravel Walks, the dryness of these should be relieved with Fountains, and the plainness of those with Statues.*[51]

Temple's Moor Park, as shown in a view attributed to Leonard Knyff, was an exercise in the Dutch mode, highly ordered, bounded by two canals and adorned with statues, which apparently were once part of the Arundel Collection.[52]

Yet, in a passage which is justifiably famous and which established resonances throughout the eighteenth century, Sir William Temple explored the aesthetic possibilities of irregularity.

*What I have said of the best Forms of Gardens, is meant only of such as are in some sort regular; for there may be other Forms wholly irregular, that may, for ought I know, have more Beauty than any of the others; but they must owe it to some extraordinary dispositions of Nature in the Seat, or some great race of Fancy or Judgment in the Contrivance, which may reduce many disagreeing parts into some Figure, which shall yet upon the whole, be very agreeable. Something of this I have seen in some places, but heard more of it from others, who have lived much among the Chineses; a People, whose way of thinking, seems to lie as wide of ours in Europe, as their Country does. Among us, the Beauty of Building and Planting is placed chiefly, in some certain Proportions, symmetries, or Uniformities; our Walks and our Trees ranged so, as to answer one another, and at exact Distances. The Chineses scorn this way of Planting, and say a Boy that can tell an hundred, may plant Walks of Trees in strait Lines, and over against one another, and to what Length and Extent he pleases. But their greatest reach of Imagination, is employed in contriving Figures, where the Beauty shall be great, and strike the Eye, but without any order or disposition of parts, that shall be commonly or easily observ'd. And though we have hardly any Notion of this sort of Beauty, yet they have a particular Word to express it; and where they find it hit their eye at first sight, they say the* Sharawadgi *is fine or is admirable.*[53]

In Raywood, Lord Carlisle was faced by *'extraordinary dispositions of Nature'*. Did he perhaps try to create a *'Sharawadgi'* and base the idea of artfully winding gravel paths, of summerhouses under dripping boughs, of pretty little artificial eminences and of water running in a cascade, not on some specific model, but on a vision culled from Sir William Temple's evocation of the effect of fancy and imagination in a Chinese garden?

## ESTATE IMPROVEMENT

The next phase in the development of the land surrounding Castle Howard is slightly obscure. What appears to have happened is that, having concentrated on the ornamentation of Raywood immediately to the east of the house, Lord Carlisle's interest in the estate shifted westwards to the park. Having extended the architectural apparatus of passages and statuary to create an ornamental pleasure ground, full of winding paths and unexpected surprises, he became concerned about the approach to the house, anxious that it should have the same effect of controlled magnificence.

Lord Carlisle had acquired with the lease for the house at Henderskelfe a certain amount of the surrounding land, which included a large area to the west of the old village described on the estate map of 1694 as the Park. This was presumably an old deer park, with a clearly defined boundary on its western perimeter, a few sparse trees, some moorland, and a lodge and kennels. There are periodic references to the planting of trees in the park during the period when the house was being built, as, for example, in February 1704, when labourers were paid *'for Seting Trees in ye Park'*.[54] But the first evidence of more grandiose plans in the area of the surrounding estate occurs in a letter that Lady Robinson, the wife of Sir William Robinson, MP for York, wrote to her son on 2 January 1714, in which she mentioned that *'Mr Vanbrook is at Castle Howard, my Lord is about erecting a noble piller in memory of ye Duke of Marlborough'*.[55]

In late October 1713 Vanbrugh had travelled up to Castle Howard in order to enjoy staying in the new house which was now more or less complete. In November Lady Mary Wortley Montagu described how he had fallen for a local lady, Henrietta Maria Yarburgh, of Heslington Hall outside York: *'Heaven no doubt*

PLATE 33

The great obelisk designed by Vanbrugh in 1714 to commemorate the Duke of
Marlborough's victories and erected at the junction of the two grand avenues leading
up to the house.

*compassionateing our Dullness has inspir'd him with a Passion that makes us all ready to die with laughing.*[56] In January he was still at Castle Howard and it was during this time that he drew up plans for the great obelisk to mark the westward access to the house, ostensibly to commemorate the Duke of Marlborough's victories, but also as a way of marking the completion of the house. On 29 May 1714, Vanbrugh was able to write to the Duke of Marlborough:

*I send with this a Draught of the Obelisk my Lord Carlisle is raising to express his grateful sense as an Englishman, of what he thinks the Nation owe your Grace. it is in all, a hundred Feet high. There is a great deal of the Material prepared, and I have writ this night, to direct the laying the foundations, my Lord Carlisle having given me leave to do so.*[57]

The obelisk is, indeed, on a completely different scale from anything which had been considered in Raywood and marks a shift in emphasis to a much larger conception of embellishing the estate with monuments which might be redolent of ancient Rome (*Plate 33*).

The next step in the development of the ceremonial route of access to the house was in planning an architectural entrance to the courtyard in front of the house. This courtyard had been levelled in the autumn of 1711 and on 26 September 1711 Matthew Nettleton, who was in charge of the labourers, was paid '*upon Acctt of ye Cort Wall*'.[58] On 20 December 1716 a further payment was made to the masons on account of '*Measurement of One of The Gateways Into ye Inner Court*'.[59] This must refer to the remarkable gateways which controlled access to the front of the house and which are shown prominently in the foreground of the engraving which was published in the third volume of Colen Campbell's *Vitruvius Britannicus* in 1725 (*Plate 1*).[60] These powerfully monumental and highly abstract entrance archways were described in 1725 by a Cambridge undergraduate as '*two heavy bulky Arches, each on four pillars, under them a Coachway into the park, these have cisterns on the top, to supply the House with water*';[61] in 1732 John Tracy Atkyns called them '*heavy Stone Arches with a monstrous Quantity of Stone pil'd up to a great Height without any Beauty*'.[62] It is not known when they were demolished.

Congruent with the entrance archways to the front courtyard was the Pyramid Gate, which was planned on a straight line with the obelisk to mark the entrance to what had been the old deer park. The Pyramid Gate, with its combination of an ancient Egyptian form superimposed on a vaguely medievalizing cubic base, punctured by a long, thin arch leading into the distance, could not be a more

PLATE 34

The pyramid gate signalling the entrance to the house and with a vista through
to the obelisk.

PLATE 35

One of the fine corner turrets terminating the curtain wall alongside the Carrmire Gate, showing Vanbrugh's liking for abstract castellation.

aggressive statement of territorial defence. In case arriving visitors were unaware of whose land they were entering, it was made superabundantly clear by the coat of arms above the archway and the inscription immediately above it, CAROLUS HOWARD COMES CARLEOLENSIS HOC CONDIDIT ANNO DNI MDCCXIX (*Plate 34*). The monumental effect of this gateway was further emphasized by the planting of an avenue leading up the hill to it, which, according to the Earl of Oxford in 1725 *'does not seem to thrive well'*.[63]

The final stage of the improvement of the park west of the house was the decision to surround it with a massive curtain wall, punctuated at intervals by various forms of turret. It is not known when these exterior fortifications were planned. They are likely to have been begun some time between 1719, when the Pyramid Gate was complete, and 20 August 1723, when Vanbrugh wrote to the Duke of Newcastle from Castle Howard:

*Great improvements have been made Since I was here last, And much greater, we are now setting Out, for Next years Operation. I hope I shall find the Walls at Claremont, as much to my Satisfaction (and your Graces too) as those are here. I find the more my Lord Carlisle sees of them, the more he is pleas'd with them, And I think all that come here, are Surpris'd at their Magnificent Effect.*[64]

PLATE 36

The Carrmire Gate, the most aggressive of the medievalizing outworks, described in 1732 as *'too much in the Vanbrugh Taste Clumsy and heavy'*.

In Vanbrugh's last surviving letter dated 8 March 1726, he wrote to Lord Carlisle:

*I told your Lp in my last, how much I found the Duke of Grafton pleas'd with Castle Howard. I have since Seen my Lord Bathurst, who declares himself quite as much, my Lord Binny do's the Same, and I think my Lord Stairs, but I have not spoke with him himself. They are all vastly Surprised and taken with the Walls and their Towers, which they talk much of. I always thought we were sure of that Card.*[65]

These two letters suggest that the great bastion wall forming the boundary to the estate was being built, and being much admired not only by Lord Carlisle but by all his visitors as well in the early part of the 1720s.

In the two surviving estate maps, it is possible to see the transformation which had been made to the park west of the house by the time Ralph Fowler came to draw up his survey of the estate in 1727.[66] In the estate map of 1694, the road from York crossed an area described as '*The Common*' in a more or less direct line of access to the village of Henderskelfe (*Plate 4*). By the time that the next estate map was drawn up in 1727, this route had been realigned so that it climbed the steep hill up to the Pyramid Gate and beyond along a further avenue to the obelisk. At the obelisk, this north–south avenue met at a rond-point another long avenue of double planted trees, which led eastwards up to the front of the house and westwards into the distance towards another rond-point near the edge of the estate. Like the planning of the interior of the house, this line of approach was very carefully organized to create a maximum visual effect with the minimum means, arranging distant views of architectural monuments to make the arriving traveller feel as if there were an infinite extent of surrounding parkland.

At the time of the estate map of 1727, the so-called Carrmire Gate at the bottom of the hill leading up to the Pyramid Gate does not appear to have been built (*Plate 36*). The first mention of it in any visitor's description appears in John Tracy Atkyns's *Iter Boreale* of 1732. He wrote of his approach to the house:

*when you come within a Mile of the House, you descend a steep Hill which gives you a View of the Park and of several Buildings, that are of the same Nature with some in my Lord Cobham's Gardens, too much in the Vanbrugh Taste Clumsy and heavy, the Entrance to the Avenue is a large Gate built of Stone the Work of the Rustic kind.*[67]

Although Atkyns identified them as being '*in the Vanbrugh Taste*', in other words heavy, pugnacious fortifications, the fact that the gate was built after his death suggests that it may have been designed by Hawksmoor in a style faithful to Vanbrugh's other designs for the outworks.

When John Tracy Atkyns visited Castle Howard in 1732, he not only recorded the appearance of the Carrmire Gate, but also the many improvements to the parkland:

*The park is laid out into several divisions, when my Lord came to it first, it was a very barren piece of ground, the greatest part of it warren, but by enclosing a number of acres at a time . . . and burning it, and laying it down with grass seeds he has improved it greatly, it cannot be very bad land, because his Lordship keeps above 200 oxen, a large number of sheep, several horses, besides no small stock of deer. It is about ten miles in circumference, the wall is not quite finish'd I believe what is done reaches at least seven miles.*[68]

Atkyns did not view the landscape with a Claude glass and a stock of apt poetic quotations, but rather with a sharp eye to potential profitability, to the quality of the soil and the possibilities of crop yield. Equally, Lord Carlisle must have been animated, in his improvements to the park, at least as much by the desire to improve the hunting and farming, as to reincarnate Poussin or Claude Lorraine.

## ARCHITECTURAL PARTERRE

The next phase in the development of the garden after the completion of the Pyramid Gate in 1719 was the planning of the parterre immediately in front of the south-facing façade of the house.

On 21 February 1721 Vanbrugh wrote to Lord Carlisle:

*I rec'd the Designs Mr Etty sent me, wch are very well; But I think any thing of frost work or Rock work, may be more a propo, in some other parts of the Garden, more retir'd and Solemn; or where there is Water: and therefore wou'd rather advise a fluted Pillar only and that of the Dorick Order, because it is the Shortest in proportion to its height, & in that regard is best to Stand alone – I have therefore drawn one, with its finishing on the Top, and its Peidestal, but 'tis to so large a Scale I can't send it in a Letter – But it shall come with Some things I have to send to Mr. Etty very Soon of Admll: Delavals. As to the Obelisks, I believe one may Venture at sight, as I find yr Ldship Inclines. But on farther thought, I am a little fearfull of venturing at any new Stroaks as to their form, in this place, but wou'd rather reserve that Liberty for Single ones, that may be Scatter'd up and down the Woods. I therefore send your Ldship here, what I wou'd recomend to you for the Parterre if you approve them. The Smallest to stand, at the 4 Lowest Angles, and the Largest on the higher or Inmost Angles. The Pillar I propose to stand rais'd on a Square bank above the division of the 4 Inmost Obelisks, and I think four Vases may be very well plac'd to attend it, at the four Corners, of that Bank, But this shall be farther describ'd with the Pillar, which shall be sent next Week if not Sooner.*[69]

This letter demonstrates that, probably during his visit to Castle Howard in November 1720, Vanbrugh had suggested to Lord Carlisle that the area in front of the house should be planted with a forest of obelisks, which would extend the spiky and sculptural feeling of the exterior of the house into the area of lawn immediately in front of it.

The exact design and positioning of these obelisks were to prove continually problematic. On 25 March 1721 Vanbrugh wrote to Lord Carlisle to say that

*Mr Etty will probably have shewn yr Lordship ere this, a Design I sent him of a Dorick Column for the Parter, which I think will do better only fluted, than with more embellishments. I have made the Piedestal Spread a little more than the Rule, which I think is quite reasonable, and will have a right effect, where a Pillar Stands Single, The Rule being Calculated for Pillars that stand in lines, which alters the Case much. I would propose this Pillar (if yr Ldship approves of it) to stand elevated upon a Square Bank, at least two foot higher than the upper Division. And I think it might be very handsomely accompany'd, by four Vases upon the four Corners of that Bank. I am very much affraid of Venturing to Flute the Obelisks: But the Balls upon them, I think will make them Gay, without being Tawdry. The Venturing at one fluted, in a Flower Garden, might be well enough, but I doubt going farther wou'd not be lik'd which I think the Whole Decorations of the Parterre will be extreamly, if rightly and Properly hit off.[70]*

Yet in May 1722 Lord Carlisle had evidently complained that, because the ground was not level, the obelisks appeared to be of slightly different heights. Vanbrugh wrote:

*I don't apprehend anything amiss, from the Obelisks falling gradually with the ground from North to South as long as those which are on the Same line from East to West stand on the Same Levell; The Case being no more than in a regular plantation up a Hill, where nothing more is endeavour'd or wish'd, than that the Trees may grow of a pretty equal height in regard to one another; but not that the Tops of them shou'd be of one dead level; nor wou'd they be half so beautifull if they cou'd be so, their rising one above another having a much better effect.[71]*

In July 1722 the size of the obelisks was causing trouble:

*In the last Letter I rec'd from your Ldship you seem to think, the four Obelisks might have been bigger, which 'tis very probable they wou'd not have been the Worse for. however considering how many there are of them, and how near the House; I hope they won't be much objected to, especially when the Pillar is up when it will be Seen, that they are only design'd as a sort of attendants to it.[72]*

Eventually, Vanbrugh was compelled by Lord Carlisle to redesign the obelisks. On 18 February 1724 he wrote:

*As to the Obelisks, I think as your Ldship do's, they are too small, I believe one may make use of the Stone as it is now wrought from about the middle downward so that the loss will be the Stone from the middle upwards; which can however, with very little working, be us'd as ashler anywhere. But I will consider this matter farther, and give your Ldship a more certain account.[73]*

The obelisks were, as recommended by Vanbrugh, accompanied by large stone vases, designed by Daniel Hervé, placed on frost-work pedestals, and gilt with leaf gold which had to be specially procured in London.[74] But the central pillar was not, as Vanbrugh wanted, a plain, fluted Doric column, but instead, as described by both Lord Oxford and John Tracy Atkyns and as shown in later eighteenth-century illustrations, '*a pillar of the Ionick order [fluted] with the entablature upon it*' and '*with a gilt vase on the top of it*'[75] (*Plate 16*).

Besides the obelisks, each 40 foot high, the Ionic pillar of 50 foot and the four large gilt vases, there were, according to John Tracy Atkyns, '*six statues of the heathen deities two groupes are a [Hercules and] Anteus, and the other the shape of Proserpine, a Turkish slave, and a sitting Venus, Saturn with the figure of a boy in his arms, Faunus with a kid*'.[76] The sitting Venus was among the four lead statues supplied, according to a bill dated 13 July 1723,[77] by Andries Carpentière, who, at least as early as 1714, had established a yard on Piccadilly, close to Hyde Park Corner, where Ralph Thoresby admired the '*curious workmanship of his in marble and lead*'.[78] It was probably a version of the so-called Crouching Venus, which, at the time, was in the Villa Medici and which had been copied by Coysevox in 1686 for the gardens of Versailles.[79] The other groups described by Atkyns were likewise copies of famous classical antiques: Hercules and Antaeus, under the loggia of the Palazzo Pitti, were universally admired and attributed to Polyclitus; Saturn with the figure of a boy in his arms should properly have been known as Silenus with the Infant Bacchus (*Plate 37*); Faunus with a kid had formerly belonged to the Queen of Sweden, and had also been frequently copied (*Plate 38*).[80] These lead reproductions on the parterre were, almost certainly, all supplied by Carpentière, who was known to specialize in the genre: he had sent Lord Carlisle a long price list of the various statues he sold and, besides the sitting Venus, had also sent, in July 1723, copies of the Farnese Hercules and Dancing Faun which can still be identified.[81]

Beyond this great mass of obelisks and lead statuary was an area which was planted more or less as shown in the double-page illustration in the third volume of Colen Campbell's *Vitruvius Britannicus, or The British Architect* (London, 1725) (*Plate 1*).[82] That Henry Hulsbergh's plate in *Vitruvius Britannicus* was not a fantasy, although shown in sharply elided perspective, is demonstrated by the estate map of 1727, which shows a similar layout of an evergreen plantation, cut through by walks and with a clearly delineated boundary of walls ending at the corners in circular bastions. This was what Vanbrugh referred to, in a letter dated 16 December 1725, as '*the New Plantations of Firs to the Southward*' with '*two little Turrets at the Angles to the Parterre*' and '*Round Bastions at the*

PLATE 37

Silenus with the Infant Bacchus, one of the many copies of well-known classical statues supplied by Andries Carpentière from his yard on Hyde Park Corner.

PLATE 38

The Faun with Kid, which, along with other lead statues by Carpentière and Vanbrugh's obelisks, adorned the parterre immediately in front of the house.

*Southernmost Angles Those being outwards, as Considerable ornaments and distinguish'd terminations of the Garden'.*[83]

While all this work was being carried out, it not surprisingly attracted a good deal of curiosity. In the years between 1721 and 1725 Lord Carlisle was more hospitable than usual and a succession of visitors went to Castle Howard in the summer to see what had been done. In August 1721 Philip, Duke of Wharton, arrived for the York races, where, according to Lady Lechmere, he *'added to the life of the place, for he has a great deal of gaiety, and everybody allows him wit, and those are two things that do mighty well upon such occasions'.*[84] In a letter to Lord Cowper dated 9 August 1721, the Duke of Wharton wrote from Castle Howard, *'This is the finest seat in England & both Nature & Art have employ'd their utmost efforts to Imbellish it. I believe it has cost an immense summ of money but I must say I think it well laid out.'*[85]

On 23 August 1721 the Earl of Essex told Lord Carlisle, *'I should have seen Castle Howard Last. for itt, without the Least Compliment Spoilt me for seeing Mr Aisleby's, & has put me quite out [of] Taste with Cashiobury'*[86] – Mr Aisleby's being John Aislabie's park, which was then being laid out at Studley Royal, and Cassiobury being Lord Essex's own house, with an elaborate garden laid out by Moses Cook, outside Watford. On 24 April 1722 Vanbrugh reported that *'Tyrril,*

*Gives people a mighty good Acct: of Castle Howd: especially the out Works'*:[87]
Tyrril was Colonel James Tyrrell, whose own house at Shotover was described by
Lord Egmont in August 1724 as having *'a large Octogon bason on the west, and
two Canals on the East, the walks, parterres, terraces, and avenues are agreeably
seperated by groves of reverend Oak beech & elm trees'*.[88] On 20 August 1723
Vanbrugh wrote to the Duke of Newcastle from Castle Howard: *'Here has been
a great deal of Company of Late, And Lord Halifax, Lady Halifax, Lord
Binny and Mr Montague (Westminster) are here still: And profess themselves
prodigiously pleas'd.'*[89] In December 1724 James Johnston, who was regarded by
Defoe as *'a master of gardening, perhaps the greatest master now in England'*,[90]
had supper with the King. According to Vanbrugh, they *'talkt much of Castle
Howard, and Mr Johnston I find set it out to all advantage Giving it a Preference
(in taking it all together) to anything he had ever met with consider'd as the
Dwelling of a Subject'*.[91]

From Vanbrugh's voluminous correspondence which survives from this period
between 1721 and his death on 26 March 1726, it is possible to gain a strong
impression of what animated Vanbrugh and, by implication, Lord Carlisle as
well, in the layout of the parterre. The first impression was that the garden was
to be an elaborate recreation and consolation at a time of public unrest. As
Vanbrugh wrote to Lord Carlisle, *'I hope however, neither the Publick nor Family
Misfortunes, will be able much to allay the Tast you have of reasonable amusemts:
Since they are really, our best Support in this Life'*;[92] and, on another occasion,

*I, without the Gout to incline my Philosophy, have every day of my Life Since
twenty years old, grown more and more of opinion, that the less one has to do,
with what is call'd the World, the more Quiet of mind; and the more Quiet of
mind, the more Happyness. All other delights, are but like debauches in Wine;
which gives three days pain, for three hours pleasure.*[93]

The second impression to be derived from Vanbrugh's correspondence is that
the layout of the parterre was not, in any possible meaning of the word, natural.
It was not in any way concerned with a view of the landscape or a notion of the
picturesque. It was in the highest degree artificial, ornamental, contrived. As the
Earl of Oxford wrote in May 1725, *'It must be easy to guess what a figure this
must make except to those who are in love with Obelisks.'*[94] Or, as Philip Yorke
wrote on the occasion of his visit in 1744, *'In general the gardens are overcrowded
with Vanbruggian statues and obelisks, particularly a lawn before the house.'*[95]

141

PLATE 39

The terrace looking
westwards towards the
domes and pinnacles of
the house and flanked by
lead statuary supplied by
Andries Carpentière.

## GARDEN BUILDINGS

The fifth and final phase in the development of the Castle Howard gardens was
the decision to extend the sense of physical manipulation of the landscape into
the open fields south and east of the parterre.

Throughout Vanbrugh's correspondence in the early part of the 1720s, it is
evident that he and Lord Carlisle had grandiose plans beyond the parterre. On
8 August 1721 Vanbrugh described to the Duke of Newcastle how '*Many new
Charms open this Year, that never appear'd before. And many more will next;
that people do not dream of now; If I take in, what a Third will produce, (bar
more Southsea Storms) I believe here will be, (beyond all contest), the Top Seat,
and Garden of England*';[96] on 26 August 1721 he told Brigadier Watkins how
'*Two Years more, 'tho they won't compleat all the Building, will so Beautify the
Outworks, of Gardens, Park &c, That I think no Place I ever Saw, will dispute
with it, for a Delightfull Dwelling in generall, let the Cricks fish out what
particular faults they please in the Architecture.*'[97]

The first indication of an extension of the garden beyond the parterre appears
in the decision to put a lake in the area of sunken ground between the far end of
the parterre with its corner bastions and the higher ground of Raywood. A lake

PLATE 40

The view along the
terrace towards the
temple and the
mausoleum, watched
over by a lead copy of
the Belvedere Antinous.

in this area was mentioned by Nicholas Hawksmoor in a letter dated 3 March
1724, in which he wrote, '*I hope your Lordship has, by this time seen a good
effect of ye Lake under Wray Wood*';[98] on 19 March 1724 he added, '*Your
Lordship may also see by the Lake (as it is at present) how Beautifull a Body of
Water at Connysthorp would look to ye North front.*'[99] On 26 March 1724
Vanbrugh wrote that '*The rising of the Water in so hopeful a manner, is indeed a
Cordial to me*';[100] and on 20 November 1725 Viscount Morpeth, Lord Carlisle's
eldest son, wrote, following an unprecedentedly wet summer, '*this very wett year
has I suppose considerably hindred the carr[y]ing on off your works, but it must
have filld your Lake if it holds the water.*'[101] The lake is shown on the estate map
rather unsatisfactorily; and it may have caused problems because a visitor wrote
in 1741 that '*On the Right hand side of the Gardens is a large piece of Water,
which when finished, will be a very great Ornament.*'[102]

The next stage in the development of the area beyond the parterre was the
decision to place within the landscape three small but significant buildings. The
first of these buildings was the so-called Temple of the Four Winds at the south-
east corner of Raywood along what had been the road from Henderskelfe to the
local town of Malton. On 7 January 1724 Hawksmoor wrote to Lord Carlisle:

*What I have sent you, here enclosed, are more Ideas, or Scizzas of ye Turret at ye Corner of Wray Wood, intended to be built with rough stone, except only a bandage about ye Windows, and something better to cope ye Walls withall. I propose it one Roome, (with a cellar and small waiting roome under it) as your Lordship may see in each of ye Scizza's or Draffts. Either of these woud make a very good Studdy, the small recesses taken out of the Wall would be very convenient for sundry purposes. I send you this for your amusement, for I know Sr. J. Vanbrugh is for a Temple of smooth freestone with a portico each way, and Dom'd over ye Center, & it woud indoubtedly doe beyond all Objection, but as yr Lordship desired a drafft of one, made of ye common Wall stone, I have drawn this accordingly, and this might be changed 100 Severall ways, if one had time and health.*[103]

Evidently the two architects had discussed the various forms that a small garden building might appropriately take and Hawksmoor had been asked to draw up plans which would be more economical than Vanbrugh's – as always – ambitious ideas.

Vanbrugh stuck to his guns and on 11 February 1724 wrote to Lord Carlisle:

*I still flatter my Self, nothing of this plain or Gothick Sort will be determin'd on at last. One thing among the rest, I believe will contribute to the changing your Ldships present inclination in this matter is, That I believe, when the Estimates come to be made, The first Design I sent, with the 4 Porticos will be found very near (perhaps quite) as cheap, as any Gothick Tower, that has yet been thought of. My Lord Morpeth about a Month ago, View'd all the Designs I had sent, He declar'd his thoughts utterly against anything but an Italian Building in that Place, and entirely approv'd the first Design.*[104]

Here is the first indication of Lord Carlisle's eldest son, Viscount Morpeth, having an influence on what was planned. Full of the experience of his Grand Tour and aware, no doubt, of the increasingly purist tendencies in the architecture of the early 1720s, he was in favour of an Italian building. By 18 February 1724 Lord Carlisle had accepted Vanbrugh's original proposal for '*the Temple with the four Porticos*'.[105]

The building which Vanbrugh had designed was indeed, as remarked by Lord Morpeth, extremely Italian, a highly reduced, miniaturized version of Palladio's Villa Rotonda (*Plate 41*). The Temple of the Four Winds demonstrates the extent to which Vanbrugh had absorbed the lessons to be learned from Palladio: it is,

PLATE 41

The Temple of the Four Winds, designed by Vanbrugh in late 1723 or early 1724
and demonstrating his much greater maturity as an architect.

especially in contrast to the architecture of the house, very precise, controlled and fastidious, suggesting Vanbrugh's much greater maturity as an architect, his understanding of the proper relationship of detail to the geometry of the whole, and his ability to create a building which makes allusion to Italy, without being too precise a copy. Hawksmoor had wanted the building to be known as the Belvedere, which, according to John James's definition in *The Theory and Practice of Gardening* (London, 1712) *'signifies a beauteous Prospect, which is properly given to these Pavilions: for that they being always built upon some Eminence, they open and command the Country round about'*;[106] but Vanbrugh had

*some doubts about the Name of Belvedere, which is generally given to some high Tower; and such a Thing will certainly be right to have some time and in Some Place, tho' I can't say I do at present think of one about the Seat, where the View is better than this, But this Building I fancy wou'd more naturally take the Name of Temple which the Situation likewise is very proper for.*[107]

Progress on the Temple was slow, in spite of the fact that Vanbrugh wished it might be finished quickly, in order that work could begin on the west wing of the house. At the time of Vanbrugh's death in March 1726, the exact scale had still not been finally settled and he was anxious about the niches.[108] When John Baker of Penn visited the house in June 1728, the Temple was still said to be *'now building'*;[109] and it was left to Hawksmoor to settle the details of the working of the masonry inside, the carving of the mouldings and the entablature, and to make *'a Small alteration, in the Cap, and thats all I differ from Sr John'*.[110] In spite of lengthy discussions about the finishing of the inside, whether it should be painted or stucco, and, if it were painted, whether it should be by Jean Hervé or Giacomo Amigoni, this had still not been decided in 1736, when, on 7 September, Lord Carlisle paid two guineas *'to Varcelli for drawing a design for ye finishing ye Temple in Stucco, & artificial marble'* and, on 6 October, a further two guineas *'Given to Altari for drawing designs for finishing ye Temple in Stucco'*.[111] Eventually the commission was given to Francesco Vassalli, who received his first payment of £42 in May 1737.[112] The four Sibyls standing outside were probably the four statues commissioned from Andries Carpentière in 1731, of which three had been finished by 16 December 1731 and were ready to be *'well cased and securely nailed up'*.[113]

Immediately to the north of the Temple of the Four Winds, down a slope along the side of Raywood, another temple was planned subsequent to Vanbrugh's death. The first mention of this building appears in Hawksmoor's bill submitted after his death by his widow, in which there is an entry dated December 1731 for *'Drawing several Plans & Uprights for the Octagon Turrett'* at a cost of four guineas; on 28 December 1731 he *'Sent down another Drawing of the Octagon Temple'*.[114] On 4 January 1732 Hawksmoor wrote to Lord Carlisle:

*There might be placed in the middle of this Turret a round ara and upon it a statue, I don't mean on the outside cap, but in ye middle, of ye floor below; as has bin often practiced. There is one famous Antiquity of this sort, cut out of a sollid rock of white marble, so that ye pillars, cap and entablature are all in one solid piece, remaining to this day.*[115]

Eventually, after Hawksmoor had suggested that it might contain *'A handsom statue of Diana, or any Godess you please, Gilded'*,[116] the building became known as the Temple of Venus. On 19 July 1735 Hawksmoor wrote to Lord Carlisle,

*I have sent you downe by this post, what your Lordship Mentiond in Your Last vizt the Sketch of the Cieling of ye Octogon; the pavement of the floor, and the pedestall or ara upon which a figure may be placed, I think the Greek Venus Gilt, woud do very well, but that I Leave to your Lordships great wisdom, and the Tast of the fam'd vertuosi. but cannot help mentioning, that the proposition is according to what Vitruvius mentions & directs in this Sort of Temple which he calls monopter.*[117]

In 1931 the Temple of Venus was described as very ruinous, and now only the foundations remain.[118]

The third of the major buildings in the fields beyond the parterre is the pyramid, which stands in full view of the front of the house on the horizon *(Plate 42)*. On 3 June 1728 Hawksmoor wrote to Lord Carlisle, *'I have sent the Drawing of the pyramid to Mr Etty at York.'*[119] This pyramid was erected to commemorate the founding of the fortunes of the third Earl of Carlisle's family by his ancestor, Lord William Howard. Its inscription records that *'In grateful Remembrance therefore of that noble and Beneficent Parent and of his pious and Virtuous Lady, this Monument is erected by Charles the Third Earl of Carlisle, of the Family of the Howards, their Great, Great, Great Grandson, Anno Domini 1728'*.

PLATE 42

A distant view of the
Pyramid showing its
relationship to the
surrounding landscape.

## LANDSCAPE INTERPRETATION

Visiting Castle Howard today, it is hard not to be impressed by the views along
what was the old village street towards the Temple of the Winds (*Plate 40*); by
the way the Temple itself sits in a rural landscape with fields and woodland
stretching out in all directions; and by the fact that two centuries have softened
and blurred the contours of the landscape and made it into an archetypal English
parkland scene. Two centuries of cultural conditioning have taught us to view
this type of landscape as if it had been deliberately composed to resemble a Poussin
or a Claude, with strong echoes of arcadianism.

The idea of Castle Howard as an early example of an English landscape garden,
consciously modelled on pictorial precedents, has entered into the secondary
literature, most notably in Ronald Paulson's *Emblem and Expression: Meaning
in English Art of the Eighteenth Century*. He has written of the garden as follows:

These are the elements and the structure of a Claude landscape, and they carry
its associations of Roman ideals and of an art which unites landscape and
history painting . . . The garden I have described can be located somewhere
between the formal – classical, geometrical – garden the English imitated from
the French and England's own unique contribution to European art, the so-

148

called English Landscape Garden of 'Capability' Brown. The intermediate garden developed by Englishmen in the first half of the eighteenth century might be called either the poetic garden or the emblematic or learned garden.[120]

Yet the evidence which is supplied, first by the detailed accounts which were kept during the course of making the gardens, second by the lengthy instructions which were provided by Vanbrugh during the course of construction of particular architectural features in the garden, third by the contemporary maps, and fourth and most importantly by contemporary visitors does not support a complex iconographic reading of the Castle Howard gardens.

What the detailed accounts supply is the sense of the garden not as a single fully fledged entity which sprang completely formed from the visual or iconographic imagination of either Lord Carlisle or his architect, Vanbrugh, but a complicated and continuous process, which was begun right at the beginning of the construction of the house and which developed as and when workmen or funds permitted: the garden did not derive from a single coherent scenic idea, but was the result of a series of expedients, of ideas applied comparatively piecemeal to different areas of the surrounding topography. The first necessity was to establish a good walled kitchen garden. The next decision was to adapt Raywood for purposes of recreation, and here the principal attitude appears to have been one of playful diversification, incorporating as many unusual and surprising features as possible in a comparatively small area of woodland. The third decision was to provide an appropriately grandiose means of access to the house through what had been the deer park. The fourth decision was to extend the carved decoration of the house into the parterre immediately in front of it. Here the motive seems to have been the simple one of trying to elaborate the visual approach to the main garden façade in order to provide a complex view out of the main sequence of rooms. It was only once these discrete areas immediately contiguous to the house had been treated that Lord Carlisle, prompted by Vanbrugh at his right hand, began to grow more ambitious and to absorb more of the surrounding landscape into the garden by the construction of a temple which could look out over the surrounding countryside.

In trying to decipher what prompted Lord Carlisle and Vanbrugh to look beyond the narrow boundaries of the garden in the immediate vicinity of the house, it is impossible to be sure what was in their minds. Vanbrugh, certainly, was not the type of architect who went round the estate with a copy of learned classical tomes in either hand, pondering on the precise symbolic reference which

PLATE 43

The view out into the landscape from the Temple of the Four Winds.

might be conjured up in the imagination of late twentieth-century professors. On the contrary, the language which he uses to describe his intentions consistently refers not to the symbolic effects of what he proposed but to its visual appearance, whether the obelisks should be fluted or not, and how to make them look '*Gay, without being Tawdry*'. Vanbrugh's greatest pleasure derived from imagining how visitors would be pleased and impressed and surprised by the various architectural features of the garden; these were to be items of entertainment, uncontaminated by complex iconographic references. Vanbrugh's last letter might form an appropriate epitaph to the garden: the comment '*I always thought we were sure of that Card*',[121] with its image of the aristocracy seated round the gambling table and deliberately and calculatedly outbidding each other, is entirely apposite. Scale, ambition and ostentation are the essential animating ideas behind his architecture: he takes pleasure in the fact that other members of the aristocracy had been to Castle Howard to compare its gardens to their own.

The only way that it is possible to derive some idea of what the third Earl of Carlisle thought about the gardens is from a curious, previously unpublished poem he wrote, which survives in manuscript at Castle Howard. To judge from the number of corrections in Lord Carlisle's hand and their evidently different dates, it was a composition he laboured over and repeatedly revised.[122] The poem begins:

> *A milk white Heifer, darling of my Herd,*
> *Nurst up with care, indulg'd with too much ease,*
> *(By which grown wanton, & ungratefull too,)*
> *Broke thro' my Folds, & from my grounds did stray,*
> *In quest of her, as o're ye feilds I rang'd.*
> *Lowdly complaining of Fate's hard decree,*
> *A beauteous Nymph most charming to ye sight,*
> *Who's radiant looks who's gracefull poise, & air*
> *Spoak her Immortal, & of race Divine,*
> *Me thus forlorne, thus mournfull did accost.*
> *Cease, Shepherd cease, thy vain pursuit she cry'd,*
> *Far from these fields thy darling Heifer roves*
> *Nor will she ever to thy folds return &*
> *By too much fondness, & indulgent care, loved*
> *Lost, & undone, these complaints she makes*
> *Cold are thy grounds, & barren is thy soil*

*Bleak are ye winds, which from ye hills do blow*
*No joy, or comfort do thy lands afford.*
*A richer pasture, & a warmer Sun*
*Now glad her heart, from Thee she's gone for ever.*

Although the image is not the happiest, the milk-white heifer who had left his herd is likely to have been Lady Carlisle, who had, as the poem describes, grown wanton and ungrateful and gone for ever. The beauteous Nymph then leads him to 'ye Seat of her abode':

*Hither arriv'd, with wonder I beheld*
*The severall beautys of this Statly Pile.*
*A work stupendious, dazzling to ye sight,*
*Beyond conception to a mortal eye,*
*Immortal Artists did ye Fabrick raise*
*And such alone can ye description make.*
*Thro' severall Gates most beautyfull, & strong,*
*Thro severall Courts magnificent, & great,*
*Into a spacious, & most sumptuous Hall,*
*Adorn'd by ye most curious hand of Art.*

This image of a stupendous stately pile with its several gates most beautiful and strong would seem sufficiently clearly to describe Castle Howard, whose essential visual features are of gates and courtyards and a most sumptuous hall. The nymph, now turned into a goddess, next opens up various tempting scenes. The first was the offer of unlimited wealth *'Great as ye Eastern Monarks do possess'*. This was refused:

*I lowly bow'd, my humble thanks return'd*
*And beg'd to be excus'd from such a weight.*
*A portion fair, unenvy'd, or dispis'ed,*
*Such as ye wants of nature can supply*
*I now enjoy, I ask, or wish no more.*

The second scene to open up was *'ye tempting scene of Power'*. This, too, was refused:

*O sacred Deity, most generous, & kind,*
*Hold not thy Son unworthy of thy love,*
*If thus unmov'd, insensible he stands,*

*Far from ye noise & grandeur of a Court,*
*Far from ye cares, & troubles yt attend,*
*Uneasy greatness, & unweildy Power,*
*My choice I make an easy safe retreat*
*Where bounteous Nature dos for life provide*
*And anxious cares do not perplex ye Mind.*

The third scene to open up was '*a garden of delight*'.

*Where Pleasure undisturb'd by busy cares,*
*In sensual joys, kept her luxurious Court.*

This scene of shaded alleys and orange groves, of myrtle hedges and terrace walks, Lord Carlisle could not resist:

*Here at ye end of a green Terrace walk*
*Where statly beaches in due order rang'd,*
*Did from ye rageing, & ye scortching Sun*
*A pleasing Canopy, & shelter make,*
*A statly beauteous Bower was plac'd, where at her ease*
*And crown'd with mirth, & joy, Luxury sat.*

Lord Carlisle evidently enjoyed the pleasures of carnal sensuality:

*Further, & more retire'd within this Bower,*
*Where richest Odours did perfume ye air,*
*On beds of roses wantonly were lay'd,*
*The brightest Nymphs, yt Mortal 'ere beheld.*
*A flowing mantle yt to ye view expos'd*
*The naked beautys of ye female sex*
*Their heaving brests, short breath, & languid eyes*
*Declar'd their longings, & their soft desires.*

Eventually, even the joys of sensual pleasure began to cloy:

*Already all ye pleasures of yon Bower*
*Have lost their relish, & do hatefull look.*
*No happyness can true, or lasting be,*
*If from ye rules of vertue wee do stray.*
*Since freely thus thou hast declar'd thy mind,*
*And I ye wishes of thy Soul doe know,*

*The Goddess said, this hour shall bring Thee peace.*
*With yt she led me to a flowry Lawn*
*Unknown to art, by nature pleasant made,*
*The seat of Innocence, & harmless Love.*
*Under ye shade there of a spreading beech,*
*Tending her flocks & harmless as her lambs,*
*The fair, ye gentle, charming Celia sat.*

Although this poem is unexpected, it is none the less important evidence – the only evidence – of Lord Carlisle's state of mind at the time when the gardens were being extended into the landscape. It is a literary fantasy, in which Lord Carlisle examines his various preoccupations, first with money, then with power, and, third, with sensual pleasure enjoyed among fountains and statues, only to be dismissed for the sake of a pastoral dream of a fair shepherdess called Celia. It suggests that there was an element of psychosexual projection involved in the extension of the garden into the surrounding landscape, so that Lord Carlisle could wander round it in his gout-ridden old age and believe it to be populated by young classical nymphs, wearing alluringly little.

If one is going to see the gardens as they were originally laid out, it requires a strong effort of the historical imagination to strip the landscape of its later connotations, to tear away the accretions of two centuries of vegetation, and to return the open hillside to an appearance which was much barer, bleaker and rawer, but filled with a complex cacophony of gilded statuary, imitations of well-known antiques. The essential feature of both Raywood and the parterre in front of the house was the great profusion of statuary, a different god round every turn of the path, and the front of the house an ornamental sculpture park, stuffed with huge obelisks and gilded urns. The layout was not prompted by any very sophisticated view of the meaning of classical statuary, which was, instead, viewed as gilded souvenirs of the Grand Tour, three-dimensional reminiscences of Rome.

There has long been a tendency for garden history to be written by literary historians. There has, therefore, inevitably been a tendency for them to look for an essentially literary significance and meaning in eighteenth-century gardens, to view them in terms of particular Virgilian or Horatian ideals.[123] Yet in recent years there has been a substantial historiographical shift in the interpretation of Walpole's England away from what Sir John Plumb described as the politics of stability towards a much more active view of conflict and political repression, represented at its most extreme by E. P. Thompson in his *Whigs and Hunters*. He has written:

> Political life in the 1720s had something of the sick quality of a 'banana republic'. This is a recognised phase of commercial capitalism when predators fight for the spoils of power and have not yet agreed to submit to rational or bureaucratic rules and forms. Each politician, by nepotism, interest and purchase, gathered around him a following of loyal dependants. The aim was to reward them by giving them some post in which they could milk some part of the public revenue: army finances, the Church, excise. . . The great gentry, speculators and politicians were men of huge wealth, whose income towered like the Andes above the rain-forests of the common man's poverty. Status and influence demanded ostentatious display, the visible evidence of wealth and power: Blenheim, Caversham, Cannons, Stowe, Houghton. Deer-parks were part of this display.[124]

Although more recent interpretations of the 1720s have not been as brutal as E. P. Thompson's, his ideas remain a useful corrective to the romanticization of the politics of eighteenth-century stability.[125] It is in the context of this debate that the Castle Howard gardens need to be interpreted, as a place not of good taste and Augustan peace and refined sensibility, but, instead, of fantasy and wealth and ostentation.

## LITERARY CLASSICISM

It remains, in concluding this chapter, to consider the emotions and sensations aroused by the Castle Howard gardens in the genre of poetry which flourished round country houses, particularly during the 1730s.

On 13 December 1731 Pope's *Epistle to Burlington* was first printed.[126] Although the poem was almost immediately taken – probably unjustly – to refer to the Duke of Chandos's new house at Cannons, its criticism was sufficiently generalized to apply to any contemporary great house:

> *Lo, what huge heaps of littleness around!*
> *The whole, a labour'd Quarry above ground.*
> *Two Cupids squirt before, a Lake behind*
> *Improves the keenness of the Northern wind.*

*His Gardens next your admiration call,*
*On ev'ry side you look, behold the Wall!* [127]

On 4 January 1732 Hawksmoor wrote to Lord Carlisle to say that he hoped '*the poet Mr. Pope will not set his satire upon us*'.[128] Later in 1732 a poem entitled *Castle Howard* was published by the third Earl of Carlisle's daughter, Lady Anne Irwin, in which she defended her father from Pope's accusations:

*How can I best describe your gen'rous Mind,*
*To ev'ry Social Act of Life inclin'd.*
*Numbers from you their daily Bread receive,*
*Th'afflicted Heart – through you forgets to grieve:*
*To serve Mankind is your peculiar End,*
*And make those happy who on you depend.*
*Your Children, Servants, Friends, this Blessing share,*
*And feel the Bounty of your constant Care.*
*Through various Paths to Happiness you've try'd,*
*But ever follow'd a falacious Guide,*
*Till from the Court and City you withdrew,*
*A Life of rural Pleasure to pursue.* [129]

Lady Anne's poem is the first indication of a different sensibility in appreciating the landscape at Castle Howard. She was alert to the possibility that '*You view gay Landskips, and new Prospects rise*' and she gave Nature her due:

*These Inequalities delight the Eye,*
*For Nature charms most in Variety.*
*When ev'r her gen'ral Law by Arts effac'd,*
*It shows a Skill, but proves a want of Taste.*
*O'r all Designs Nature shou'd still preside;*
*She is the cheapest, and most perfect Guide.* [130]

At the same time, Lady Anne demonstrates the extent to which Castle Howard was saturated with classical references:

*Diana more to bless her fav'rite Grove,*
*Added this other Mark of partial Love,*
*That no unruly Passions shou'd invade*
*The Breast of those who wander in this Shade:*
*No jealous Thoughts, nor no corroding Care,*

*Nor Politicians Schemes shou'd enter here.*
*If Love sometimes – as Love will oft intrude,*
*No Place so Sacred can that Pow'r exclude.*
*The Heav'nly Venus only here inspires*
*All modest Wishes, and all chaste Desires.*[131]

Lady Anne was pleased with, and commended for, her literary performance which certainly is superior to her father's. On 6 January 1732 she wrote to him:

*I have heard some observations since I writ to yr Lrdshp upon Castle Howard to its advantage; Mr West who writ Stow told one yt inform'd me of it that he lik'd the Poem extreamly and thought there was a great many good things in it. It has been borrow'd by two or three people of me since I came to town but I have not yet seen 'em to know their thoughts of it. I am pleas'd to remain an unsuspected person; tis thought a Masculine performance no body believing I have any other Concern in it than my fondness to the place.*[132]

Later in the same month, she sent him a copy of the *Epistle to Bathurst*, adding:

*I can't help making one observation upon Mr Pope's poem which I omitted in my letter. The Man of Ross is his hero; the lines which describe him are the best, in my opinion, of any in the poem; he is there celebrated for the same virtues that Castle Howard mentions your Lordship for; and though your circumstances and his are different, social virtues are the same in all people, and if worthy of commendation in him, why not in you?*[133]

This theme of Lord Carlisle as the Man of Ross dispensing hospitality and charity to the poor reappears in a poem published in *The Gentleman's Magazine* in August 1737, which describes an occasion when several sports were held in the grounds of Castle Howard:

*See how luxuriant plenty, gayly crown'd,*
*Show'rs with a godlike hand her favours round;*
*The guests now seated at the fearful board*
*With grateful glee confess the lib'ral lord.*
*The sparkling wine to Howard's health went round,*
*Long live great Howard! willing echos found,*
*Each rose from table with a chearful face,*
*The sounding bell proclaim'd th'approaching race,*

*The eager multitudes now form'd a lane*
*From Howard's palace to the sacred Fane.*[134]

Finally, the various recurrent themes of a life of rural retirement, of an insistent classicism, and of an ordered estate reappear in Thomas Gent's *Pater Patriae: Being, An Elegiac Pastoral Dialogue occasioned by the most lamented Death of the Late Rt. Honble and Illustrious Charles Howard* (York 1738):

*Ah, me! dear Strephon! Is my Lord then dead!*
*That God-like Soul, with Astraeal Virtues, fled!*
*Is he, whose Looks were, as in Darkness, Light,*
*Hence ever vanish'd from our mortal Sight!*
*Mourn all ye Virgins of this beauteous Wood:*
*Join, join with us to raise a briny Flood!*[135]

What this survey of the poetry inspired by Castle Howard suggests is that the sentiment of literary arcadianism, of seeing the grounds as a classical landscape, was, almost certainly, *ex post facto*, inspired not so much by visual imagery as by saturation in Virgil and Horace. At the same time, it demonstrates the reality and incredible power of the mythographic imagination in the early eighteenth century, which was able to lock a landscape behind high walls and then repopulate it with nymphs and dryads, with temples and obelisks, with Venus and Diana, so that the classical statuary appears not so much as the sediment of aesthetic taste, but alive and lurking in the grove.

PLATE 44

A woodcut of the grounds at Castle Howard, used to illustrate Thomas Gent's *Pater Patriae* (York, 1738).

158

CHAPTER SIX

# The Mausoleum

## ORIGINAL IDEA

Sometime in the early 1720s, when Vanbrugh was staying with the third Earl of Carlisle, they conceived together the idea of the grandest and noblest of all the garden monuments, a great mausoleum. The idea of such a burial place was clearly already in their minds at the time of the death of the Duke of Marlborough on 16 June 1722. As Vanbrugh wrote to Lord Carlisle on 19 June 1722:

*It having been referr'd to my Ld Godolphin with the other Executors, Clayton & Guidot, to consider about the Dukes funeral and place of burying I have taken the liberty, to mention to my Lord what your Ldship designs at Castle Howard, and has been practic'd by the most polite peoples before Priestcraft got poor Carcasses into their keeping, to make a little money of. Sure if ever any Such thing as erecting Monuments in open places was right, it wou'd be so in this Case. But I fancy the Dutchess will prevent his lying near her, tho' twou'd not make her very melancholy neither. The Place I propose, is in Blenheim Park with some plain, but magnificent & durable monument over him.[1]*

Vanbrugh was right to think that the idea would not appeal to the Duchess of Marlborough, who had an eminently practical mind and detested Vanbrugh's architectural extravagances. As he reported to Lord Carlisle on 19 July 1722:

*I believe my Lord Godolphin would have likt very well to have had the Duke of Marlbh: buryed in the Park, with a Very good Monument over him; but the Duke directs in his Will that they shou'd bury him in the Chappell at Blenheim. Here is a Pompous funeral preparing, but curb'd and Crippl'd by her Grace; who will govern it by her fancys, amongst which, there is but one good one, and that is that She'll pay for it. I don't know whether it won't cost her Ten Thousand pounds. What a Noble monument wou'd that have made, whereas this Idle Show, will be*

159

*gone in half an hour, and forgot in Two days. The other, wou'd have been a Show, and a Noble one, to many future Ages.*[2]

It is easy to understand why the idea of a great monument in the park at Blenheim should have so appealed to Vanbrugh. Like many Whigs, Vanbrugh had no love for the institutions of the Church of England and, in particular, for the clergy. Throughout his plays, he had systematically lampooned them and, though it might be argued that the sentiments of his characters were not his own, he wrote with an authenticity which makes it possible to deduce his own beliefs, or lack of them, through the plot. In *The Relapse*, Young Fashion, on being accused of inability to take the Army's oaths as a Jacobite, retorted that *'Thou may'st as well say I can't take Orders because I'm an Atheist.'*[3] Lord Foppington declares Sunday a vile day and attendance at Church nothing but an excuse for ogling;[4] and Bull the chaplain is the single most unsympathetic character, whose every appearance is marked by sarcastic references to the worldliness and self-interest of the Church. He is described as loving *'Eating more than he loves his Bible'*[5] and loving the Nurse *'better than he loves his Pulpit'.*[6] He marries Young Fashion and Hoyden secretly and then agrees to her bigamy on the specious grounds that the sin of disobedience would be greater.[7] The promise of Fat-goose living encourages him to confess, in spite of simony, because *'What Providence orders, I submit to.'*[8] *'For as Chaplains now go, 'tis probable he eats three Pound of Beef to the reading one Chapter – This gives him Carnal Desires, he wants Money, Preferment, Wine, a Whore . . . give him fat Capons, Sack and Sugar, a Purse of Gold, and a Plump Sister . . . and I'll warrant thee, my Boy, he speaks Truth like an Oracle.'*[9] As Nurse declares, he is *'a Priest of Baal'* whose *'Absolution is not worth an old Cassock'.*[10]

In *The Provok'd Wife*, Vanbrugh was still more outspoken against priestcraft. He suggested that there might be errors in the Bible's translation;[11] that *'Religion's out of Fashion'*[12] and *''Tis a damn'd Atheistical Age';*[13] that a mad parson is likely to be a good preacher;[14] and that, *'were there no Men in the World . . . adieu going to Church, for Religion wou'd ne'er prevail with us.'*[15] Moreover, he made the fatal error of dressing the drunken Sir John Brute in the garb of a priest and making him behave in a way which was clearly intended to shock religious sensibilities.[16]

If one reason for building a mausoleum was to keep one's carcase from the clutches of the Church, another was that it should be *'a Show, and a Noble one, to many future Ages'.*[17] This was a recurrent theme in Vanbrugh's beliefs about architecture: that it should be able to transcend history, through a sense of scale, of solidity, and of duration. When Vanbrugh proposed to the Duchess of Marlborough that the Old Manor of Woodstock should be preserved, his reasons were partly visual; but they were also associational, because he was aware of the evocative power of antique remains.

*There is perhaps no other thing, which the most Polite part of Mankind have more universally agreed in; than the Vallue they have ever set upon the Remains of distant Times nor amongst the Severall kinds of those Antiquitys, are there any so much regarded, as those of Buildings.*[18]

He then goes on to imagine '*Travellers many Ages hence*' coming to visit Blenheim. There could be no clearer evidence of Vanbrugh's understanding of building as a fortification against the corruption of time and as a monument of an individual life.

If the idea of monumental architectural commemoration did not appeal to the Duchess of Marlborough, it evidently did to Lord Carlisle. For in a letter to the Duchess of Marlborough dated 23 July 1722, as well as apologizing for not attending the Duke of Marlborough's funeral, he reiterated Vanbrugh's proposal, in almost identical phraseology:

*I take this occasion to condole with your Grace upon my Ld. Duke's death, who's name will bee transmitted down to Posterity in ye most honourable Manner not only for his great & glorious Actions but for ye real services he did his Country. It is very worthy, & commendable in your Grace to shew ye respect you have for this great Man's memory, by ye great & Pompous Funeral you design to make for him, but as things of yt nature are but shews for a day, & forgot in a week, I hope your Grace will reserve some part of ye expence yt you design to bee at upon this occasion for a noble & lasting Monument erected to his Memory.*[19]

## RATIONAL THEOLOGY

In his letter of 19 June 1722 Vanbrugh makes explicit reference to '*what your Ldship designs at Castle Howard*', which suggests that, by June 1722, the idea of building a mausoleum had been discussed and that, even if Vanbrugh originally suggested it, Lord Carlisle was sufficiently enamoured of the proposal to regard it as his own. Moreover, in order to refer so derisively to priestcraft, Vanbrugh must have known that Lord Carlisle would not object to a hint of anti-clericalism.

In fact, there is evidence to suggest that, if Vanbrugh's objection to priestcraft was contingent, Lord Carlisle's was more clearly worked out and deeply conceived.

There exists at Castle Howard a manuscript, hitherto unregarded, described as an *Essay on God and his Prophets* and written in Lord Carlisle's hand.[20] There is every evidence to suggest its authenticity: there are innumerable drafts besides the fair copy; throughout there are constant corrections indicating that it was composed with care and not simply copied from other authorities; there is a certain mannered awkwardness of style and, ultimately, a vigour and idiosyncrasy of argument which reveal that it was not a casual production. That it has survived at all, the longest and most articulate of Lord Carlisle's writings, shows that he valued it. Indeed, once deciphered and once the argument has been disinterred from its prolix and haphazard accretions, it emerges as a document of great interest.

The *Essay on God* begins with historical precedents for the misuse of ecclesiastical authority:

*examine ye Pagan Governments with respect to their Institutions, & laws, & you will find, yt most of them stand upon this foundation; their Rulers pretended, yt they receiv'd their directions from ye Gods, in order undoubtedly ye better to enforce ye observance of ye laws they gave to their People.*

He goes on to suggest that the peculiarity of the Christian gospel is precisely that it has no secular application:

*ye Author of yt doctrine had no such views; he declares his Kingdom is not of this World, yt his people were not to expect from him honours, riches or power; but on ye contrary, he tells them, yt those who will follow him, those, who will be obedient to his laws, must not only refrain from gratifieing their sensual appetites, & renunce ye pleasures of this World, but must expect to suffer all manner of evil treatment, indignities, persecutions, & even death itself.*

The source of corruption is revealed as the priesthood, which has assumed an unjust authority in the interpretation of scripture for purely worldly purposes:

*upon all such occasions they assert, yt they are, & ought to be ye only Expounders of those sacred Oracles, & yt Man must submit his judgment in all things relateing thereunto to their superior understandings & integrety in ye explanations they make theiroff.*

The *Essay* ends with a spirited and vitriolic denunciation of Moses, the first to misuse revelation and miracles:

*In ye beginning of his administration, till he was well fix'd in his Government, it may reasonably be suppos'd, yt he acted with great caution, yt he endeavour'd to make ye people as easy & happy as he could, & yt he exerted his authority more for their service & good, than for ye aggrandiseing of himself & Family, but when he found himself well establish'd, & his authority submitted to, it will appear yt he acted quite otherwise.*

The *Essay* finishes thus as abruptly as it begins, its purpose and implications unexplained.

What are we to make of this, a peer of the realm undermining the authority of the established Church and indulging in complex and heterodox theological speculation? The principal influence on Lord Carlisle's attitudes appears to have been Thomas Hobbes, among whose works he possessed not merely a first edition of *Leviathan* but also *Behemoth* and his popular translation of Thucydides, as well as Lord Clarendon's *Brief View and Survey of the Dangerous and pernicious Errors to Church and State in Mr. Hobbes's Book, entitled Leviathan* (Oxford, 1676) and John Eachard's *Mr. Hobb's state of nature considered* (4th edn, London, 1696).[21]

There are certain specific references that indicate Lord Carlisle's debt to Hobbes. Lord Carlisle states that '*all ye accounts wee have of Fairies, witches & spirits in former times are now generally exploded*': they had been most powerfully exploded by Hobbes, who wrote of '*the opinion that rude people have of Fayries, Ghosts, and Goblins; and of the power of Witches*'.[22] Lord Carlisle writes of the Pentateuch:

*An other observation may be made yt will likewise draw ye validity of Moses's writings into question; he himself gives an account of his death & burial with this remarkable passage, yt no man knoweth of his Sepulchre unto this day; it is most certain yt Moses could not write an account of his own death, & burial; it is therefore strongly to be presum'd, yt yt passage (wherein it is said, yt no Man knoweth of his Sepulchre unto this day) must have been writ long after his death, & if one thing has been added, no body can be certain what has or has not been added throughout all his books.*

It was Hobbes who, according to Leland, had first made this observation, subjecting scripture to the test of criticism:[23]

*We read in the last Chapter of Deuteronomie, ver. 6, concerning the sepulcher of Moses, that no man knoweth of his sepulcher to this day, that is, to the day wherein those words were written. It is therefore manifest, that those words were written after his interrement. For it were a strange interpretation, to say Moses spake of his own sepulcher (though by Prophecy), that it was not found to that day, wherein he was yet living.*[24]

Like Hobbes, Lord Carlisle believed that, in antiquity, priests pandered to the populace in order to keep the peace: as Hobbes wrote,

*being entertained with the pomp, and pastime of Festivalls, and publike Games, made in honour of the Gods, [the common people] needed nothing else but bread, to keep them from discontent, murmuring, and commotion against the State.*[25]

Or, as Lord Carlisle wrote,

*what was ye intent, & to what purpose were ye institutions of ye several Oracles yt were read of in ye Pagan story, it plainly appears yt ye Rulers & Governours in those days made use of them to prevaile with ye People to submit to what they thought most proper & necessary.*

Like Hobbes, Lord Carlisle thought that priests should confine themselves to proclaiming morality and the Kingdom of God for the good of the commonwealth: according to Hobbes, '*by precepts and good counsell, to teach them that have submitted, what they are to do, that they may be received into the Kingdom of God when it comes*';[26] or, according to Lord Carlisle,

*I do believe many of them are of great use to Mankind, by their preachings & exhortations, seting forth ye necessity & great advantage of a true Christian life, & by shewing to Man of what infinite Benefit it is to him strictly to perform all moral dutys, than ye due performance of which nothing can contribuit more to ye good, & prosperity of all Societies in which cheifly consists Man's happyness in this life . . . Great was ye Superstition of ye People in those days, but yet greater was ye Knavery of ye Priests.*

More generally, it seems to be to Hobbes that Lord Carlisle owed the most formidable of his arguments. Lord Carlisle wrote in his *Essay on God* of the fallibility and frailty of man before miracles and revelation: '*As man is not infallible, as he is subject to human frailties, & too frequently govern'd by his passions, & interest, ye truth of what Man has asserted upon such occasions, has ever been more, or less question'd*'; elsewhere,

*Ye nature of Man may be prevail'd upon to believe not only ye grossest absurdities, ye highest improbabilities, but even direct impossibilities, when designing, & artfull Men make use of those never failing means, pretended inspirations, Revelations, & declarations of ye Will of ye Deity to bring about their ambitions, & wicked purposes.*

The only true test for revelation, Lord Carlisle argued, was the test of reason and social usefulness. It is worth quoting the relevant passage at length to obtain the full force and texture of his ideas:

*There can not be a better, or a more certain rule to trye ye truth of all Revelations, than by examineing ye doctrine & purport ye Revelation deliver'd; if it contains instructions for ye good conduct of Man's life, inforceing all moral duties, by ye due observance of which Man will ever acquit himself to God, & to his Neighbour; if ye said Revelation enjoyns no arbitrary commands, grounded upon will & pleasure, & not upon reason; if it inforces no useless or unnecessary Ceremonies which ever have been invented by ye Priests to amuse & delude Man. if it directs nothing contradictary or inconsistant to ye known, & allow'd attribuits of yt Being, from whence it is suppos'd, it is diriv'd; if it is agreable in all things to reason, which must always direct Man in ye judgment he makes in these, & in all other cases whatsoever; in short if it tends solely to ye good, & happyness of ye People to whom it is declar'd, & not to ye raiseing ye power or answering ye private views of those, who declare it then & in yt case such Revelation may (altho it dos not positively follow, yt it do) proceed from God.*

The argument is that of *Leviathan*: submit all things to the test of reason and social usefulness, for man is weak and brutish.

The *Essay on God* is not the only evidence that, during the 1720s at least, Lord Carlisle had grown fond of heterodox theological speculation. Something of his interest can also be gleaned from the *Journal of the Life of Thomas Story*, published in 1747.[27] Story was a prominent Quaker, who came from a well-established Cumberland family, whose elder brother had been chaplain to the first Earl of Carlisle, and who met the third Earl as a youth.[28] On his return from America, Story renewed his acquaintance with Lord Carlisle, lent him a copy of Robert Barclay's *Apology for the True Christian Divinity, as the same is held forth, and preached, by the People, called in Scorn, Quakers* (London, 1678) and promised to expound Quaker beliefs.[29] In 1726 Story visited Castle Howard and it appears that he and Lord Carlisle embarked on a wide-ranging discussion which included

'*The Kingdom of Antichrist, being a false Shew, Counterfeit, and Pretence of Christianity, under which all Cruelties and Oppressions are, and have been acted, to the Destruction of Life, Limb, Property and Religion: And the Children of this Kingdom are Priests*'.[30] Story returned to Castle Howard '*and dined with the Earl of Carlisle and his Family; the Lord Cornbury being likewise there*'. This time, Lord Carlisle initiated '*Discourse about the Ceremonies of the National Church*' and showed himself sympathetic to the idea of Church unity. '*These Things are no way essential to Religion, and may well be spared; and we have no Foundation in Scripture for them, and some other Things we use.*' The third Earl's chaplain retorted, '*Things innocent in their own Nature may be enjoined by the Church and the Legislature; and thence arises a Duty of Obedience.*' Lord Carlisle replied, '*That whatever is invented and imposed by Man, in Matters of Religion, more than what was ordained by CHRIST, and taught by him and his Apostles, is vicious, and ought not to be regarded; (O noble Confession!) and dismissed his Chaplain with a frown.*'[31] Throughout, Lord Carlisle showed himself a keen pundit on ecclesiastical practice and biblical authority, eager to comprehend the ideas of the Quakers – he admitted to having attended Quaker meetings and read their books[32] – strongly aware of his inability to control his natural inclinations, and able to conduct an argument with Lord Cornbury '*concerning the Meaning of John the Baptist*'.

The combined evidence of Lord Carlisle's own ideas as expressed in the *Essay on God* and Thomas Story's testimony to the strength and independence of his religious views in discussion suggests that, by 1720, if not before, Lord Carlisle had read widely in theological literature and been deeply influenced by the broad tradition of rational theology which stemmed from Hooker in the sixteenth and Chillingworth in the seventeenth century, through the writings of Locke and Lord Halifax, to the writings of the Deists in the first decade of the eighteenth century.[33] This evidence is supported by examination of the *Catalogue of the R[igh]t Honble Charles Earle of Carlisle's Books In His Lordships Library att Castle Howard Taken in February 1716*, which survives in manuscript.[34] Purely statistically, Lord Carlisle's library abounded in works of theology. Of 353 books which were listed in all, a total of 221 can be readily identified from the casual method of listing titles. Of these, 98 can be categorized as theological or philosophical. Amongst more recent works, which were acquired, if not read, by Lord Carlisle were Locke's *Essay concerning Human Understanding* (5th edn, London, 1706), Pierre Bayle's *Historical and Critical Dictionary* (London, 1710) and, perhaps most strikingly, Matthew Tindal's *The Rights of the Christian Church asserted against the Romish and all other Priests who claim an independent power over it* (London, 1706). Tindal, a worldly Fellow of All Souls, masked a straightforward attack on ecclesiastical pretension with a considerable display of historical learning, ample quotation, an apparent grasp of the theoretical dimension and an occasional straightforward jibe, as when he described Dodwell publishing '*a Piece to justify Musick in Churches; as tho' when he destroy'd 'em for better Uses, he wou'd still employ 'em as places to fiddle in*'.[35] The book caused hysterical dismay amongst High Church divines; but it found a place in Lord Carlisle's library.

The evidence that Lord Carlisle had come into contact with – and may have been influenced by – the writings of the Deists, and that he certainly held strong and independent views about the role of the Church and of the priesthood provides an appropriate context for understanding the decision to build a mausoleum at Castle Howard. For a mausoleum was a singularly appropriate expression of Lord Carlisle's particular brand of religiosity. He would probably have been aware of the Deist argument that superstition had arisen around funeral rites for the dead. As John Toland, the best-known Deist author, wrote in his *Letters to Serena* (London, 1704),

*This new Idolatry of the Christians is altogether grounded, as that of the ancient Heathens, on the excessive Veneration of dead Men and Women; but improv'd by degrees to such a pitch by the Artifices of Priests, who allure others by this example to follow their Directions, which always tend to the Increase of their own Glory, Power and Profit.*[36]

Lord Carlisle would equally have known about Epicurean beliefs in the extinction of the soul: as Joseph Glanvill had written, '*these things hang together in a Chain of Connexion, or at least in these Mens Hypothesis; and 'tis but an unhappy chance, if he that hath Lost one Link holds another*'.[37] Certainly, he possessed William Coward's eccentric tract, *Second Thoughts concerning the Human Soul, demonstrating the notion of the human soul, as believ'd to be a spiritual immortal substance, united to human body, to be a heathenish invention and not consonant to the principles of philosophy, reason or religion* (London, 1702), in which Coward cited the text of the Book of Wisdom: '*The Potter maketh a God of the same Clay, that a little before he was made of Earth himself, and within a while after returneth to the same, when his life that was lent him shall be demanded.*'[38]

The mausoleum was to be an emblem, like the frontispiece of Henry Pemberton's *A View of Sir Isaac Newton's Philosophy* (London, 1728), of a universe that was rational, lucid and mathematical. It was to be bereft of conventional symbols of

PLATE 45

The frontispiece to
Henry Pemberton's *A
View of Sir Isaac
Newton's Philosophy*,
showing the image of a
temple surrounded by
appropriate devices.

the resurrection and free from the jurisdiction of the priesthood (*Plate 45*). It was
to ensure an afterlife in a monument and, as Vanbrugh wanted it to be, '*a Noble
one, to many future Ages*'.

## CLASSICAL ANTECEDENTS

When Lord Carlisle came to draw up his will, some time prior to Vanbrugh's
death, he wrote in it:

*I do design to build a burial place near my seat of Castle Howard, where I desire
to be lay'd, My Funeral to be very private, I would have no body invited, desireing
only to be attended to my grave by such of my Children as shall happen to be with
me at ye time of my death, & my Servants my Chaplain to preach a sermon
exhorting to repentance & a good life, for I take it yt upon such occasions & at
such times people are generally better dispos'd to receive good impressions for
which last service of my Chaplains, I leave him ten pounds. but in case this burial
place which I propose to build should not be finish'd at ye time of my death, I
then desire yt my Body may be deposited in B[ul]mer Church, to remain there till
such time as my Son shall build a Burial place & when such Burial place is finished
then my Body to be remov'd & lay'd therein & in case this Burial place for ye
Family is not finished by me, I recommend it to my Son to be performed by him*

*as a thing very proper nay absolutely necessary & in ye erecting of this Building as well as in all his other works of Architecture, I recommend to my Son & desire yt he will consult & take ye opinion of Sr John Vanbrugh, & Mr Hawksmore, with who's performances I am very well satisfied & I believe they are very skillfull & knowing in ye science of Architecture. I think this Burial place should be built in ye form of a little chapple to hold about 40 or 50 people with a Cupola, or Tower upon it & placed upon Lody Hill over against ye Hill where ye two high Beaches stand whereby it may be an ornament to ye Seat. I would have no other inscription upon ye stone under which my Body shall be lay'd than this, here lyes Charles ye 3d. Earl of Carlisle of ye Family of ye Howards who built this house called Castle Howard & made ye plantations yt belong thereunto.*[39]

This draft of Lord Carlisle's will demonstrates the importance he attached to the construction of an appropriate funeral monument, and that he had spent a considerable amount of time thinking about its appropriate position and appearance, even to the extent of composing in his mind an epitaph for himself.

Following Vanbrugh's death in March 1726, it was left to Nicholas Hawksmoor to interpret Lord Carlisle's commands. From an architectural point of view, this was, in many ways, fortunate. For although Vanbrugh had developed into a much more sober and reflective architect than he had been at the outset of his career, more concerned with what Hawksmoor described as 'Strong Reason', as well as 'good fancy',[40] he lacked the *gravitas* necessary for the design of a funeral monument. Hawksmoor, on the other hand, was passionately interested in antique antecedents, in the scholarship of architecture. Perhaps because of his training under Wren or because of his more professional temperament, Hawksmoor liked to be able to cite appropriate recondite sources, to discuss the design of a building in his library and to show Lord Carlisle relevant books. Always more taciturn than Vanbrugh and, by 1726, slightly embittered by repeated disappointments in the Office of Works, Hawksmoor responded to the idea of building a mausoleum with the full power of a highly developed architectural intelligence.

On 3 September 1726, Hawksmoor wrote to Lord Carlisle from Greenwich:

*Touching the other Building your Lordship mentions and the use you intend it for, (I wish there was noe occasion for it but since it must be) I suppose it is to be placed upon the hill in Yeomans Close, not farr from the Lake. To make it in the form of a Greek Temple, with great submission, I must differ from your thoughts. the Gentiles, Jews, or any other polite people had either Magnificent piles for Sepulture, but never buryed near their temples, or built their tombs in the form of any temple dedicated to divine honours. I therefore humbly Advise that we may take the form of one of ye Greek or Latin Examples, for such a Structure as your Lordship speaks of, for I know your Lord'p is not Supestitious, and I am only for following architectonricall method, and good Reason, in Spite of evill Custom, and pernicious practice.*[41]

This part of the letter demonstrates the extent to which Lord Carlisle had a clear idea of what he wanted and Hawksmoor's characteristic tendency to blind a client with his vastly superior archaeological expertise.

Hawksmoor then goes on to quote suitable precedents. The first of these was the original Mausoleum at Halicarnassus in modern-day Turkey in which both he and, before him, Wren had long been interested. In *Parentalia*, first published in 1750 from papers collected by Wren's antiquarian son, there appears a long discussion '*Of the Sepulchre of Mausolus King of Caria*', concerning its description by Pliny and Martial and its possible reconstruction.[42] This passage was presumably familiar to Hawksmoor, because, in a subsequent letter to Lord Carlisle, he declared how '*Sr. Christopher Wren, contemplated with great exactness this Fabrick according to the measures given by Pliny, and declared, by his calculation; it could be nothing but the Dorick Sistyle.*'[43] Hawksmoor had recently made himself the laughing-stock of London by basing the steeple of St George's, Bloomsbury on a reconstruction of the Mausoleum of Halicarnassus and planting George I on top.[44]

The second precedent cited by Hawksmoor in his first letter about the mausoleum was '*the Monument of Porsenna ye king of Tuscany, if I may be allowed to call it among the Latins, being in ye Early days of Rome however it was in Italy*'.[45] This, too, was one of the buildings which had intrigued Wren and which he had discussed with Robert Hooke in October 1677.[46] In the *Discourse on Architecture*, which appears interleaved in the Heirloom copy of *Parentalia*, Wren described how '*Another stupendious Fabrick, of I think, also Tyrian Architecture, was the Monument of Porsenna, King of Etruria. This Sepulchre we have describ'd by Pliny, wth the particular Dimension's in Feet which I have accordingly Delineated.*'[47] A reconstruction also appears in John Greaves's *Pyramidographia: or a Description of the Pyramids in Aegypt* (London, 1646) on page 66.

Hawksmoor continued his first letter about the Castle Howard mausoleum as follows:

*The manner, and form of either of these fabricks, may be imitated, in Little, as well as at a great Expence, and I will draw up a Scheme for your Lordship accordingly. There are many forms of this nature of fabrick, built to ye Memory of illustrious persons, the designs of which are published in ye Books of Antiquity, that your Lordship may see at pleasure.*

In the event, neither the Mausoleum of Halicarnassus nor Porsenna's tomb provided the model for the Castle Howard mausoleum as it was built.

On 11 July 1728 Hawksmoor wrote to Lord Carlisle that he had

*sent you Sundry Drafts of your Mausausoleum, and now I send you the designe your Lordship, Ld Morpeth, and I last talked of, when you were in London. it is upon the Designe of the Capo di Bove, as they now call it or ye Tomb of Metella, a Noble person of Rome. And indeed it was a Noble Monument, and durable, (if anything can be sayd to be so in this world) it was also great, for ye Square Basment, in which was ye Sepulcral chamber was on each side (if we are rightly informed) 100 fot English and the round part or Tamburo. 90 foot. the whole hight was, 100 foot.*[48]

The tomb of Cecilia Metella, known in the eighteenth century as the Capo di Bove because of its frieze of bulls' skulls, is a vast Roman drum monument half-way up a rising slope on the Appian Way. Lord Carlisle would presumably have remembered it from his visit to Rome in the early 1690s. Certainly the monuments on the Appian Way, stretching out south of Rome, made a deep impression on him, since he wrote in one of the drafts of his will,

*ye practice of ye Romans was very right in erecting ye Monuments they raised for their dead near ye high ways & in ye most frequented places in order as I suppose yt ye liveing might thereby be put in mind of ye worthy actions of their Ancesters & likewise of their own Mortality.*[49]

Hawksmoor, on the other hand, must have known of the physical appearance of the tomb of Cecilia Metella from archaeological publications.[50] For example, in 1726, John Breval, a former fellow of Trinity College, Cambridge, and subsequently travelling companion to George, Viscount Malpas, published his *Remarks on several Parts of Europe: Relating chiefly to the History, Antiquities and Geography, of those Countries Through which the Author has travel'd.* In this he finished

*this Part of my Observations upon Rome with two or three Words upon the Sepulchres and Mausoleums, which alone make a vast Branch of Learning, and are perhaps as great an Instance of the rich and luxuriant Genius of the Antients in Point of Architecture as the World can produce. Most of the considerable Avenues to Rome, for some Furlongs before you arrive at the Gates, are cover'd with the Vestiges of these Tombs; which, in their entire State must have spread an Air of Horrour and Melancholy over the Places they took in, notwithstanding the Pleasure the Eye could not but receive from the Vanity and Splendour of so many sumptuous Monuments.*[51]

The most likely visual source for the tomb of Cecilia Metella is provided by Breval, who concluded his account of Roman mausolea by saying that '*BARTOLI, who has given us Draughts of some of these Mausoleums, has represented them rather like what we may suppose they were in the Roman, than what they really are in these present Times.*'[52] When Hawksmoor described '*the Designes of the Capo di Bove, as they now call it or ye Tomb of Metella*', he is likely to have been referring to the marvellously atmospheric, crisp engravings which appear in Pietro Santi Bartoli's *Gli Antichi Sepolcri, overo Mausolei Romani, et Etruschi* (Rome, 1697), of which several plates show the plan and elevation of the '*Sepolcro di Cecilia Metella detto volgarmente Capo di Bove*'.[53] (*Plate 46*).

The tomb of Cecilia Metella provided the idea of a large, circular drum. To it, Hawksmoor, in consultation with Lord Carlisle and Viscount Morpeth, decided to add an arcade (*Plate 47*). On 1 October 1728 (*not* 1729, as transcribed by Geoffrey Webb) Hawksmoor wrote:

*What your Lordship sent me, I hope will be right as to ye Mausoleum, which I take to be that with ye Arcade round it, which cannot miss of having an admirable appearance. I am affray'd it will be expensive, but then you may take a Little more time in doing it. What I desire, is that Mr. Etty will send me a full account of what you have pitch'd upon, and all ye Dimensions, and alterations, in ye Drafft your Lordship, Ld Morpeth, and I, talked on when your Lordship was in Londn. Last time, and I will send you my thoughts and assistance as well as the distance of Lond from York will permit, till I can get to C. Howard.*[54]

By the following spring, it had been decided to adopt Viscount Morpeth's suggestion of '*a collonade round the Temple or Mausoleum; instead of an Arcade.*'[55]

On 6 May 1729 Hawksmoor was able to report to Lord Carlisle that,

*According to your Lordships order, I have attended Ld Morpeth with ye Designs of ye Mausoleum, and he is entirely for the Colonade, he mention'd Ionick colums, but I told him ye the difficulty of ye Entablement, was what we most apprehended*

*Alzata del Sepolcro di Cecilia Metella detto Capo di Boue*

1. *Basamento quadrato ora spogliato della cortina di grossi trauertini che lo cingeuano in torno* 2. *Terra pieno che copre gran parte del detto basamento, e l'antica porta di efso* 3. *Corritore largo palmi 12. alto palmi 40.* 4. *Stanza doue era l'Arca Sepolcrale di Cecilia che ora da l'andito nella fabrica* 5. *Finestra o porticella oue e la scala per salire alla sommità del Sepolcro* 6. *Muro antico moderno con merli attorno ad uso di roccha o Fortezza*

PLATE 46

The Tomb of Cecilia Metella, as illustrated in Pietro Santi Bartoli's *Gli Antichi Sepolcri, overo Mausolei Romani, et Etruschi.*

*and therfor I recommended ye Dorick Order and I have drawn it accordingly.
His Lordship desires that in ye portico that runs round, there may be neeches in
ye wall answering ye Ring of Columns; I have drawn neeches, in 2 severall
positions which ye Designe shows, in ye plan. His Lordship does not approve of
ye Step which runs round ye colonade because he thinks it will soon Lye ruinous
and I am of ye same opinion. Therfor I have put a Round Basment (in immitation
of Bramante) under ye Colonade. The designe of this Temple will answer all the
Beautys of ye Antique and will be truly magnificent, convenient and Durable.*[56]

The source for Lord Morpeth's proposal of a circular colonnade was, as
mentioned by Hawksmoor, Bramante's Tempietto at S. Pietro in Montorio, which,
as is clear from a subsequent letter, Hawksmoor knew from its engraving by
Palladio;[57] only, because of the necessity of finding stones large enough to bridge
the space between the columns, it was necessary to reduce the proportions of
Bramante's intercolumniation, since *'if the [Tempietto] had bin with 4 foot
Columns it would have required another sort of Division, the bended Sally of the
Architrave would have bin so large'.*[58]

On 7 July 1729 Lord Morpeth told Lord Carlisle that he had *'call'd several
times upon Mr. Hawksmore but he was in Hertfordshire I think the last time I
was with him we settled almost every part of the Mausoleum for your approbation
and I wrote to him my thoughts about the steps'.*[59] So, by the summer of 1729,
the design of the Castle Howard mausoleum had been established.

The letters which were sent by Hawksmoor from his house on Millbank in
Westminster, where he was surrounded by the resources of an ample architectural
library which enabled him to examine and carefully consider all the appropriate
antique precedents for a mausoleum, to the third Earl of Carlisle, ensconced in
his private apartments, looking out over the Yorkshire countryside and brooding
over the idea of a monument to himself, make it possible to observe as it were in
slow motion the gestation of a great architectural idea.

Hawksmoor attached to his letters detailed drawings, which, like the letters,
show his mind turning over different alternatives, submitting the various precedents to the discipline of a rigorous sense of architectural geometry. The first
proposals show a building which was lower and squatter than the one built, with
proposals for a circular arcade, which was clearly the way the building was
conceived up until the spring of 1729.[60] Some time during the first half of 1729,
Hawksmoor sent to the third Earl of Carlisle a drawing which showed in cross-
section the different ideas of an arcade and a colonnade compared (*Plate 47*).[61]

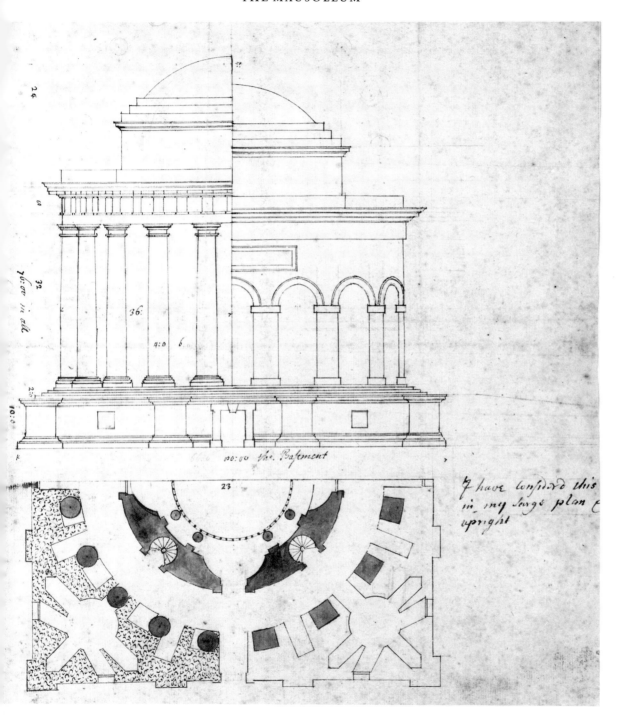

PLATE 47

A drawing by Nicholas Hawksmoor of alternative schemes for the mausoleum,
showing, on the right-hand side, the early idea of an arcaded drum.

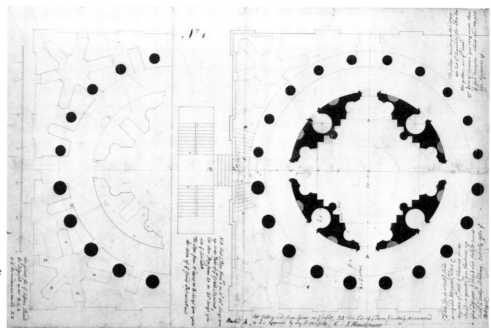

PLATE 48

Hawksmoor's drawing of the ground plan of the mausoleum showing his care and precision in working out the proportional geometry.

The effect of the colonnade was to raise the whole physical profile of the building and to make it taller and squarer: it is not surprising that this was the version that Viscount Morpeth preferred, and the one which Lord Carlisle selected.

In a further ground plan, Hawksmoor showed the various proposals for the spacing of the columns (*Plate 48*).[62] The drawing is characteristic of Hawksmoor's care and precision in working out the geometry of the building and it is peppered with annotations, including the recommendation that the left-hand side is '*what I shwd to my Lord Morpeth, he likes & Approves of it, with 5 Columns in an Angle, or quarter as you Sent me up in your Designe, I think Lord Carlisle cannot have a Nobler Building; entirely Affter ye Antique*'.[63] It shows in particular the way that he enjoyed geometrical play, inscribing a square within a circle and using circles of different diameter.

It is clear from both the correspondence and the drawings that the final form of the mausoleum was the result of long discussion and much careful thought. The power of the building as it was executed derives from the fact that it has a sense of finality, of ideas which have been fully integrated into an appropriate order. It gives the impression that if one dimension were shifted, then the clarity of the whole design would collapse, so that the whole building is sustained by a carefully articulated tension. It is possible to interpret this clarity and precision of form in the light of the long hours which Hawksmoor spent poring over architectural books, trying out different ideas, putting his taut personality into the search for a solution.

## BURLINGTONIAN INTERVENTION

The foundations of the mausoleum were already being laid by April 1729, when the form of the columns had still not been finally decided.[64] On 26 October 1729 Hawksmoor wrote to Lord Carlisle:

*I hope your Lordship has made a considerable advance in ye Basment of ye Mausoleum, and then it will Lessen in bulk in its upper part, except that the stones will of necessity grow larger, and where your Lordship will get them I am at a Loss to know, only thus much I know that they may be had. I heartily wish it was up, but I much approve, of your Lordships sentiments, not to go on too fast, but to take time; for that will be better, both for ye Building itself, and not worse for yr Lordships affairs, for indeed it is a great undertaking and I would not have you hurt yrself for ye world.*[65]

On 16 February 1731 Hawksmoor wrote to Lord Carlisle from Greenwich to say that he had '*a great desire to see what your Lordship has done, and May is the most proper time if I am but able to Stand upon my Leggs*'.[66] On 5 April 1731 he sent several drawings, '*the sections of the inside Wall, the outside Wall, the Plan & the Cell, & a large Plan a quarter of the round also the Moldings & Cornices*';[67] on 14 July 1731 he made two further drawings '*of the Mosoleum, one round Plan, one inside*';[68] on 5 September 1731 an entry in Lord Carlisle's private account book records that fifty guineas were '*Given to Mr. Hawksmoor as a present for his trouble, & expence in coming down to examine my works & in order to give further directions for ye carrying them on*'.[69] In his letter of thanks dated 4 October, Hawksmoor described how he and his son-in-law, Nathaniel Blackerby, had been to various houses on their return journey, including Thoresby, Wollaton and Blenheim and how '*Upon the whole I must declare (without flattery) that Castle Howard takeing all its noble qualifications and Beautys; promises much more than any thing one can see, and I must needs congratulate your Lordships happy Genius that has so well conducted this magnificent undertake-ing.*'[70] On his return to London, the Hon. Richard Arundell, who had been appointed Surveyor-General at the age of thirty, '*askd me after the Mausoleum; which I finde begins to be much talked of*'.[71] In a letter dated 12 December 1731,

Sir Thomas Robinson (*Plate 50*), Lord Carlisle's son-in-law, described how he had been told that Castle Howard '*improves in beauty every day, and that the mausoleum begins to have a very magnificent appearance*'.[72]

In the summer of 1732 fashionable society migrated to York for the opening of the newly built York Assembly Rooms, designed by the third Earl of Burlington and subscribed to by all the Yorkshire nobility and gentry.[73] According to the Countess of Strafford,

*There was a vast deal of company this year at the races. Lord Burlington received great applause upon the opening of the great room and I really think with justice, for 'tis certainly a very fine performance. My Lady was also extremely liked for her easy civilities to every body. They brought all their plate and kept a constant table and indeed a very good one. The principal people at York besides the above-mentioned were, Duke of Rutland, Lord and Lady Faulkonbridge, Lord and Lady Widdrington, Lord Carlisle and all his daughters, Lord Malpas, Lord Lonsdale, Lord Mountcastle, Lord Irwin, all Lady Ramsden and Winn's family, General Churchell, Mr. Conoly, Mr. Bows and a vast many more fine men I have forgot.*[74]

Lord Burlington brought the opera singer Francesco Bernardi, known as Senesino, to perform; Sir Thomas Robinson was required by the gentry to give a speech of thanks; even Hawksmoor wished he could have been there and longed to hear how the rooms were approved.[75]

One of the topics of conversation at the opening of the York Assembly Rooms must have been the Castle Howard mausoleum. On 26 July 1731 the Duchess of Marlborough wrote to her granddaughter from Scarborough how

*My Lord Carlisle is laying out a mint of money on making an extraordinary place to bury his own family in a fine manner than I have ever heard of and for a great number of them, which are yet to be born. At the same time none of his children are easy and Lady Mary can't be married for want of a good fortune.*[76]

Another more influential critic was the Earl of Burlington himself, who, over the previous decade, had become an increasingly powerful authority on matters architectural, to whom Hawksmoor's grand and beautiful *'plan for building the new parliament house'* had been submitted *'for his approbation'* earlier in the year,[77] and who pointed out that there was no antique precedent for the intercolumniation proposed by Hawksmoor for the Castle Howard mausoleum, since it was a circular, not a square, building.

Poor Hawksmoor! After years of deep professional experience, stretching back to his long and faithful service under Wren, having several times been passed over in the Office of Works by political placemen, and now, in his early seventies, suffering severely from gout, he was criticized by Lord Burlington in the area about which he felt most pride, his tremendous knowledge of antique sources and (as his son-in-law, Nathaniel Blackerby, wrote in his obituary notice) *'of all the famous Buildings, both Antient and Modern, in every part of the World, to which his excellent Memory, that never fail'd him to the last, greatly contributed'*.[78] His letter to Lord Carlisle, dated 3 October 1732, is a masterpiece of aggrieved self-justification, in which he quotes successive architectural authorities in his defence, Vitruvius, Perrault, Palladio, *'Mr Evelyn in his addition to the Parallel of Monsr. Chambray'*, Wren, Henry Maundrell, author of *A Journey from Aleppo to Jerusalem* (London 1702), and Samuel Lisle, who, like Maundrell, was a former chaplain to the Levant Company.[79] Two days later, Hawksmoor clarified his views in a more temperate fashion:

*I am very uneasy to find you so much concerned, but I assure your Lordship you need not; for I am certain the disposition we have made is right, and warrantable, and you have it in your power to give it what Entablement you please. I esteem'd the Dorick most suitable to the Masculin strength we wanted, and, as your*

*Lordship did seem to apprehend that the Cell, of the Temple would rise too high, I thought the Dorick, woud help us also in that case. but what a sad sight it wou'd be to see the Entablement crack and settle by the large spaces of the intercolumniations, for the Entablement is the grand beauty of this magnificent structure. I must once more beg that we may make proper modells for what is to come, I wish also it was possible to have the opinions of the criticks before we begin the work, rather than to put us into concern when it is too late.*[80]

As Hawksmoor must have known, Lord Burlington was, from a strictly pedantic point of view, correct; the real reason for the proposed spacing of the columns was the difficulty of finding stones large enough to bridge the gaps.

Sir Thomas Robinson, Lord Carlisle's son-in law, was an acquaintance of Lord Burlington. Robinson was a tall, gangling Yorkshire landowner, who had a high opinion of his own architectural knowledge and was a frequent unwanted guest at Lord Burlington's villa at Chiswick.[81] He had consulted Lord Burlington about the design of the hall of his house at Rokeby.[82] In a letter of thanks to Lord Carlisle, dated 25 October 1732, he wrote how he had:

*talk'd with Ld. Burlinton about the intercolumniation of the Mausoleum, he alld. a Diameter & a half had been practised in sqr. Buildings but no instance of a Circular Colonade of that proportion in the Dorick order, as your Ldp. proposes seeing him your self, I think it needless to give further p(ar)ticulars on this subject, but I must say, if the Building was mine, considering how farr it is advanced, the intention of the Fabrick, and the difficulty & expence might attend an alteration, I shou'd finish according to the first plan with a compleat Dorick entablature, and tho' it may have some faults (as I believe 'twill be very difficult to find one, that has entirely escaped the censure of Criticks) yet I will venture to affirm there will be no such Building when 'tis finish'd in Europe.*[83]

In November 1732 Sir Thomas Robinson again talked with Lord Burlington and reported that '*The reason Ld B — gave why a Diameter & half for the Dorick order, was not proper in a round Building, because from the Nature of a Circular Colonade the Columns must appear to stand closer, let the Spectator examine it from what point of view he will, then they wou'd do in a Square Building.*'[84]

Worse was to follow Lord Burlington's criticism of the intercolumniation. In November 1732 Hawksmoor heard that ominous cracks had begun to appear in the outer wall of the basement of the mausoleum and that there were '*some failings in ye walls of ye inward part of ye Vault of the Mausoleum*'.[85] He did his best to reassure Lord Carlisle, but neither Sir Thomas Robinson nor Lord Burlington was prepared to be charitable. According to Sir Thomas Robinson,

*There are five things this misfortune may be attributed to, unskilful or Careless Masons, Negligent Overseers, bad Materials, Boggy foundation or fault in the design, I think yr Ldp. shews great justice & command of temper not to lay the blame on any one, till 'tis thoroly examin'd, as you have always paid those concern'd in yr. works so punctually & in so generous a Manner, let the fault fall on whom it will, I think they are unpardonable.*[86]

In December 1732 Lord Burlington dined with Sir Thomas Robinson *'and says he heard the Loculys were not arched, & the vacancies between the Ashler work of the walls were fill'd up with rubble stones without Mortar, I hope he was wrongly inform'd in both, otherwise I wish all repair don't prove ineffectuall'.*[87]

Burlington's report was no more than ill-informed gossip, but Hawksmoor was clearly extremely worried by what he was told and it is evident from his letters that there were defects in the masonry, for which he – unjustifiably – received the blame. On 13 March 1733, Lady Anne Irwin, Lord Carlisle's daughter, wrote to her father:

*Mr Hawksmore was with me ye other day and made many enquiries after the Mauseleum, the state of which I believe he is better acquainted with than I coud inform him but an eye witness is allways preferable to a report, I told him yr Lrdshp expected him down in the Spring & when I came away was determin'd not to proceed till he had thoroughly examin'd it; he seem'd undetermin'd as to his journey but said he woud if possible wait upon you, the board of Works he says are going to engage in a large undertaking which is a new Parliament House design'd by my Ld Burlington   he as a Member of yt board will have some business upon that occasion, wch may possibly interfere with his attendance upon you.*[88]

In the event, gout in both hands prevented Hawksmoor from travelling to Yorkshire, as he intended, in June 1733. Instead, he was forced to rely on letters from William Etty and a visit from Mr Doe, the Studley Royal mason, in order to understand what had been done wrong. Much of the rest of 1733 was spent making good the workmanship, reinforcing the masonry in the corridors, and underpinning the walls.

Construction in 1733 ended at the level of *'ye heads of ye Great columns that the Worke may drye and consolidate'.*[89] The incomplete shell was covered over with boards for the winter, to protect it from frost, while the capitals inside were modelled on the Arch of Titus.[90] On 6 February 1734 Hawksmoor '*Sent down a Scheme and Modell of the Grand Entablemt of the Mausoleum*'[91] and on 25 June he sent a more confident letter to William Etty:

*I had your Letter from Castle Howard 6 days ago, by which I understand, all affairs there, go on well, in relation to the Mausoleum. And that, what you did Last Summer, answers expectation, and that no more fractures, failings or other disapointments, shew themselves; so that I hope the fabrick will be everlasting.*[92]

Soon after, he heard that Etty was dead, just at the moment when the architrave, frieze and cornice were due to have been completed.

On 20 July 1733 Sir Thomas Robinson had written to inform Lord Carlisle that he had '*spent this whole morn with Mr Hawksmoor & have shewn him my design for the Basemt. of the Mausoleum, he flatters me with the approbation of it. I am sorry I can't return him the complymt. by approving the scheme he shew'd me for finishing the entableture of the Colonade.*'[93] They spent the rest of the morning examining '*all the Designs of the Antients of these kind of Buildings*' and Hawksmoor was forced to agree to Sir Thomas Robinson's proposal to abolish the plinth over the entablature, which would '*undoubtedly be more in the true Antique taste*', as well as cheaper. Sir Thomas Robinson ended his letter with the patronizing comment, '*I must say one thing in favr. of Mr Hawksmoor I never talk'd with a more reasonable Man, nor with one so little prejudic'd in favour of his own performances, in this instance he has given a proof, acknowledging what I have proposed wou'd have a very good effect.*' Although Hawksmoor agreed, he found it difficult to conceal his irritation in his future letters to Lord Carlisle, writing on 1 August 1734:

*Sr Thomas Robinson has half a score of papers for your Lordship which I hope he has shewn My Lord Burlington. they concern the Mosoleum. I woud rather have all ye World see the designe before the thing is done, and finde all the faults, they can (possibly) rather than condemn when 'tis too late.*[94]

During 1735 there was further discussion about the appropriate form of the attic storey and dome of the mausoleum, about whether Lord Burlington's suggestion of Diocletian windows should be adopted, and where the gutters should be placed. Hawksmoor's letters have a tone of weary fatalism, and on 30 September 1735 he wrote of '*the great fatigue, Length of time and expence*'.[95] His last letter to Lord Carlisle, dated 17 February 1736, said that he had had '*a sad*

*Winter*' and that '*the World is determined to starve me. for my good services*'.[96]
On 22 March 1736 Lady Anne Irwin wrote:

*I am very glad the Mausoleum has stood this Winter without any further failure. I hope you have secur'd it. Mr Hawksmore appears to be so very feeble I think tis odds he cant attend you, and I should be glad upon yt account the Apothecaries in Architecture were sufficient to cure the distemper without the help of a Doctor.*[97]

On Saturday 27 March 1736 *Reads Weekly Journal* announced that '*Thursday morning died, at his House on Millbank, Westminster, in a very advanced Age; the learned and ingenious Nicholas Hawksmore Esq.; one of the greatest Architects this or the preceding Century has produc'd.*'[98]

Sir Thomas Robinson did not mourn Hawksmoor's death. On 24 April 1736 he wrote to Lord Carlisle:

*I was very sorry on your Lordship's account for poor Mr. Hawksmoor's death, and as in my opinion nothing will more add to the grandeur and magnificence of your Lordship's Mausoleum, than a proper out-wall and court round the building, I hope he had drawn a design for completing the necessary work before his death.*[99]

Hardly had Hawksmoor breathed his last than Sir Thomas Robinson saw it as an opportunity to interfere with his designs and to recommend that the mausoleum should be provided with a surrounding set of walls. By August 1736 Sir Thomas Robinson was negotiating with Henry Flitcroft, a former carpenter who had become one of Lord Burlington's favoured architects, as to whether he would oversee the completion of the mausoleum; Lord Carlisle rejected Flitcroft's services and Robinson then proposed that Daniel Garrett, another disciple of Lord Burlington, would be more suited to the task.[100] As he wrote to Lord Carlisle on 24 December 1736:

*My Ld. Burlington has a much better opinion of Mr. Garrets knowledge & judgmt. than of Mr. Flitcrofts, or any Person whatever, except Mr. Kent, he lives in Burlington house, & has had the care & conduct of the D. of Richmond's house my Ld. Harrinton's & all my Lds. designs he ever gave; I have talk'd with this Gentleman what he wou'd expect to go down with me the next Year & to be absent from London 5 or 6 weeks, his demand is 30 guineas & fall expences bore up & down.*[101]

On 15 March 1737 Lord Morpeth wrote to Lord Carlisle, '*I suppose you will soon sett about the Mausoleum and easily gett the cap finishd this year.*'[102] On 16

March Sir Thomas Robinson declared that he was '*extreamely glad Mr. Garrets designs meet with yr. approbation*'[103] and, on 7 April, '*I fancy 'ere this yr Ldp. has begun to work again on the roof of the Mausoleum.*'[104] On 19 October two guineas were '*Given to Mr. Garret for examineing my works at ye Mausoleum*';[105] and on 24 January 1738 Sir Thomas Robinson wrote:

*Enclosed are Mr. Garrets designs for the outward Court of the Mausoleum wch. have been approved att Chiswick, in my own opinion he has shewn great skill & judgemt. in what he has on this occasion perform'd, & the little Poggio att the going into the vault, will not only have a very good effect there, but be of great use to make a fine Landing above, & make the entrance into the Chappell more agreable and solemn – The staircase is the same as Ld B — at Chiswick, & I think very well adapted to this Building, in short I think the whole is according to the antient taste, & I hope yr Ldp will approve of these designs.*[106]

Thus Hawksmoor's designs for the Castle Howard mausoleum, over which he had laboured so long and thought so carefully, which he had discussed in every detail with Viscount Morpeth and Lord Carlisle, were, in the course of execution, dogged by bad luck and subjected at every point to the sniping and superior criticism of Sir Thomas Robinson and the Earl of Burlington. In the end the building was completed, not as Hawksmoor had intended, isolated and free-standing on its hill, but anchored in the landscape by steps which were copied from the Earl of Burlington's villa at Chiswick, and by outer walls and bastions by the Earl of Burlington's *protégé* Daniel Garrett (*Plate 51*).

## AESTHETIC RESULT

Of all the buildings at Castle Howard, the mausoleum is the most impressive, a monument of huge dimensions, but simple in its profile, dominating the surrounding landscape. Among the great architectural buildings in England, the Castle Howard mausoleum is one of the least known, the most secretive, isolated on the Yorkshire hillside, visible from all sides, but curiously aloof and self-contained, retaining within its form a sense of secrecy; a shrine to an unknown cult, a monument to a forgotten man. Nobody ever goes in; nobody comes out; its appearance is identical from whatever direction one is looking; huge and Cyclopean when one is standing close to it (*Plate 51*); miniaturized and austere from far away. It is a building which exerts a deep fascination.

In order to interpret the architectural form of the mausoleum, it is important

PLATE 51

A view of Hawksmoor's great mausoleum showing the force of the main structure and the slightly irrelevant steps added by Burlington's *protégé*, Daniel Garrett.

to place it in the context not only of the development of Hawksmoor's architectural career, an opportunity for Hawksmoor to design a building precisely attuned to his archaeological passions, but also of the changing desires and circumstances of the third Earl of Carlisle, for whom it was built.

It should be recognized that when the house at Castle Howard was first conceived, the third Earl was a comparatively young man, proud, arrogant, full of self-confidence, with the expectation of a successful political career ahead. It did not matter to him too much what other people thought of the designs, whether they were precisely correct in every detail. He and his architect, Vanbrugh, were principally interested in producing an effect of display and building a house which would be both enjoyable to live in and impressive to visitors. It is a house which succeeds in being immensely entertaining, vivid and, in many respects, superficial, concerned with outward magnificence and slightly disappointing when it comes to the rooms inside.

By the time it came to the plans for the mausoleum, the third Earl was a disappointed man. His political career had been short-lived. He and his fellow members of the Whig party had not enjoyed the same political influence with Queen Anne as they had under William III. The construction of the house had turned out to be not so much a celebration of political power as a long-drawn-

185

PLATE 52

Henry Howard,
Viscount Morpeth,
the third Earl of
Carlisle's eldest son and
heir, painted at the time
he went on the Grand
Tour in 1715.

out and financially difficult labour of love. His wife had decided that she did not like the cold Yorkshire weather and that she would live in Watford instead. They had separated. By the time George I succeeded to the throne and there was the possibility that the Earl of Carlisle would, once again, enjoy a position of political influence and prestige, his health had begun to deteriorate and he had decided that he preferred the isolation of Yorkshire, where he could live in an environment entirely of his own creation, rather than having to suffer the soot and political intrigues of London.

Lord Carlisle's children were a terrible disappointment to him. His son and heir, Viscount Morpeth, was a valetudinarian with a taste for antique busts, who wrote uninteresting letters to him concerning the state of his health (*Plate 52*). His eldest daughter, Lady Elizabeth (*Plate 49*), insisted on marrying against his wishes a prominent but bad-tempered Worcestershire lawyer, Nicholas Lechmere. In September 1725 she hit the gambling tables at Bath and was rumoured to have lost gigantic sums of money. According to Lady Mary Wortley Montagu,

*The discreet and sober Lady Lechmere has lost such Furious summs at the Bath that 'tis question'd whether all the sweetness that the Waters can put into my*

*Lord's blood can make him endure it, particularly £700 at one sitting, which is aggravated with many astonishing Circumstances. This is as odd to me as Lord Tenham's shooting himselfe, and another Demonstration of the latent Fire that lyes under cold Countenances.*[107]

In early February 1726 Lady Lechmere took a dose of laudanum, but failed to kill herself.[108] Both Lord Carlisle and Lord Lechmere refused to pay her gambling debts. In August 1726 Lord Carlisle received an unusual letter from his son-in-law:

*The Distress, wch my Wife remains under, is greater yn I can express in Words, And such as would move the Compassion of the Hardest Heart Towards Her. The afflictions I am bro[ugh]t Under, are very Heavy, But I ask no Compassion from You, for my self. The Regard You have shewn to me, since I marry'd Your Daughter, Ever taught me to expect None.*[109]

Soon afterwards Nicholas Lechmere died and, on a visit to Castle Howard to recover, Lady Elizabeth married Sir Thomas Robinson.

Lord Carlisle's second daughter was more amusing and regaled her father with entertaining letters full of London gossip. She married Viscount Irwin of Temple Newsam, who, to judge from his letters, was a scamp, whose primary interest was fornication. As he wrote to his brother Henry just before the wedding:

*Possibly you may have heard of my intentions of entring into the holy state of Matrimony, all preliminaries are agreed to & in a little time I shall be turn'd of, but the day of execution is not yet fix'd, if you make but a short stay att Paris you may divert yourself with a country dance amongst us; I come now to begg a favour of you that is to buy a ffan it must be a very good one being a present for my Doxy, the woman you know.*

He added that

*The ladies of Castle Howard are all in town & your Brother Irwin: I believe I shall swive my little Nymph before his hore getts into possession of his mannor of Tufton & Cufton, they all goe into Yorkshire in about 20 days & in a short time after follows consummation, Your brother Arthur is no changling he drinks & fucks dans toutes les bourdelles de la ville, Charles designs to gett into the Gards & fucks as often as his mighty Member can be raised which wee hear his women cannot always prevail with to a stiff erection.*[110]

Lord Carlisle's third daughter, Lady Mary Howard, never could find a husband,

PLATE 53

The third Earl of Carlisle in the full splendour of his coronation robes with a
backdrop of the north front of Castle Howard,
painted by William Aikman in 1728.

which was perhaps just as well, because her father was reputed to dislike having to provide a suitable dowry.

By the late 1720s when the mausoleum was being planned, Lord Carlisle was a comparatively old man, crippled by gout. He appears to have abandoned the majority of his contacts in London, only venturing down very occasionally to eat syllabubs with Lady Grisell Baillie.[111] Instead, he appears to have lived a carefully regulated life, mostly at Castle Howard in the company of his chaplain, with visits from his children.

So when it came to the design of the mausoleum, it was not only Hawksmoor who projected the long-pent-up frustrations of a difficult professional career into the making of a final and definitive architectural masterpiece: the third Earl of Carlisle had time and freedom to ponder his last great work, to look out to the distant horizon and to imagine a huge and noble architectural form, which would carry with it memories of his Grand Tour and which would provide an image of antique *dignitas*. It was to be a symbol laden with cultural resonances in a world which he regarded as being irredeemably corrupt. It was to be a place where he could contemplate his future without the thought of interfering priests.

On 1 January 1738 Lord Carlisle wrote to the Duke of Newcastle:

*The Older I grow the more I suffer from Age and infirmities; the Pains in my Stomach increase upon me, the least motion now (even that of a Coach) raises the humour in my Stomach; and gives me Pain; my happyness now consists not only in a quiet mind but likewise in a quiet Body.*[112]

On 21 February he again wrote, '*I find my self under a necessity of going to The Bath this Spring, altho' I much apprehend the difficulties and fatigue of the journey.*'[113] He reached Bath, but there, on 1 May, he died.

According to the *Political State of Great Britain*:

*On Saturday, May the 6th. the Corpse of the late Earl of Carlisle was carried from the Bath to his fine Seat at Castle Howard, to be interr'd in the Mausoleum there, built by his Lordship for the Burial-place of his Family; it consists of seventy Cells built of Stone; each of them is to hold one Coffin, and over them is a fine Chapel, in the Center of which, by his Lordship's Will, a Monument is to be erected to his Memory. These Edifices in the Neighbourhood of Castle Howard, are admired by Persons of Taste, as the most polite and elegant Structures in England.*[114]

This report was inaccurate. The mausoleum at Castle Howard was not ready to receive the third Earl's mortal remains until 1745. He was buried, for the time

PLATE 54

A detail of the columns of the mausoleum, demonstrating the overwhelming scale
of the building and its immensely powerful geometry.

PLATE 55

A view of the interior of the mausoleum showing the crisp stonework and the ceiling
modelled on the Pantheon in Rome.

being, in the local parish church at Bulmer, where an inscription in the sanctuary records:

*Charles Howard IIId Earl*
*Of Carlisle Intered May 14*
*1738 Removed Into The*
*Mausolaeum June 28*
*MDCCXLV*[115]

At the time of his death, the third Earl of Carlisle could look back on a long and, in some respects, a curious life, consisting of a rapid rise to a position of influence in the circle surrounding William III, and the rest of it deliberately withdrawn from London and the Court, devoted to building a succession of spectacular architectural monuments. Of these monuments the greatest is, undoubtedly, the mausoleum: a building which, in spite of the difficulties in its construction and the repeated changes in the evolution of the design, manages to transcend its circumstances by the form and vision of the original idea, by its layers of resonance into the classical tradition, by its very tight and carefully worked-out architectural geometry, by its wonderful light and still pristine, interior, whose crisp stonework stretches up into a dome modelled on the Pantheon in Rome (*Plate 55*).

It is a moot question how far aesthetic appreciation of a building is assisted or hindered by a more complete knowledge of the circumstances which led to its creation; but a knowledge of the circumstances undoubtedly enables the historical imagination to comprehend the physical structure of the building with a richer understanding of the ideological and cultural aspirations of its past.

# Conclusion

This has been a book about a historically specific and unusually well-documented group of buildings; but it has also implicitly been a book about how to look at and think about those buildings in terms of their original conditions of production. There has been a tendency in much architectural history to investigate buildings as if they were the products of the free volition of individual architects, to look at them from the outside and within the long perspective of history, not as configurations which were the result of accident and changes of mind and conflicts of desire. Yet it makes it easier to understand the physical form of a building if one can reconstruct the lost aspirations which lay behind the decision to build. Architecture is not only a form of sculpture; it also concerns the life of the people who lived in it and gave it meaning.

So, standing beside the Castle Howard mausoleum, it is possible to look back over the landscape and to see just below the surface an archaeology of feeling, of a self-important man travelling up to Yorkshire to survey a small village and contemplate its destruction; of William Talman, arriving in his carriage; Vanbrugh, laughing and forever ebullient, enjoying Castle Howard as a place where he could come and stay when life in London became difficult; workmen struggling with the preposterous complexities of constructing a palace on a bleak, open hillside; Hawksmoor diligently measuring everything up and looking forward to the day when he would have full executive responsibility; Sir Thomas Robinson wandering around, finding fault and pontificating on what should be done.

These images make it possible to strip back the foliage of intervening centuries, to regild the statuary, and to reinstate the sense of astonishment that at the end of the seventeenth century someone should have decided to build a palace on such a scale in such a place. Instead of being absorbed into the landscape as if it were a natural emanation of a forgotten historical conjuncture, it is possible to see it with the eyes of contemporaries, stark and startling. The feeling that it has of being a lost kingdom, under the control of some hidden articulating hand, becomes more comprehensible when it is seen as a place of highly projected fantasy and psychological retreat, where the third Earl of Carlisle and his architects, Sir John Vanbrugh and Nicholas Hawksmoor, were able to realize a set of complex architectural dreams, which remain as monuments to forgotten afternoons wandering round the estate and imagining the future.

# Notes

## ABBREVIATIONS USED IN THE NOTES

BL                British Library
CH                Castle Howard MSS.
*CSP (Dom.)*      *Calendar of State Papers (Domestic)*
CROC              Cumbria County Record Office, Carlisle
CROK              Cumbria County Record Office, Kendal
*CTB*             *Calendar of Treasury Books*
*DNB*             *Dictionary of National Biography*
HMC               Historical Manuscripts Commission Reports
H of N            Howard of Naworth MSS, Department of Palaeography and Diplomatic, University of Durham
H of PT           History of Parliament Trust
HRO               Hertfordshire Record Office
LAD               Leeds Archives Department
NPG               National Portrait Gallery, London
NYRO              North Yorkshire Record Office
PHA               Petworth House Archive
PRO               Public Record Office
RIBA              Royal Institute of British Architects
SNPG              Scottish National Portrait Gallery
SRO               Scottish Record Office
TCC               Trinity College, Cambridge
V&A               Victoria and Albert Museum, London
Webb, *Letters*   Webb, Geoffrey (ed.), *The Complete Works of Sir John Vanbrugh*, 4, *The Letters*, London, 1928.
Webb, *Mausoleum Letters*   Webb, Geoffrey (ed.) 'The Letters and Drawings of Nicholas Hawksmoor relating to the Building of the Mausoleum at Castle Howard', *Walpole Society*, XIX, 1931.
Wren Soc.         *Volumes of the Wren Society I-XX*, Oxford, 1924–43

CHAPTER ONE: THE PATRON

1 – For life at Naworth, see Lady Anne Halkett, *Memoirs*, ed. J. Loftis, Oxford, 1979, and Edmund Sandford, *A Cursory Relation of all the Antiquities & Familyes in Cumberland circa 1675*, ed. R. S. Ferguson, Cumberland and Westmorland Antiquarian and Archaeological Series no. 4, Kendal, 1890, p. 47.

2 – J. Hodgson, *A History of Northumberland*, Newcastle, 1832, II, ii, p. 402.

3 – G. J. W. Ellis (ed.), *Letters written during the years 1686, 1687, and 1688, and addressed to John Ellis, esq.*, London, 1829, II, pp. 45–6.

4 – *CSP (Dom.), 1687–9*, p. 356.

5 – H. F. Brown, *Inglesi e Scozzesi all'Università di Padova*, Venice, 1921, p. 36.

6 – E. Brown, *A Brief Account of Some Travels in divers Parts of Europe*, London, 1685; other contemporary descriptions of Vicenza appear in G. Burnet, *Some Letters containing an Account of what seemed most remarkable in travelling through Switzerland, Italy, some parts of Germany &c. in the Years 1685 and 1686*, Amsterdam, 1686, pp. 123–4; W. Acton, *A New Journal of Italy, containing What is Most Remarkable of the Antiquities of Rome, Savoy and Naples*, London, 1691, p. 68; and M. Misson, *A New Voyage to Italy*, London, 1695, p. 128.

7 – CH J8/35/1.

8 – CH J8/35/4.

9 – Information about the Grand Tour is contained in W. E. Mead, *The Grand Tour in the Eighteenth Century*, Boston, 1914; P. Kirby, *The Grand Tour in Italy 1700–1800*, New York, 1952; L. Schudt, *Italienreisen im 17. und 18. Jahrhundert*, Vienna, 1959; E. Chaney, *The Grand Tour and the Great Rebellion: Richard Lassels and 'The Voyage of Italy' in the Seventeenth Century*, Geneva, 1985; and J. Black, *The British and the Grand Tour*, London, 1985. Among contemporary guidebooks Viscount Morpeth is likely to have used R. Lassels, *The Voyage of Italy, or a Compleat Journey through Italy*, Paris, 1670, a standard and racy account of what to see, and the works of Brown and Burnet, copies of which were catalogued in his library in 1698.

10 – John Macky, *A Journey through England. In Familiar Letters From A Gentleman Here, To His Friend Abroad*, London, 1714, I, p. 120. The position of Carlisle House is established by George Clinch, *Soho and its Associations, Historical,*

*Literary and Artistic*, London, 1895, pp. 24–5, by H. Phillips, *Mid-Georgian London*, London, 1964, p. 297 and by *Survey of London: The Parish of St Anne, Soho*, XXXIII, London, 1966, p. 44. Confusingly, there was another Carlisle House to the west of Soho Square in what is now Carlisle Street. This is much better documented and became the assembly rooms of Mrs Cornelys in the late eighteenth century.

11 – CROK Rydal MSS WD/Ry Box 25. Information about Cumberland elections is contained in R. S. Ferguson, *Cumberland and Westmorland MPs from the Restoration to the Reform Bill of 1867*, London, 1871, and, especially, in R. Hopkinson, 'Elections in Cumberland and Westmorland 1695–1723', Ph.D. dissertation, University of Newcastle, 1973, and R. Hopkinson, 'The Electorate of Cumberland and Westmorland in the Late Seventeenth and Eighteenth Centuries', *Northern History*, XV, 1979, pp. 96–116. I am greatly indebted to Dr Hopkinson for his assistance and advice and for allowing me to consult his transcriptions of the ciphered Lowther correspondence; and to Dr Eveline Cruickshanks for permitting me to consult unpublished entries for the History of Parliament.

12 – CROC D/LONS/W/2/1/no. 13.

13 – HMC 10 IV Bagot, p. 331.

14 – Details of Lord Carlisle's expenditure in the late 1690s are contained in 'Mr. Nevil Ridley's Accounts 1692 to 1701' (CH H1/1/3). Information about Henry Cook appears in R. de Piles, *The Art of Painting, and The Lives of the Painters*, London, 1706, pp. 408–9, in *Dictionarium Polygraphicum: Or, The Whole Body of Arts Regularly Digested*, London, 1735, in George Vertue, *Notebooks*, II, Walpole Society, XX, 1932, pp. 134–5, and in E. Croft-Murray, *Decorative Painting in England, 1537–1837*, I, *Early Tudor to Sir James Thornhill*, London, 1962, p. 245; about Louis Chéron in George Vertue, *Notebooks*, III, Walpole Society, XXII, 1934, p. 22, in E. K. Waterhouse, *Dictionary of British 18th Century Painters*, Woodbridge, 1981, p. 79, and in Tessa Murdoch, 'Huguenot Artists, Designers and Craftsmen in Great Britain and Ireland, 1680–1760', Ph.D. dissertation, University of London, 1982, pp. 49–50 and 61–2; and about Thomas Highmore in Waterhouse, p. 171.

15 – CH H1/1/3; Rupert Gunnis, *Dictionary of British Sculptors 1660–1851*, London, n.d., rev.

typescript ed. John Physick (V&A 37.V.137), IV, pp. 1036–7.

16 – Gerrit Jensen and Joel Lobb are documented in G. Beard and C. Gilbert, *Dictionary of English Furniture Makers 1660–1840*, Leeds, 1986, pp. 551 and 485–7.

17 – CH H1/1/3.

18 – The date of his journey to Yorkshire is contained in a letter from Sir John Lowther to William Gilpin dated 23 July 1698 (CROC D/LONS/W2/1/38); the layout of Henderskelfe is shown on a map dated 1694 in the Castle Howard archive; the fire is referred to in a letter from Hugh James to James Grahme dated 7 April 1693, printed in Annette Bagot and Julian Munby (eds.), '*All Things is Well Here': Letters from Hugh James of Levens to James Grahme, 1692–5*, Cumberland and Westmorland Antiquarian and Archaeological Society, X, 1988, p. 33. I am indebted to Julian Munby for this reference.

19 – CH A5/41.

20 – CROC D/LONS/W/2/1/no. 26.

21 – CROC D/LONS/W/2/1/no. 54.

22 – CROC D/LONS/W/2/1/no. 58 and CROC D/LONS/W/2/2/no. 2.

23 – CROC D/LONS/W/2/2/no. 14.

24 – For previous suggestive investigations of the circumstances of building country houses, see H. J. Habbakuk, 'Daniel Finch, 2nd Earl of Nottingham: His House and Estate', in *Studies in Social History*, ed. J. H. Plumb, London, 1955, pp. 141–78; J. Summerson, 'The Classical Country House in 18th-Century England', *Journal of the Royal Society of Arts*, CVII, July 1959, pp. 539–87; L. and J. C. F. Stone, 'Country Houses and Their Owners in Hertfordshire, 1540–1879', in *The Dimensions of Quantitative Research in History*, ed. W. O. Aydelotte *et al.*, London, 1973, pp. 56–123; M. Girouard, 'A place in the country', *Times Literary Supplement*, no. 3859, 27 February 1976, pp. 223–5; and, especially, M. Girouard, *Life in the English Country House: A Social and Architectural History*, New Haven, 1978. Reviews of Girouard's *Life in the English Country House* include L. Stone in *Times Literary Supplement*, no. 3997, 10 November 1978, p. 1298 and J. H. Plumb in *New York Review of Books*, XXV, no. 16, 26 October 1978, pp. 6–9.

25 – The inscription is recorded in Thomas Gent's *Pater Patriae: Being, an Elegiac Pastoral Dialogue occasion'd by the most Lamented Death of the Late Rt. Honble. and Illustrious Charles Howard, Earl of Carlisle*, York, 1738, p. 14; John Tracy Atkyns commented in his *Iter Boreale* (MS Yale Center for British Art, p. 27) 'that Nothing but the highest Strain of Generosity could tempt a Man to expose himself by such wretched Stuff in Order to preserve the Memory of an Ancestor'.

26 – The draft for the inscriptions to the portraits was clearly carefully composed by the third Earl and survives (CH J8/35/12). The purpose of the mausoleum is described in one of the drafts of his will (CH J8/14B).

27 – For the history of the Howard family, there is the Hon. C. Howard, *Historical Anecdotes of the Howard Family*, London, 1769; and G. Brenan and E. P. Statham, *The House of Howard*, London, 1907.

28 – The principal sources for the life of Lord William Howard are *DNB*; G. Ornsby, *Selections from the Household Books of the Lord William Howard of Naworth Castle*, Surtees Society, LXVIII, Durham, 1878; D. Mathew, 'The Library at Naworth', in *For Hilaire Belloc*, ed. D. Woodruff, London, 1942, pp. 117–30; A. L. Rowse, 'Nicholas Roscarrock and his Lives of the Saints', in *Studies in Social History*, ed. J. H. Plumb, London, 1955, pp. 3–31; P. Williams 'The Northern Borderlands under the Early Stuarts', in *Historical Essays 1600–1750 presented to David Ogg*, ed. H. E. Bell and R. L. Ollard, London, 1963, pp. 1–17; and, especially, the works of Professor Howard Reinmuth: 'Lord William Howard, 1563–1640; A Great Border Magnate', Ph.D. dissertation, University of Minnesota, 1958; his article, 'Border Society in Transition', *Early Stuart Studies: Essays in Honor of David Harris Willson*, ed. H. S. Reinmuth, Minnesota, 1970, pp. 231–50; and an unpublished biography which he kindly allowed me to consult.

29 – Evidence for the sale of Lord William Howard's books appears in E. G. Millar, 'A MS from Waltham Abbey in the Harleian Collection', *British Museum Quarterly*, 7, 1933, p. 113, and C. E. and R. C. Wright, *The Diary of Humphrey Wanley 1715–1726*, London, 1966, p. 58; and for the dereliction of the Naworth garden in W. Stukeley, *Itinerarium Curiosum: or, An Account of the Antiquities, and Remarkable Curiosities in Nature or Art, Observed in Travels in Great Britain*, 2nd. edn, London, 1776, II, p. 58.

30 – Sources for the life of the first Earl of Carlisle

include *DNB*; B. Henning, *The House of Commons 1660–1690*, London, 1983, II, pp. 588–91; G. Miège, *A Relation of Three Embassies from his Sacred Majestie Charles II to the Great Duke of Muscovie, the King of Sweden and the King of Denmark perform'd by the Right Hoble the Earle of Carlisle*, London, 1669; G. Burnet, *Bishop Burnet's History of His Own Time*, 6 vols., Oxford, 1823; C. R. Hudleston (ed.), *Naworth Estate and Household Accounts 1648–1660*, Cumberland and Westmorland Antiquarian and Archaeological Society Record Series, IX, 1958; and H. Reinmuth, 'A Mysterious Dispute Demystified: Sir George Fletcher vs. The Howards', *Historical Journal*, 27:2, 1984, pp. 289–307.

31 – Burnet, II, p. 265.

32 – Burnet, II, p. 265.

33 – Henning, II, p. 590.

34 – Burnet, II, p. 265.

35 – J. Wilkinson, *The History of Carlisle House Soho*, London, 1939, p. 13.

36 – HMC *Ormonde* VII, p. 61.

37 – CH H2/3/8 'A Catalogue of the Right Honble Charles Earl of Carlisle's Books in the Library in his Lsps House in Soho Square London Taken in March 1698'.

38 – HMC *XI Report VII*, p. 42.

39 – CH J8/35/13.

40 – N. Tindal, *The History of England, by Mr Rapin de Thoyras, Continued from the Revolution to the Accession of George II*, London, 1745, XIX, p. 345.

41 – The link between heraldry and architecture is made by R. Blome, *Gentleman's Recreation*, London, 1686, which links both HERALDRY and ARCHITECTURE under ETHICKS. An excellent account of attitudes to genealogy is provided by A. Wagner, *English Genealogy*, Oxford, 1960.

42 – Abel Boyer, *The History of King William the Third*, III, London, 1703, p. 451; G. P. R. James, *Letters Illustrative of the Reign of William III from 1696 to 1708 Addressed to the Duke of Shrewsbury by James Vernon Esq., Secretary of State*, London, 1841, III, p. 94; N. Luttrell, *A Brief Historical Relation of State Affairs from September 1678 to April 1714*, Oxford, 1857, IV, p. 659; HMC *Carlisle*, p. 10.

43 – The complex electoral politics of this period are explored by J. H. Plumb, *The Growth of Political Stability 1675–1725*, London, 1965; G.

S. Holmes and W. A. Speck, *The Divided Society: parties and politics in England 1694–1716*, London, 1967; G. S. Holmes (ed.), *Britain after the Glorious Revolution*, London, 1969; W. A. Speck, *Tory and Whig: The Struggle in the Constituencies 1701–1715*, London, 1970; G. S. Holmes, *The Electorate and the National Will in the First Age of Party*, Lancaster, 1976; and G.S. Holmes, *British Politics in the Age of Anne*, rev. edn, London, 1987.

44 – CROK Levens MSS Graham correspondence.

45 – CROK Rydal Hall MSS 5547; *HMC XIV Bagot*, p. 335.

46 – PHA 15.

47 – CROK Rydal MSS WD/Ry Box 25.

48 – CROC D/LONS/W/2/3/no. 109.

49 – Walter Harris, *A Description of the King's Royal Palace and Gardens at Loo, Together With a Short Account of Holland*, London, 1699; Boyer, III, p. 495; [James Ralph], *The History of England during the Reigns of K. William, Q. Anne, and K. George I*, London, 1744, II, p. 978; A. W. Vliegenthart, 'Het Loo', *William and Mary and their House*, Pierpont Morgan Library, New York, 1979, pp. 43–6; John Dixon Hunt and Erik de Jong (eds.), 'The Anglo-Dutch Garden in the Age of William and Mary', *Journal of Garden History*, 8, nos. 2 and 3, April–September 1988, pp. 144–59.

50 – Ralph, III, p. 1000; Mark Noble, *A Biographical History of England from the Revolution to the End of George I's Reign*, London, 1806, II, pp. 38–9; Henry Horwitz, *Parliament, Policy and Politics in the Reign of William III*, Manchester, 1977, pp. 295–7.

51 – CROC D/LONS/W/2/4/no. 87.

52 – CROC D/LONS/W/2/4/no. 88.

53 – CROC D/LONS/W/2/4/no. 100.

54 – CROC D/LONS/W/2/4/no. 101; Luttrell, V, p. 123; Horwitz, p. 299.

55 – CROC D/LONS/W/2/4/no. 105.

56 – CROC D/LONS/W/2/4/no. 110.

57 – For this episode, see Burnet, V, p. 15; Luttrell, V, pp. 169–70; Keith Feiling, *A History of the Tory Party 1640–1714*, Oxford, 1924, pp. 364–5; Edward Gregg, *Queen Anne*, London, 1980, pp. 133–4, 152–8; Holmes, 1987, pp. 367–8.

58 – J. J. Jusserand, *A French Ambassador at the Court of Charles II*, London, 1892, p. 128. See also, S. Pepys, *Diary and Correspondence*, ed. R. Braybrooke, London, 1858, II, p. 212. Lord

Clarendon's own attitude towards the error of building Clarendon House is recorded in *The Life of Edward Earl of Clarendon Written by Himself*, Oxford, 1827, III, pp. 456–8.

59 – Burnet, I, p. 431.

60 – Pepys, III, p. 155. A popular squib is recorded in R. Gunther (ed.), *The Architecture of Sir Roger Pratt*, Oxford, 1928, p. 135.

61 – Roger North, *Of Building*, ed. H. Colvin and J. Newman, Oxford, 1981, p. 142. Euston is described by John Evelyn, *Memoirs, comprising his Diary from 1641 to 1705–6 and a Selection of his familiar letters*, ed. W. Bray, II, London, 1827, pp. 428–9; North pp. 142–3; C. Fiennes, *The Illustrated Journeys of Celia Fiennes 1685–c.1712*, ed. C. Morris, London, 1982, p. 139; and by Sir John Perceval, later first Earl of Egmont, in his 'Journal of a Tour of England, from London to Carlisle and return 14 July–28 October 1701', BL Add. 47057, f. 12.

62 – For Cliveden, see Evelyn, III, pp. 13–14; S. Markham, *John Loveday of Caversham 1711–1789: The Life and Tours of an Eighteenth Century Onlooker*, Wilton, 1984, p. 177; G. Jackson-Stops, 'The Cliveden Album: drawings by Archer, Leoni and Gibbs for the 1st Earl of Orkney', *Architectural History*, 19, 1976, pp. 5–16.

63 – C. Deering, *Nottinghamiae Vetus et Nova; Or an Historical Account of the Ancient and Present State of the Town of Nottingham*, Nottingham, 1751, p. 186; D. Defoe, *A Tour through the Whole Island of Great Britain*, ed. P. Rogers, Harmondsworth, 1971, p. 453.

64 – BL Add. 5238, no. 60; P. Leach, 'Ragley Hall', *Archaeological Journal*, CXXVIII, 1971, pp. 230–3.

65 – *The Complete Letters of Lady Mary Wortley Montagu*, ed. R. Halsband, Oxford, 1967, III, p. 162.

66 – G. Webb, 'The Letters and Drawings of Nicholas Hawksmoor relating to the Building of the Mausoleum at Castle Howard, 1727–1742', *Walpole Society*, XIX, 1930–1, p. 126 (henceforth Webb, *Mausoleum Letters*); G. S. Thomson, *Letters of a Grandmother 1732–1735*, p. 53. See also John Harris, 'Thoresby House, Nottinghamshire', *Architectural History*, 4, 1961, pp. 11–21.

67 – G. P. R. James (ed.), *Letters Illustrative of the Reign of William III from 1696 to 1708 Addressed to the Duke of Shrewsbury by James Vernon Esq., Secretary of State*, London, 1841, II, p. 108.

68 – D. Defoe, *A Tour thro' the Whole Island of Great Britain, divided into Circuits or Journies*, 2nd edn, London, 1738, II, p. 330.

69 – Lord Carlisle is known to have visited Chatsworth from an undated letter to the Duke of Wharton, in which he says, 'I went from Holm P. to Chatsworth, ye Duke is very well, & dos not design to leave yt place, till Newmarket meeting, where I hope to kiss your hands' (CROC D/LONS/L1/1) His brother William was staying there in August 1699 when Castle Howard was being planned (CH H1/1/3).

70 – Bishop White Kennet to Rev. Samuel Blackwell of Brampton (BL Lansdowne 1013, f. 290). I am greatly indebted for this reference to Dr Clyve Jones. Details of the fight are contained in John Lowther, Viscount Lonsdale, *Memoir of the Reign of James II*, York, 1808, p. 33; Evelyn, III, pp. 165–7; Colley Cibber, *An Apology for the Life of Colley Cibber*, London, 1925, I, p. 42; and Lord Macaulay, *The History of England from the Accession of James the Second*, ed. C.H. Firth, London, 1914, II, pp. 896–8. See also F. Thompson, *A History of Chatsworth*, London, 1949 and O. R. F. Davies, 'The Dukes of Devonshire, Newcastle and Rutland 1688–1714: A Study in Wealth and Political Influence', D.Phil. dissertation, University of Oxford, 1971.

71 – In August 1697 Lord Carlisle is known to have been at Petworth, since he paid out five shillings 'to ye Pheasant keeper att Pettworth' (CH H1/1/2). And, according to James Lowther, he was in Sussex again hunting in February 1699 (CROC D/LONS/W/2/1/no. 54).

72 – For Petworth, see John Macky, *A Journey through England. In Familiar Letters From a Gentleman Here To His Friend Abroad*, London, 1724, I, pp. 103–5; Defoe, 1738, I, pp. 201–2; and G. Jackson-Stops, 'The Building of Petworth', *Apollo*, May 1977, pp. 324–33.

73 – Boyer, III, p. 517. Similar views are expressed in M. Noble, *A Biographical History of England from the Revolution to the End of George I's Reign*, London, 1806, I, p. 9, and J. Dallaway, *Anecdotes of Painting in England*, London, 1828, III, pp. 215–16. For modern views of William and Mary's attitudes to the arts, see Stephen Baxter, *William III*, London, 1966, especially pp. ix, 37, 135, 144, 302; J. G. van Gelder, 'The Stadholder-

King William III as Collector and "Man of Taste" ', *William and Mary and their House*, Pierpont Morgan Library, New York, 1979, pp. 29–41; and J. R. Jones, 'The building works and court style of William and Mary', *Journal of Garden History*, 8, nos. 2 and 3, April–September 1988, pp. 1–13.

74 – N. Luttrell, *A Brief Historical Relation of State Afairs from September 1678 to April 1714*, Oxford, 1857, I, p. 504.

75 – E. Law, *The History of Hampton Court Palace*, London, 1891, III, p. 39; Burnet, IV, p. 3. The best modern account of Hampton Court appears in H. Colvin *et. al.*, *The History of the King's Works*, V, 1660–1782, pp. 153–74.

76 – Luttrell, I, p. 549.

77 – Fiennes, pp. 200–1; W. A. J. Prevost, 'A Journie to Carlyle and Penrith in 1731', *Transactions of the Cumberland and Westmorland Antiquarian and Archaeological Society*, LXI, 1961, pp. 210–14; H. Colvin *et. al.*, *Architectural Drawings from Lowther Castle, Westmorland*, Architectural History Monographs: no. 2, Society of Architectural Historians of Great Britain, 1980.

78 – Fiennes, pp. 153–4; Lord Egmont's 'Journal', f. 13; Letter Books of 1st. Lord Egmont, CXI (BL Add. 47030, f. 96).

79 – Duke of Leeds MSS, Yorkshire Archaeological Society.

80 – Lord Egmont's 'Journal', f. 23. See also 'Tour of several English counties in 1725 by a Cambridge Undergraduate' (Bath Public Reference Library MS 38:43 pp. 25–8); Defoe, 1738, II, pp. 352–3; P. Finch, *History of Burley-on-the-Hill*, London, 1901, and Habbakuk, pp. 141–78.

81 – HMC 12 V Rutland II, p. 148.

82 – *The Royal Progress: or, a Diary of the King's Journey, from His Majesty's setting out from Kensington till his return*, London, 1695, pp. 5–8.

83 – The classic account of the sociology of taste appears in T. Veblen, *The Theory of the Leisure Class*, New York, 1899; more recent investigations include Mary Douglas and Baron Isherwood, *The World of Goods: Towards an Anthropology of Consumption*, London, 1978; Mihaly Csikszentmihalyi and Eugene Rochberg-Halton, *The Meaning of Things*, Cambridge, 1981; and P. Bourdieu, *Distinction: A Social Critique of the Judgement of Taste*, London, 1984.

84 – J. Griffith, *A Sermon occasion'd by the Death of the late Duke of Devonshire*, p. 15.

85 – Macky, I, pp. 103–5.

86 – *Memoirs of the Life, Family, and Character of Charles Seymour, Duke of Somerset*, London, [1749], p. 65.

87 – CROC D/LONS/L2/6.

88 – CH G2/1/1.

89 – Andrea Palladio, *The Architecture of Andrea Palladio in Four Books*, ed. Giacomo Leoni, London, 1715, 2, p. 1.

90 – For the politics of this period, see the works listed in note 43 above. In addition, mention should be made of L. Stone, 'The Results of the English Revolutions of the Seventeenth Century', in J. G. A. Pocock (ed.), *Three British Revolutions: 1641, 1688, 1776*, Princeton, 1980, pp. 23–108, and G. S. de Krey, *A Fractured Society: The Politics of London in the First Age of Party 1688–1715*, Oxford, 1985.

91 – P. G. M. Dickson, *The Financial Revolution in England: A Study in the Development of Public Credit 1688–1756*, London, 1967; W. A. Speck, 'Conflict in Society', *Britain after the Glorious Revolution, 1689–1714*, ed. G. S. Holmes, London, 1969, pp. 135–54; D. C. Coleman, *The Economy of England 1450–1750*, Oxford, 1977; G. Holmes, *British Politics in the Age of Anne*, rev. edn, London, 1987, pp. xliv-lxi.

92 – The 'impeach'd Lords' were Lord Somers and the Earls of Orford and Halifax, whom the House of Commons had attempted to impeach in June 1701, but who had been acquitted by the House of Lords.

93 – CROC D/LONS/L13.

94 – For the attitudes of country opposition to the Court in the reign of William III, see D. Rubini, *Court and Country, 1688–1702*, London, 1968; and, especially, David Hayton, 'The "Country" interest and the party system, 1689–c.1720', in Clyve Jones (ed.), *Party and Management in Parliament, 1660–1784*, Leicester, 1984, pp. 37–74.

95 – J. R. Magrath (ed.), *The Flemings in Oxford being Documents selected from the Rydal Papers in illustration of the Lives and Ways of Oxford Men 1650–1700*, III, 1691–1700, Oxford, 1924, pp. 93–4.

96 – For this literary tradition, see G. R. Hibbard, 'The Country House Poem of the Seventeenth Century', *Journal of the Warburg and Courtauld Institutes*, 19, 1956, pp. 159–74; Raymond Williams, *The Country and the City*, London,

1973; V. C. Kenny, *The Country House Ethos in English Literature 1688–1750: Themes of Pastoral Retreat and National Expansion*, Brighton, 1984; D. E. Wayne, *Penshurst: The Semiotics of Place and the Poetics of History*, London, 1984.

97 – Ben Jonson, *The Works*, London, 1716, III, pp. 177–8.

98 – *Ibid.*, p. 179.

99 – [Mary Evelyn], *Mundus Muliebris: Or, the Ladies Dressing-Room Unlock'd, And her Toilette Spread*, London, 1690, preface.

100 – This literature is surveyed in J. Sekora, *Luxury: The Concept in Western Thought, Eden to Smollett*, Baltimore, 1977.

101 – *A Brief History of Trade in England*, London, 1702, p. 43.

102 – C. Davenant, *True Picture of a Modern Whig, Set Forth in a Dialogue between Mr Whiglove and Mr Double, Two Under-Spur-Leathers to the Late Ministry*, London, 1701, p. 31.

103 – North, p. 3.

104 – [J. Pomfret], *The Choice. A Poem*, London, 1700, p. 3.

## CHAPTER TWO: THE ARCHITECT

1 – CROC D/LONS/L/W/2/2/no. 25.

2 – CH G2/2/1.

3 – NYRO Worsley MSS ZON/13/1/226.

4 – CH H1/1/2.

5 – G. Webb (ed.), *The Complete Works of Sir John Vanbrugh*, 4, *The Letters*, London, 1928, p. 5 (henceforth Webb, *Letters*).

6 – Information about Talman's visit is contained in a letter written by Vanbrugh to the Duke of Newcastle dated 15 June 1703 (West of Alscot MSS Box 12) and printed in Lawrence Whistler, *The Imagination of Vanbrugh and His Fellow Artists*, London, 1954, pp. 35–8.

7 – For Talman's work for the Crown see H. Colvin *et. al., The History of the King's Works*, V, 1660–1782, pp. 33–5, 163–6.

8 – BL Add. 20101, f. 69. Talman's practice as a country-house architect is discussed in M. D. Whinney, 'William Talman', *Journal of the Warburg and Courtauld Institutes*, XVIII, 1955, pp. 123–39; H. Colvin, *A Biographical Dictionary of British Architects 1600–1840*, London, 1978, pp. 803–7 and J. Harris, *William Talman: Maverick Architect*, London, 1982.

9 – Whistler, p. 36.

10 – These plans are discussed in Whinney, pp. 133–4; M. D. Whinney and O. Miller, *English Art 1625–1714*, Oxford, 1957, p. 223; *Catalogue of the Drawings Collection of the Royal Institute of British Architects*, T–Z, ed. Jill Lever, Farnborough, 1984, p. 10; and Harris, *Talman*, pp. 35–6.

11 – Whistler, pp. 36–7.

12 – Charles Ford, 'Vanbrug's House' (Rothschild MS 2257, Trinity College, Cambridge); Jonathan Swift, *Miscellanies in Prose and Verse*, London, 1711, p. 389; Lawrence Whistler, *Sir John Vanbrugh, Architect and Dramatist 1664–1726*, London, 1938, p. 49; Lawrence Whistler, *The Imagination of Vanbrugh and His Fellow Artists*, p. 26; Kerry Downes, *Vanbrugh*, London, 1977, pp. 14–15; Kerry Downes, *Sir John Vanbrugh. A Biography*, London, 1987, p. 202.

13 – P. Hopkins, 'John Vanbrugh's Imprisonment in France, 1688–93', *Notes and Queries*, 224, 1979, p. 534. The standard account of Vanbrugh's time in France is now Downes, *Sir John Vanbrugh*, 1987, pp. 63–76.

14 – Downes, *Vanbrugh*, 1977, p. 249.

15 – HMC. *Finch*, IV, p. 416.

16 – Suggestions of French sources for the design of Castle Howard are provided by Whinney and Miller, p. 336 and Whistler, *Sir John Vanbrugh, Architect and Dramatist*, p. 50.

17 – S. Pepys, *Letters and the Second Diary of Samuel Pepys*, ed. R. G. Howarth, London, 1932, p. 36.

18 – C. Cibber, *An Apology for the Life of Mr. Colley Cibber, Comedian and later Patentee of the Theatre Royal. With an Historical View of the Stage during his Own Time*, Dublin, 1740, p. 125; M. Summers, *The Restoration Theatre*, London, 1934, p. 190; Downes, *Sir John Vanbrugh*, 1987, pp. 118–31.

19 – Cibber, 1740, p. 126.

20 – Macky, 1724, I, p. 188.

21 – J. Wright, *Historia Histrionica: An Historical Account of the English Stage*, London, 1699, pp. 10–11.

22 – Cibber, 1740, p. 241.

23 – Rev. J. Spence, *Anecdotes, Observations and Characters of Books and Men. Collected from the Conversation of Mr Pope*, ed. S. W. Singer, London, 1820, p. 46.

24 – J. H. Jesse, *Memoirs of the Court of England*

*from the Revolution in 1688 to the Death of George the Second*, London, 1843, II, p. 353.

25 – Webb, *Letters*, p. 5.

26 – Lord Egmont, 'Journal', f. 23.

27 – 'Tour by a Cambridge Undergraduate', p. 25.

28 – M. Misson, *A New Voyage to Italy. With Curious Observations on several Other Countries*, 4th edn., London, 1714, II, part I, p. 101.

29 – For contemporary descriptions of Chatsworth, see Fiennes, pp. 105–7; Joseph Taylor, *A Journey to Edenborough in Scotland by Joseph Taylor, Late of the Inner Temple, Esq.*, ed. W. Cowan, Edinburgh, 1903, pp. 30–9; BL Lansdowne MS 1014, f. 75; Stukeley, II, p. 26; 'Manuscript Observations of a Traveller in England principally on the Seats and Mansions of the Nobility and Gentry from 1722–1745, attributed to William Freman of Hamells, Hertfordshire' (Soane Museum AL 46a), ff. 58–61; 'Tour by a Cambridge Undergraduate', pp. 64–75.

30 – Charles Leigh, *The Natural History of Lancashire, Cheshire and the Peak, in Derbyshire: with an Account of the British, Phoenician, Armenian, Greek and Roman Antiquities in those Parts*, Oxford, 1700, III, p. 45.

31 – Misson, p. 101.

32 – Taylor, p. 35.

33 – Lord Egmont, 'Journal' f. 23.

34 – CH H1/1/3.

35 – For London's career, see Stephen Switzer, *Ichnographia Rustica: Or, the Nobleman, Gentleman, and Gardener's Recreation*, London, 1718, I, pp. viii-ix, 80–1; J. Gibson, 'A short Account of several Gardens near London, with remarks on some particulars wherein they excel, or are deficient, upon a View of them in December 1691', *Archaeologia*, XIII, 1796, p. 189; John Harvey, *Early Nurserymen*, Chichester, 1974, pp. 55–6.

36 – V&A E433–1951 and E434–1951. E434–1951 is the earlier and is inscribed on the back 'Maps for My Ld Carlisle'. These drawings were sold by the Marquess of Bute at Sotheby's on 23 May 1951, lots 19.16 and 19.17. See Whistler, *The Imagination of Vanbrugh and His Fellow Artists*, pp. 31–3, plates 21 and 22; and Downes, *Vanbrugh*, 1977, pp. 29–31.

37 – I am inclined to think that Professor Downes's introduction of a drawing at Welbeck Abbey (*Vanbrugh*, 1977, p. 29) at this point is a canard. The drawing is much more developed and

sophisticated than the early drawing in the Victoria and Albert Museum; and there is no evidence that it relates to Castle Howard, being labelled simply 'Mr Vanbrooks draft of a great house'.

38 – V&A E425–1951, inscribed on the back 'North Front Imperfect'; Whistler, *The Imagination of Vanbrugh and His Fellow Artists*, pp. 45–6, plate 4.

39 – V&A E425–1951; Whistler, *The Imagination of Vanbrugh and His Fellow Artists*, plate 6.

40 – V&A E420–1951; Whistler, *The Imagination of Vanbrugh and His Fellow Artists*, plate 3; Downes, *Vanbrugh*, 1977, plate 20.

41 – V&A E418–1951; Whistler, *The Imagination of Vanbrugh and His Fellow Artists*, pp. 41–4, plate 11, Downes, *Vanbrugh*, 1977, plate 21

42 – CH H1/1/2.

43 – CH G2/1/2.

44 – BL Add. 20101, f. 69.

45 – Webb, *Letters*, pp. 75–6.

46 – V&A E423–1951; Whistler, *The Imagination of Vanbrugh and His Fellow Artists*, p. 45, plate 12.

47 – Joseph Addison, *Critical Essays from the Spectator*, ed. Donald F. Bond, Oxford, 1970, p. 189.

48 – H. S. Goodhart-Rendel, *Nicholas Hawksmoor*, London, 1924, p. 13.

49 – Goodhart-Rendel, p. 14.

50 – K. Downes, *Hawksmoor*, London, 1959, p. 71.

51 – K. Downes, *Hawksmoor*, London, 1969, p. 51.

52 – Downes, *Vanbrugh*, 1977, p. 27.

53 – Downes, *Sir John Vanbrugh*, 1987, pp. 193–203. See also Charles Saumarez Smith, 'Battle of the Giants', *Building Design*, 16 October 1987, pp. 38–9. Although I disagree with aspects of Professor Downes's interpretation, I should emphasize that his studies are the single most indispensable source for any study of Castle Howard and that I am indebted to them throughout this book.

54 – Webb, *Letters*, pp. 6–7.

55 – W. R. Chetwood, *A General History of the Stage*, Dublin, 1749, pp. 202–3; Downes, *Sir John Vanbrugh*, 1987, p. 178.

56 – CH G2/2/3.

57 – CH H1/1/3 and CROC D/LONS/L3/nos. 72 and 73.

58 – CH J8/3/1.

59 – Downes, *Hawksmoor*, 1979, pp. 234–5.
60 – Webb, *Letters*, p. xii.
61 – Colen Campbell, *Vitruvius Britannicus, or The British Architect, Containing The Plans, Elevations, and Sections of the Regular Buildings, both Publick and Private, in Great Britain*, I, London, 1715, p. 63.
62 – Webb, *Letters*, p. 71.
63 – Ephraim Chambers, *Cyclopedia: Or, An Universal Dictionary of the Arts and Sciences*, London, 1728, S, p. 12.
64 – For discussion of the principles of late seventeenth-century planning, see M. Girouard, *Life in the English Country House*, pp. 120–62 and P. Thornton, *Seventeenth-Century Interior Decoration in England, France and Holland*, New Haven and London, 1978, pp. 52–63.
65 – CH G2/1/1, p. 13.
66 – John Evelyn, *An Account of Architects and Architecture, together with an Historical, Etymological Explanation of certain Terms, particularly Affected by Architects*, London, 1723, p. 12.
67 – Downes, *Hawksmoor*, 1979, p. 254.
68 – *Ibid.*, p. 254.
69 – SRO GD 18/2107, pp. 50–1.
70 – Webb, *Letters*, p. 14.
71 – Downes, *Hawksmoor*, 1979, p. 254.

CHAPTER THREE: THE HOUSE

1 – CH G2/2/2.
2 – *Register of the Freemen of the City of York*, II, 1559–1759, Surtees Society, CII, 1899, p. 174; Skaife MSS, York Reference Library, I, p. 254; for the Ettys, see Colvin, *A Biographical Dictionary of British Architects*, pp. 300–1.
3 – Webb, *Mausoleum Letters*, p. 148.
4 – CH G2/1/2, f. 1.
5 – CH G2/1/2, ff. 3,4,7. John Milburn or Milbourne had previously been employed as principal joiner at Levens Hall in Westmorland, where the contract for building the south wing on 8 September 1692 described him as 'John Milburne of Henderskelfe' (Bagot and Munby, p. 173).
6 – Downes, *Hawksmoor*, 1979, p. 234.
7 – BL Portland Loan 29/113, misc. 14, 'Notes in handwriting of Edward Harley, Earl of Oxford, of his Tour in Northumberland and other Northern Counties', 1725.
8 – CH G2/1/1, f. 55; CH G2/1/2, f. 7.
9 – CH G2/2/4.
10 – CH G2/1/2, f. 18.
11 – William Leyburn, *Architectonice: Or, a Compendium of the Art of Building*, London, 1700, p. 72. See also, *The Builder's Dictionary: or Gentleman and Architect's Companion*, London, 1734, I, GLASS.
12 – CH G2/1/2, ff. 9,10,18.
13 – CH G2/2/4.
14 – CH G2/2/15.
15 – Gunnis, p. 82; Richard Hewlings, 'Ripon's Forum Populi', *Architectural History*, 24, 1981, p. 47.
16 – CH G2/2/18.
17 – CH G2/1/2, f. 18.
18 – CH G2/2/27.
19 – Gunnis, pp. 190–1.
20 – CH G2/2/21.
21 – CH G2/1/2, f. 3.
22 – CH G2/2/11.
23 – CH G2/2/4.
24 – Whistler, *The Imagination of Vanbrugh and His Fellow Artists*, p. 37.
25 – Webb, *Letters*, p. 9.
26 – CH G2/2/20.
27 – CH J8/1/564.
28 – CH G2/2/27.
29 – CH G2/2/17; CH G2/1/2, f. 32.
30 – Colvin *et al.*, *The History of the King's Works*, V, p. 158.
31 – Murdoch, p. 111.
32 – CH G2/2/32.
33 – CH G2/2/27.
34 – John Cornforth, 'Boughton House, Northamptonshire', *Country Life*, CXLVII, 17 September 1970, p. 687; CH G2/2/27.
35 – CH G2/1/1, p. 95.
36 – CH G2/1/2, ff. 32, 43.
37 – CH G2/1/2, f. 3.
38 – Webb, *Letters*, p. 24.
39 – CH G2/1/2, ff. 32,43.
40 – Habbakuk, pp. 141–78. More recent suggestive accounts of the economics of country-house building appear in L. and J. F. C. Stone, 'Country Houses and Their Owners in Hertfordshire, 1540–1879', in Aydelotte *et al.*, pp. 56–123; Lawrence Stone, *Family and Fortune: Studies in Aristocratic Finance in the Sixteenth and Seventeenth Centuries*, Oxford, 1973; L. and J. F. C. Stone, *An Open Elite? England 1540–1880*, Oxford, 1984; and J. V. Beckett, *The Aristocracy in England 1660–1714*, Oxford, 1986,

pp. 325–37. The subject is currently being actively
investigated at the level of a county study by Dr R.
G. Wilson of the University of East Anglia, who
kindly lent me a copy of an unpublished paper
'Towards an Economic History of Country House
Building: The Norfolk Example', delivered at the
Institute of Historical Research, October 1988.

41 – CH J8/28/10.

42 – CH J8/28/16.

43 – CH J8/28/19.

44 – CH J8/28/22.

45 – CH J8/28/24.

46 – H of N C709.

47 – H of N C709.

48 – CH J8/5/1.

49 – CH J8/3/1–2.

50 – H of N C245.

51 – H of N N111.

52 – H of N C245.

53 – Romney Sedgwick, *The House of Commons
1715–1754*, London, 1970, II, p. 518.

54 – Webb, *Letters*, p. 14.

55 – Sedgwick, II, p. 626.

56 – CH J8/3/1–2.

57 – Lawrence Stone, *The Crisis of the Aristocracy
1558–1641*, Oxford, 1965, p. 760.

58 – O. R. F. Davies, 'The Dukes of Devonshire,
Newcastle and Rutland 1688–1714: A Study in
Wealth and Political Influence', D. Phil.
dissertation, University of Oxford, 1971, p. 146.

59 – PHA 243.

60 – Pearl Finch, *Burley-on-the-Hill*, London,
1901, p. 194.

61 – Geoffrey Beard, 'On Patronage', *Leeds Art
Calendar*, no. 46–7, 1961, p. 5.

62 – Gregory King, *Natural and Political
Observations and Conclusions upon the State and
Condition of England 1696. To which is prefixed,
A Life of the Author by G. Chalmers*, London,
1804, appendix.

63 – Geoffrey Holmes, 'Gregory King and the
Social Structure of Pre-Industrial England', in
Geoffrey Holmes, *Politics, Religion and Society in
England 1679–1742*, London, 1986, p. 294.

64 – Francis Atterbury, Bishop of Rochester,
*Epistolary Correspondence*, London, 1787, IV,
p. 394.

65 – Finch, p. 26.

66 – Habbakuk, p. 152.

67 – CROC D/LONS/L2/6.

68 – Davies, p. 206.

69 – Mark Girouard, 'Dyrham Park,
Gloucestershire', *Country Life*, 131, 22 February
1962, p. 398.

70 – CH J8/5/2.

71 – CH H1/1/4.

72 – CH H1/1/6.

73 – CH J8/33/12–60.

74 – CH J8/3/2.

75 – CH J8/33/12.

76 – CH J8/33/17.

77 – CH J8/33/50.

78 – CH J8/33/33.

79 – CH J8/33/43.

80 – CH J8/33/16.

81 – CH J8/33/19.

82 – CH J8/33/55.

83 – CH J8/33/13.

84 – CH J8/33/50.

85 – Richard Neve, *The City and Country
Purchaser, and Builder's Dictionary: Or, the
Compleat Builders Guide*, 2nd edn, London, 1726,
ARCHITECT.

86 – Webb, *Letters*, pp. 22–3.

87 – Webb, *Letters*, p. 23.

88 – Webb, *Letters*, p. 65.

89 – CH J8/5/1–2.

90 – Webb, *Letters*, p. 31.

91 – Webb, *Letters*, p. 35.

92 – M. W. Flinn, *Origins of the Industrial
Revolution*, London, 1966, pp. 47–8.

93 – L. and J. F. C. Stone, *An Open Elite?* For
reviews of the Stones' *An Open Elite?*, see C. Clay,
*Economic History Review*, XXXVIII, 1985, pp.
452–4; H. Perkin, *Journal of British Studies*, 24:4,
October 1985, pp. 496–501; R. G. Wilson, *Social
History*, 11:1, January 1986, pp. 105–8; B. Harris,
*Journal of Social History*, Fall 1986, pp. 201–204;
and, especially, E. and D. Spring, 'The English
Landed Elite, 1540–1879: A Review', *Albion*,
17:2, Summer 1985, pp. 149–66. See also Charles
Saumarez Smith, 'Supply and Demand in English
Country House Building, 1660–1740', *Oxford
Art Journal*, vol. II, no. 2, 1988, pp. 3–9.

94 – Webb, *Letters*, p. 9.

95 – CH G2/1/2, f. 5.

96 – CH G2/1/2, f. 2.

97 – CH G2/1/2, f. 21.

98 – For reviews of this literature, see Michael
Fores, 'The Myth of a British Industrial
Revolution', *History*, 66, no. 217, June 1981, pp.
181–98; Maxine Berg *et. al.*, *Manufacture in Town*

and *Country before the Factory*, Cambridge, 1983; Maxine Berg, *The Age of Manufactures 1700–1820*, London, 1985; and L. A. Clarkson, *Proto-Industrialization: The First Phase of Industrialization*, London, 1985.

99 – The most influential text has been Neil McKendrick *et. al., The Birth of a Consumer Society: The Commercialization of Eighteenth-century England*, London, 1982; but it has been related to a more general interest in attitudes towards consumption. See Chandra Mukerji, *From Graven Images: Patterns of Modern Materialism*, New York, 1983; Colin Campbell, *The Romantic Ethic and the Spirit of Modern Consumerism*, Oxford, 1987; Lorna Weatherill, *Consumer Behaviour and Material Culture 1660–1760*, London, 1988; and for a review of the literature, Grant McCracken, *Culture and Consumption: New Approaches to the Symbolic Character of Consumer Goods and Activities*, Indiana, 1988.

100 – CH H1/1/3.

101 – CH G2/2/5.

102 – NYRO Worsley MSS ZON/13/1/226.

103 – For Bramham, see 'Manuscript Observations of a Traveller in England principally on the Seats and Mansions of the Nobility and Gentry from 1722–1745' (Soane Museum AL 46a), f. 53; *The Travels through England of Dr Richard Pococke during 1750, 1751, and later years*, ed. J. J. Cartwright, Camden Society XLII, I, Westminster, 1888, p. 61.

104 – BL Add. 38,488a, f. 45.

105 – For this circle, see P. Rogers, 'The Burlington Circle in the Provinces: Alexander Pope's Yorkshire Friends', *Durham University Journal*, LXVII, 1974, pp. 219–26.

106 – Webb, *Letters*, p. 25.

## CHAPTER FOUR: THE INTERIOR

1 – CH H1/1/6.

2 – Information about John Vanderbank is contained in W. G. Thomson, *A History of Tapestry from the Earliest Times until the Present Day*, rev. edn, London, 1930, pp. 361, 488–9; *Survey of London*, XXXIV, *The Parish of St Anne, Soho*, London, 1966, p. 515; and Wendy Hefford, 'Soho and Spitalfields: little-known Huguenot tapestry-weavers in and around London, 1680–1780' *Proceedings of the Huguenot Society of London*, 24, no. 2, 1984, pp. 103–12.

3 – CH J8/1/564.

4 – CH F4/1. This probate inventory, which is the principal source of information for the interior furnishings, is likely to have been drawn up in 1758 or 1759, following the death of the fourth Earl.

5 – Yale Center for British Art MS, p. 20.

6 – HMC *Portland*, VI, p. 183.

7 – CH G2/2/6.

8 – CH H1/1/6.

9 – CH G2/1/1, p. 111.

10 – CH G2/1/1, p. 132.

11 – CH F4/1.

12 – Yale Center for British Art MS, p. 21.

13 – CH H1/1/6.

14 – *The General Shop Book: or, The Tradesman's Universal Director*, London, 1753, UPHOLDER.

15 – Beard and Gilbert, p. 427.

16 – A. Heal, *London Furniture Makers from the Restoration to the Victorian Era 1660–1840*, London, 1953, p. 62; Tessa Murdoch, *The Quiet Conquest: the Huguenots 1685–1985*, London, 1985, p. 186; Beard and Gilbert, p. 335.

17 – CH H1/1/6.

18 – CH F4/1.

19 – For identification of textile materials, see J. Fowler and J. Cornforth, *English Decoration in the 18th Century*, London, 1974; P. Thornton, *Seventeenth Century Interior Decoration in England, France and Holland*, New Haven and London, 1978; F. M. Montgomery, *Textiles in America 1650–1870*, New York, 1984; and E. S. Cooke, Jr (ed.), *Upholstery in America and Europe from the Seventeenth Century to World War I*, New York, 1987. I am greatly indebted to Wendy Hefford and Natalie Rothstein for their comments on this section.

20 – HMC *Portland*, VI, p. 183.

21 – CH F4/1.

22 – For state beds of this period, see Thornton, pp. 166–72.

23 – For paper hangings, see Francis Lenygon, *Decoration in England from 1660–1770*, London, 1914, p. 227; A. F. Kendrick, *English Decorative Fabrics of the Sixteenth to Eighteenth Centuries*, Benfleet, 1934, p. 65.

24 – CH F4/1.

25 – CH F4/1.

26 – CH F4/1.

27 – Yale Center for British Art MS, p. 21.

28 – HMC *Verulam*, p. 236.

29 – John Loveday, *Diary of a Tour in 1732*

through Parts of England, Wales, Ireland and Scotland, Roxburghe Club, Edinburgh, 1890, pp. 187–90.

30 – Yale Center for British Art MS, p. 21.

31 – BL Portland Loan 29/113 misc. 14.

32 – For the collecting of art in the late seventeenth century, see the excellent monograph by Iain Pears, The Discovery of Painting: The Growth of Interest in the Arts in England, 1680–1768, New Haven and London, 1988.

33 – For Lord Sunderland's collection, see T. F. Dibdin, Aedes Althorpianae: Or, An Account of the Mansion, Books and Pictures at Althorp, London, 1822; E. K. Waterhouse, Exhibition of Pictures from the Althorp Collection in Aid of the Friends of the Fitzwilliam Museum, Cambridge, London, 1947; J. P. Kenyon, Robert Spencer Earl of Sunderland 1641–1702, London, 1958; and K. J. Garlick, A Catalogue of the Pictures at Althorp, Walpole Society, 45, 1976.

34 – Lord Egmont, 'Journal', f. 220.

35 – R. Cowdry, A Description of the pictures, statues, bustos, basso-relievo's, and other curiosities at the Earl of Pembroke's house at Wilton, London, 1751; J. Kennedy, A Description of the Antiquities and Curiosities in Wilton-House, Salisbury and London, 1769; A. Michaelis, Ancient Marbles in Great Britain, London, 1882; Sidney, 16th Earl of Pembroke, A Catalogue of the Paintings and Drawings in the Collection at Wilton House, London, 1968; J. Cornforth, 'Conversations with Old Heroes: The Collections of Thomas, 8th Earl of Pembroke', Country Life, 26 September 1968, pp. 748–51; J. Cornforth, 'A Virtuoso's Gallery: the 8th Earl of Pembroke's Collection of Pictures', Country Life, 3 October 1968, pp. 834–41.

36 – Henry Snyder, The Marlborough–Godolphin Correspondence, Oxford, 1975, II, p. 973. See also D. Green, Blenheim Palace, London 1951; and H. Honour, 'English Patrons and Italian Sculptors in the first half of the eighteenth century', Connoisseur, May 1958, pp. 220–6.

37 – CH H1/1/3–4.

38 – CH J8/33/53.

39 – CH H1/1/6.

40 – CH J8/33/55.

41 – CH G2/2/37.

42 – CH H1/1/6.

43 – CH G2/2/37.

44 – CH J8/33/13.

45 – D. C. Mullin, The Development of the Playhouse, Berkeley, California, 1970, p. 71. See also Philip Olleson, 'Vanbrugh and Opera at the Queen's Theatre, Haymarket', Theatre Notebook, XXVI, Spring 1972, pp. 94–101; Joseph Roach, 'Vanbrugh's English Baroque: Opera and the Opera House in the Haymarket', Ph.D. dissertation, Cornell University, 1973; and Juliet Milhous, 'New Light on Vanbrugh's Haymarket Theatre Project', Theatre Survey, XVII, no. 2, November 1976, pp. 143–61.

46 – J. Downes, Roscius Anglicanus, Or, An Historical Review of the Stage, London, 1789, p. 64.

47 – Cibber, I, p. 143.

48 – Webb, Letters, p. 16.

49 – Olleson, p. 100.

50 – Webb, Letters, p. 26.

51 – Edward Croft-Murray, Decorative Painting in England, 1537–1837, 2, The Eighteenth and Early Nineteenth Centuries, London, 1970, p. 253.

52 – For Pellegrini's career in England, see George Vertue, Notebooks, I, Walpole Society, XVIII, 1930, pp. 38–9 and E. Croft-Murray, Decorative Painting in England 1537–1837, II, The Eighteenth and Early Nineteenth Centuries, Feltham, 1970, pp. 253–6.

53 – C. Ripa, Iconologia: or, Moral Emblems, London, 1709.

54 – Tancred Borenius, 'Venetian Eighteenth Century Painters in England', Studio Fine Art, April 1931, p. 51. See also Tancred Borenius, 'Castle Howard and its Lost Treasures', Burlington Magazine, 78, 1941, pp. 3–9.

55 – CH H1/1/6.

56 – CH G2/2/37.

57 – CH H1/1/6 and 10.

58 – Alastair Laing, 'Foreign Decorators and Plasterers in England', in Charles Hind (ed.), The Rococo in England: A Symposium, London, 1986, pp. 26–7.

59 – BL Portland Loan 29/113 misc. 14.

60 – Yale Center for British Art MS, p. 19.

61 – Borenius, 'Castle Howard and its Lost Treasures', p. 4.

62 – Tancred Borenius, 'Two Venetian Pictures of Queen Anne's London', Apollo, 3, no. 16 [1926], pp. 207–9.

63 – Croft-Murray, II, p. 221.

64 – Jacop Campo Weyerman, De Levensbeschryvingen der Nederlandsche

*Konstschilders en Konstschilderessen*, The Hague, 1769, IV, pp. 431–2. This passage was translated by Ton Broos.

65 – Downes, *Vanbrugh*, 1977, p. 33.

66 – For this aspect of Versailles, see Nathan T. Whitman, 'Myth and Politics: Versailles and the Fountain of Latona', in J. C. Rule (ed.), *Louis XIV and the Craft of Kingship*, Ohio, 1969, pp. 286–301; Anthony Blunt, *Art and Architecture in France 1500–1700*, rev. edn, London, 1973, p. 337; John Rupert Martin, *Baroque*, London, 1977, pp. 148–50; Guy Walton, *Louis XIV's Versailles*, New York, 1986, pp. 80–90.

67 – André Félibien, *Description Sommaire du Chasteau de Versailles*, Paris, 1674, pp. 11–12.

68 – Downes, *Vanbrugh*, 1977, p. 33.

69 – For issues of interpretation in eighteenth-century iconography, see D. J. Gordon, 'Ripa's Fate', in S. Orgel (ed.), *The Renaissance Imagination. Essays and Lectures by D. J. Gordon*, Berkeley, California, 1975, pp. 51–74.

70 – George Sandys, *Ovid's Metamorphosis Englished, Mythologiz'd and represented in Figures*, Oxford, 1632, p. 66.

71 – *Phaeton's Folly, or, the Downfal of Pride: Being a Translation of the Second Book of Ovid's Metamorphoses, Paraphrastically and Grammatically*, London, 1655, p. 3.

72 – *Memoirs of Denzil Lord Holles, Baron of Ifield in Sussex, From the Year 1641, to 1648*, London, 1699, p. 11.

73 – Croft-Murray, 1, *Early Tudor to Sir James Thornhill*, 1962, p. 250.

74 – *Ibid.*, p. 251.

75 – *Ibid.*, p. 267.

76 – CH H2/3/8; CH H2/3/1.

77 – Colnaghi, *Exhibition of Old Master and English Drawings*, May/June 1969, no. 89. Initialled on verso: *WK*, and inscribed: *Palace of the Sun, 1st Book of Ovide*.

78 – Ovid, *Metamorphoses. In Fifteen Books. Made English by Several Hands*, 2nd edn, London, 1724. Cambridge University Library classmark 7706 d. 130.

79 – Ovid, *Metamorphoses*, I, p. iv.

80 – Sandys, p. 37.

81 – *Ibid.*, p. 44.

82 – For seventeenth- and eighteenth-century interpretations of Endymion, see François Antoine Pomey, *The Pantheon, Representing the Fabulous Histories of the Heathen Gods and Most Illustrious Heroes. In a Short, Plain and Familiar Method by Way of Dialogue*, London, 1694, p. 255; Andrew Tooke, *The Pantheon, Representing the Fabulous Histories of the Heathen Gods and Most Illustrious Heroes*, London, 1713, pp. 242–3; Gerard de Lairesse, *The Art of Painting, in All its Branches, Methodically demonstrated by Discourses and Plates*, London, 1738, pp. 97–9; and Samuel Boyse, *A New Pantheon; or, Fabulous History of the Heathen Gods*, London, 1758, p. 95.

83 – CH G2/1/2, f. 58.

84 – For information about Bagutti, see Geoffrey Beard, *Decorative Plasterwork in Great Britain*, London, 1975, pp. 54 and 203, and Laing, pp. 24–7.

85 – H. A. Tipping and Christopher Hussey, *English Homes Period IV: 2, The Work of Sir John Vanbrugh and his School, 1699–1736*, London, 1928, p. 21.

86 – CH G2/1/2, f. 61.

87 – CH G2/1/1, p. 124; Gunnis, p. 393.

88 – Werner Sombart, *Luxury and Capitalism*, Ann Arbor, Michigan, 1967, p. 101.

89 – Webb, *Letters*, pp. 55–6.

90 – Webb, *Letters*, pp. 56–7.

91 – W. Pick, *An Authentic Historical Racing Calendar of all the Plates, Sweepstakes, Matches &c. run for at York*, York, 1785, p. 5.

92 – Montagu, I, p. 213.

93 – CTB XXIX 1714–1715 p.v; Wolfgang Michael, *England under George I, 1, The Beginnings of the Hanoverian Dynasty*, London, 1936, p. 57.

94 – HMC *Carlisle*, p. 14.

95 – CROC D/LONS/W/3/no. 18.

CHAPTER FIVE: THE GARDEN

1 – For information about the life of George London, see references in Chapter 2, note 35.

2 – Switzer, I, pp. 80–1.

3 – George London and Henry Wise, *The Compleat Gardiner: Or, Diversions for Cultivating and Right Ordering of Fruit-Gardens and Kitchen-Gardens*, 2nd edn, London, 1699, advertisement. See Blanche Henrey, *British Botanical and Horticultural Literature before 1800*, Oxford, 1975, I, p. 190.

4 – V&A E433–1951 and E434–1951.

5 – BL Portland Loan 29/233, f. 89.

6 – Switzer, II, p. 198.

7 – For their association see John Harris, *William Talman: Maverick Architect*, London, 1982, pp. 43–5.

8 – CH H1/1/3.

9 – Downes, *Hawksmoor*, 1979, p. 234.

10 – Whistler, *The Imagination of Vanbrugh and his Fellow Artists*, p. 35.

11 – BL Stowe MSS 748, f. 9.

12 – Webb, *Letters*, p. 19.

13 – Webb, *Letters*, p. 30

14 – N. Hardwick (ed.), *A Diary of the Journey through the North of England made by William and John Blathwayt of Dyrham Park in 1703*, Gloucester, 1977, p. 18.

15 – CH G2/1/2, f. 20.

16 – CH G2/2/13.

17 – CH G2/1/2, f. 20.

18 – CH G2/2/14.

19 – CH H1/1/4.

20 – CH J8/33/15.

21 – CH J8/33/62.

22 – Joan Thirsk (ed.), *Agrarian History of England and Wales*, 5, *1640–1750*, Cambridge, 1984, II, p. 527.

23 – CH G2/1/2, f. 20.

24 – CH G2/1/1, f. 112.

25 – West Suffolk RO E2/44/1, pp. 117–41.

26 – Rev. W. MacRitchie, *Diary of a Tour through Great Britain in 1795*, ed. D. MacRitchie, London, 1897, p. 125.

27 – In the middle part of the century, the head gardener was Robert Teesdale, who was described by the *York Chronicle* on 9 July 1773 as 'well known for his eminent abilities in that profession'. I am grateful to Andrew Duncan for lending me a so far unpublished book, 'A Palace, A Town, A Fortified City: Castle Howard 1770–1820', which contains a chapter on the later history of the gardens.

28 – CH G2/2/20.

29 – CH G2/2/29.

30 – CH G2/1/2, f.30.

31 – CH G2/1/2, f.45.

32 – CH G2/1/2, f.47.

33 – CH G2/1/2, f.48.

34 – For Nost's career, see Gunnis, pp. 279–82; and H. Colvin *et. al.*, *History of the King's Works*, V, p. 173.

35 – CH H1/1/6.

36 – CH G2/2/32.

37 – Switzer, I, p. 87.

38 – C. Hussey, *English Gardens and Landscape 1700–1750*, London, 1967, p. 89.

39 – 'Account of my Journey begun 6 Aug 1724', Yorkshire Archaeological Society, MS 328.

40 – BL Portland Loan 29/233, f. 89.

41 – Bath Public Reference Library MS 38:43, pp. 43–6.

42 – SRO GD 18/2107, pp. 50–1.

43 – Yale Center for British Art MS, pp. 23–5.

44 – Switzer, I, p. 87.

45 – Joseph Taylor, *A Journey to Edenborough in Scotland*, Edinburgh, 1903, pp. 30–9.

46 – Stukeley, p. 52.

47 – CH H1/1/3.

48 – Sir William Temple, *Miscellanea*, London, 1697, II, p. 110.

49 – G.W. Johnson, *A History of English Gardening, Chronological, Biographical, Literary, and Critical*, London, 1829, p. 121.

50 – Temple, II, p. 127.

51 – *Ibid.*, p. 118.

52 – BL Add. 47030, f. 90. See also John Dixon Hunt and Erik de Jong (eds.), 'The Anglo-Dutch Garden in the Age of William and Mary', *Journal of Garden History*, 8, nos. 2 and 3, April–September 1988, pp. 245–7.

53 – Temple, II, p. 132.

54 – CH G2/1/2, f. 20. The estate maps of 1694 and 1727 are in the Castle Howard archive.

55 – Vyner MSS 13151, VR Correspondence file, *cit.* Richard Hewlings, 'Ripon's Forum Populi', *Architectural History*, 24, 1981, p. 49.

56 – Montagu, I, p. 201.

57 – Webb, *Letters*, p. 60.

58 – CH G2/1/2, f. 62.

59 – CH G2/1/1, p. 64.

60 – Campbell, III, pp. 5–6.

61 – Bath Public Reference Library, MS 38:43.

62 – Yale Center for British Art MS, p. 18.

63 – 'A Journey through Hertfordshire, Lincolnshire, and Notts. to the Northern Counties of Scotland, by Timothy Thomas, chaplain to Edward Harley, Earl of Oxford, 1725' (BL Portland Loan 29/233, f. 87, reprinted in HMC *Portland*, VI, p. 95).

64 – Webb, *Letters*, p. 152.

65 – *Ibid.*, p. 173.

66 – CH F4/14/12.

67 – Yale Center for British Art MS, p. 17.

68 – *Ibid.*, pp. 25–6.

69 – Webb, *Letters*, pp. 129–30.

70 – *Ibid.*, p. 131.

71 – *Ibid.*, p. 143.

72 – *Ibid.*, pp. 147–8.

73 – *Ibid.*, p. 157.

74 – Gunnis, p. 190.

75 – BL Portland Loan 29/113 misc. 14; Yale Center for British Art MS, p. 22.

76 – Yale Center for British Art MS, p. 23.

77 – CH G2/2/52.

78 – Ralph Thoresby, *The Diary of Ralph Thoresby F.R.S.*, ed. Rev. J. Hunter, London, 1830, II, p. 209. For Carpentière, see Gunnis, pp. 82–3.

79 – Francis Haskell and Nicholas Penny, *Taste and the Antique: the Lure of Classical Sculpture 1500–1900*, New Haven, 1981, pp. 321–3.

80 – *Ibid.*, pp. 211, 232–3, 307.

81 – CH G2/2/51 and 52.

82 – Campbell, III, pp. 5–6.

83 – Webb, *Letters*, p. 171.

84 – HMC *Carlisle*, p. 34.

85 – HRO, Cowper [Panshanger] MSS D/EP F57.

86 – CH J8/1/769.

87 – Webb, *Letters*, p. 142.

88 – BL Add. 47030, f. 74.

89 – Webb, *Letters*, p. 152.

90 – Defoe, 1971, p. 347.

91 – Webb, *Letters*, p. 165.

92 – *Ibid.*, p. 132.

93 – *Ibid.*, p. 135.

94 – BL Portland Loan 29/113 misc. 14.

95 – Philip Yorke, 'The Travel Journal of Philip Yorke 1744–1763', *Publications of the Bedfordshire Historical Record Society*, XLVII, 1968, pp. 130–1.

96 – Webb, *Letters*, p. 136.

97 – *Ibid.*, p. 138.

98 – CH J8/1/566.

99 – CH J8/1/567. The idea of putting a lake to the north of the house was left until the late 1790s to execute.

100 – Webb, *Letters*, p. 159.

101 – CH J8/1/507.

102 – 'Itinerary of a journey from Cambridge to Suffolk, Norfolk, Lincolnshire and Yorkshire in 1741'(BL Add. 38, 488a, f. 49).

103 – Downes, *Hawksmoor*, 1979, p. 243.

104 – Webb, *Letters*, p. 156.

105 – *Ibid.*, p. 157.

106 – John James (trans.), *The Theory and Practice of Gardening by A.J. Dezalliers d'Argenville*, London, 1712, pp. 76–7.

107 – Webb, *Letters*, p. 160.

108 – *Ibid.*, p. 172.

109 – Buckinghamshire Archaeological Society MS 195/4 no. 2. I am grateful to Peter Goodchild for this reference.

110 – CH J8/1/576.

111 – CH J8/4/7.

112 – Beard, *Decorative Plasterwork*, p. 249.

113 – CH J8/34/234.

114 – Downes, *Hawksmoor*, 1979, p. 267. A proposal for the Temple of Venus survives in the British Museum, Department of Prints and Drawings (K45.18.1).

115 – Webb, *Mausoleum Letters*, p. 129.

116 – *Ibid.*, p. 154.

117 – CH J8/1/631.

118 – Nick Helm wrote a short, but excellent, diploma thesis on the Temple of Venus for the Architectural Association in 1978, which he kindly allowed me to consult.

119 – Webb, *Mausoleum Letters*, p. 119.

120 – Ronald Paulson, *Emblem and Expression: Meaning in English Art of the Eighteenth Century*, London, 1975, pp. 19–20. See also John Dixon Hunt and Peter Willis (eds.), *The Genius of the Place: The English Landscape Garden 1620–1820*, London, 1975, p. 15.

121 – Webb, *Letters*, p. 173.

122 – CH J8,35/6.

123 – For an essentially literary view of gardens of this period, see, for example, E. Malins, *English Landscaping and Literature 1660–1840*, London, 1966; Maynard Mack, *The Garden and the City*, Oxford, 1969; John Dixon Hunt, *The Figure in the Landscape*, Baltimore, 1976; Morris Brownell, *Alexander Pope and the Arts of Georgian England*, Oxford, 1978; D. C. Streatfield and A.M. Duckworth, *Landscape in the Gardens and the Literature of 18th Century England*, Los Angeles, 1981; and Peter Martin, *'Pursuing Innocent Pleasures': The Gardening World of Alexander Pope*, Hamden, Conn., 1983. A different attitude is evident in Robert Williams, 'Rural Economy and the Antique in the English Landscape Garden', *Journal of Garden History*, 7:1, January–March 1987, pp. 73–96 and in the research being undertaken by Tom Williamson at the Centre for East Anglian Studies.

124 – E. P. Thompson, *Whigs and Hunters: The Origin of the Black Act*, London, 1975, pp. 197–8. See also E. P. Thompson, 'Patrician Society,

Plebeian Culture', *Journal of Social History*, 7, Summer 1974, pp. 382–405; and E. P. Thompson, '18th Century English Society: Class Struggle Without Class?', *Social History*, 3, 1978, pp. 133–65.

125 – For more recent interpretations of this period, see Geoffrey Holmes, 'The achievement of stability: the social context of politics from the 1680s to the age of Walpole', in J. Cannon (ed.), *The Whig Ascendancy: Colloquies on Hanoverian England*, London, 1981, pp. 1–22; Linda Colley, *In Defiance of Oligarchy: The Tory Party 1714–60*, Cambridge, 1982; Jeremy Black (ed.), *Britain in the Age of Walpole*, London, 1984, especially pp. 1–22, 45–68; and the controversy surrounding the publication of J. C. D. Clark, *English Society 1688–1832: Ideology, social structure and political practice during the* ancien régime, Cambridge, 1985 and J. C. D. Clark, *Revolution and Rebellion: State and society in England in the seventeenth and eighteenth centuries*, Cambridge, 1986. See Joanna Innes 'Jonathan Clark, Social History and England's "Ancien Regime" ', *Past and Present*, 115, 1987, pp. 165–200.

126 – Maynard Mack, *Alexander Pope, A Life*, New Haven, 1985, p. 498.

127 – Alexander Pope, *Epistles to Several Persons (Moral Essays)*, ed. F.W. Bateson, London, 1951, pp. 143–4.

128 – Webb, *Mausoleum Letters*, p. 129.

129 – Lady Anne Irwin, *Castle Howard the Seat of the Right Honourable the Earl of Carlisle*, London, 1732, p. 1.

130 – *Ibid.*, p. 3.

131 – *Ibid.*, p. 6.

132 – CH J8/1/241.

133 – HMC *Carlisle*, pp. 97–8.

134 – *Gentleman's Magazine*, VII, August 1737, p. 506.

135 – Thomas Gent, *Pater Patriae: Being, An Elegiac Pastoral Dialogue Occasioned By the most Lamented Death of the Late Rt. Honble. and Illustrious Charles Howard, Earl of Carlisle*, York, [1738], p. 4.

CHAPTER SIX: THE MAUSOLEUM

1 – Webb, *Letters*, p. 147.

2 – Webb, *Letters*, p. 148.

3 – Bonamy Dobrée (ed.), *The Complete Works of Sir John Vanbrugh*, vols. 1–3, *The Plays*, London, 1927, I, p. 24.

4 – *Ibid.*, p. 38.

5 – *Ibid.*, p. 64.

6 – *Ibid.*, p. 62.

7 – *Ibid.*, p. 79.

8 – *Ibid.*, p. 89.

9 – *Ibid.*, p. 81.

10 – *Ibid.*, p. 88.

11 – *Ibid.*, p. 117.

12 – *Ibid.*, p. 127.

13 – *Ibid.*, p. 166.

14 – *Ibid.*, p. 153.

15 – *Ibid.*, p. 149.

16 – *Ibid.*, pp. 157–9.

17 – Webb, *Letters*, p. 148.

18 – *Ibid.*, p. 29.

19 – BL Add. 61465, f. 75.

20 – CH J8/35/15.

21 – CH H2/3/8; CH H2/3/1. For the influence of Hobbes in the late seventeenth century, see Samuel Mintz, *The Hunting of Leviathan: Seventeenth-century Reactions to the Materialism and Moral Philosophy of Thomas Hobbes*, Cambridge, 1962; and John Bowle, *Hobbes and his Critics*, rev. edn., London, 1969.

22 – Thomas Hobbes, *Leviathan, or The Matter, Forme and Power of a Commonwealth, Ecclesiastical and Civill*, London, 1651, p. 7.

23 – John Leland, *A View of the Principal Deistical Writers that have appeared in England in the Last and Present Century*, 4th edn, London, 1764, I, p. 32.

24 – Hobbes, p. 200.

25 – *Ibid.*, p. 57.

26 – *Ibid.*, p. 269.

27 – Thomas Story, *A Journal of the Life of Thomas Story*, Newcastle, 1747.

28 – *Ibid.*, p. 617.

29 – *Ibid.*, p. 623. For the history of the Quakers in the early eighteenth century, see R. T. Vann, *The Social Development of English Quakerism 1655–1755*. Cambridge, Mass., 1969, pp. 158–96; and M. R. Watts, *The Dissenters: From the Reformation to the French Revolution*, Oxford, 1978, pp. 269–70, 307–8.

30 – Story, pp. 659–61.

31 – *Ibid.*, pp. 679–80.

32 – *Ibid.*, p. 618.

33 – For the background to this literature and to the growth of heterodox opinion in the early

eighteenth century, see Leslie Stephen, *History of English Thought in the Eighteenth Century*, 2nd edn, London, 1881; R. N. Stromberg, *Religious Liberalism in Eighteenth Century England*, Oxford, 1954; G. R. Cragg, *Reason and Authority in the Eighteenth Century*, Cambridge, 1964; John Redwood, *Reason, Ridicule and Religion: The Age of Enlightenment in England, 1660–1750*, London, 1976; and R. E. Sullivan, *John Toland and the Deist Controversy: A Study in Adaptation*, Cambridge, Mass., 1982.

34 – CH H2/3/1.

35 – Matthew Tindal, *The Rights of the Christian Church asserted against the Romish and all other Priests who claim an independent power over it*, London, 1706, p. lxxi.

36 – John Toland, *Letters to Serena*, London, 1704, p. 123.

37 – Joseph Glanvill, *Essays on Several Important Subjects in Philosophy and Religion*, London, 1676, VI, p. 2.

38 – William Coward, *Second Thoughts concerning the Human Soul*, London, 1702, p. 105.

39 – CH J8/14B.

40 – Downes, *Hawksmoor*, 1979, p. 40.

41 – Webb, *Mausoleum Letters*, p. 117.

42 – Christopher Wren (ed.), *Parentalia: or, Memoirs of the Family of the Wrens*, London, 1750, pp. 367–8. See also Downes, *Hawksmoor*, 1979, p. 21.

43 – Webb, *Mausoleum Letters*, p. 136.

44 – Downes, *Hawksmoor*, 1979, p. 187; also Hugh Meller, *St George's, Bloomsbury*, London, 1975, pp. 5–6.

45 Webb, *Mausoleum Letters*, p. 117.

46 – *The Diary of Robert Hooke, 1672–1680*, ed. H. W. Robinson and W. Adams, London, 1935, pp. 317, 320–2; Downes, *Hawksmoor*, 1979, pp. 20–1.

47 – Wren, *Discourse*, p. 10.

48 – Webb, *Mausoleum Letters*, p. 119.

49 – CH J8/14B.

50 – For Hawksmoor's library, see Kerry Downes, 'Hawksmoor's sale catalogue', *Burlington Magazine*, XCV, 1953, pp. 332–5; and A. N. L. Munby (ed.), *Sale Catalogues of Libraries of Eminent Persons*, 4, *Architects*, ed. D. J. Watkin, pp. 45–105.

51 – John Breval, *Remarks on several Parts of Europe: Relating chiefly to the History, Antiquities and Geography, of those Countries Through which the Author has travel'd*, London, 1726, II, pp. 269–70.

52 – Breval, II, p. 270.

53 – Pietro Santi Bartoli, *Gli Antichi Sepolcri, overo Mausolei Romani et Etruschi*, Rome, 1704, plates 35, 36, 37, 38.

54 – CH J8/1/ 578.

55 – Webb, *Mausoleum Letters*, p. 120.

56 – *Ibid.*, p. 121.

57 – Andrea Palladio, *L'Architettura, divisa in quattro libri*, Venice, 1642, p. 71.

58 – Webb, *Mausoleum Letters*, p. 135.

59 – CH J8/1/510.

60 – Webb, *Mausoleum Letters*, plate XVIII (a) and (b).

61 – *Ibid.*, plate XX.

62 – *Ibid.*, plate XIX.

63 – *Ibid.*, p. 163.

64 – *Ibid.*, p. 121.

65 – *Ibid.*, p. 124.

66 – *Ibid.*, p. 125.

67 – Downes, *Hawksmoor*, 1979, p. 267.

68 – *Ibid.*, p. 167.

69 – CH J8/4/7.

70 – Webb, *Mausoleum Letters*, p. 127.

71 – *Ibid.*, p. 127.

72 – HMC *Carlisle*, p. 88.

73 – For this episode, see R. Wittkower, 'Burlington and His Work in York', in W. A. Singleton (ed.), *Studies in Architectural History*, York, 1954, p. 53, and P. Borsay, 'The English urban renaissance: the development of provincial urban culture c.1680–c.1760', *Social History*, V, 1977, p. 582. For Burlington's career and views of architecture, see James Lees-Milne, *Earls of Creation*, London, 1962, pp. 103–56, and Jacques Carré, 'Lord Burlington (1694–1753). Le Connaisseur, le mécène, l'architecte', Ph.D. dissertation, Dijon, 1980.

74 – HMC *Hastings*, III, p. 15.

75 – Webb, *Mausoleum Letters*, p. 131.

76 – Gladys Scott Thomson, *Letters of a Grandmother 1732–1735*, London, 1943, p. 58.

77 – Colvin *et. al.*, *History of the King's Works*, V, p. 419.

78 – *Read's Weekly Journal*, 27/3/1736, no. 603.

79 – Webb, *Mausoleum Letters*, pp. 133–7.

80 – *Ibid.*, p. 132.

81 – For the career of Sir Thomas Robinson, see Sedgwick, pp. 338–9; Colvin, *A Biographical*

*Dictionary of British Architects*, pp. 702–3; and
Michael McCarthy, 'Sir Thomas Robinson: An
Original English Palladian', *Architectura*, 10:1,
1980, pp. 38–57.
82 – CH J8/1/412.
83 – CH J8/1/427.
84 – CH J8/1/429.
85 – Webb, *Mausoleum Letters*, p. 138.
86 – CH J8/1/431.
87 – CH J8/1/433.
88 – CH J8/1/205.
89 – Webb, *Mausoleum Letters*, p. 144.
90 – *Ibid.*, pp. 144–5.
91 – Downes, *Hawksmoor*, 1979, p. 268.
92 – Webb, *Mausoleum Letters*, p. 146.
93 – CH J8/1/457.
94 – Webb, *Mausoleum Letters*, pp. 150–1.
95 – *Ibid.*, p. 158.
96 – *Ibid.*, p. 159.
97 – CH J8/1/259.
98 – *Read's Weekly Journal*, 27/3/1736, no. 603.
99 – *HMC Carlisle*, p. 169.
100 – For Garrett, see Peter Leach, 'The
Architecture of Daniel Garrett', *Country Life*,
CLVI, September 1974, pp. 694–7, 766–9, 834–7;
and Colvin, pp. 332–4.

101 – CH J8/1/490.
102 – CH J8/1/524.
103 – CH J8/1/493.
104 – CH J8/1/494.
105 – CH J8/4/8.
106 – CH J8/1/504.
107 – Lady Mary Wortley Montagu, *The Complete
Letters*, ed. R. Halsband, Oxford, 1966, II, p. 57.
108 – *Ibid.*, II, p. 58.
109 – CH J8/1/375.
110 – LAD Irwin MS. 12/8.
111 – Lady Griselda Baillie, *Household Book
1692–1733*, ed. R. Scott-Moncrieff, London,
1911, pp. 300–1.
112 – BL. Add. 32,691, f.1.
113 – BL. Add. 32,691, f. 45
114 – Abel Boyer, *Political State of Great
Britain*, London, 1738, LV, pp. 448–9.
115 – I am indebted to Eeyan Hartley for drawing
this inscription to my attention. William Robinson
was paid £5 19s 4½d on 12 May 1738 'for Mason
work in Bulmer Church for ye late Earls Buriall'
(CH G2/1/4); and the last payments for the
mausoleum were to Christopher Thompson for
whitesmith work 'in ye years 1743 & 1744' (CH
G2/2/80).

# Select Bibliography

MANUSCRIPT SOURCES (listed alphabetically by repository)

Alscot Park, Warwickshire: West MSS

Bath Public Reference Library: MS.38:43 Tour of several English Counties in 1725 by a Cambridge Undergraduate

Borthwick Institute, York: Yarburgh MSS

British Library, London

  Add. 38,488a Itinerary of a journey from Cambridge to Suffolk, Norfolk, Lincolnshire and Yorkshire in 1741

  Add. 47057 'A Journey kept by the 1st. Lord Egmont of a Tour of England, from London to Carlisle and return 14 July–28 Oct 1701'

  Add. 61101–61710 Blenheim MSS

  Portland Loan 29/113 Misc. 14 Notes in handwriting of Edward Harley, Earl of Oxford, of his Tour in Northumberland and other Northern Counties, 1725

  Portland Loan 29/233 'A Journey through Hertfordshire, Lincolnshire, and Notts. to the Northern Counties of Scotland', by Timothy Thomas, chaplain to Edward Harley, Earl of Oxford, 1725

Bryn Mawr Jones Library, Hull: DP/146 Journal of Robert Broadley

Buckinghamshire Archaeological Society: MS. 195/4 no. 2 Diary of John or James Baker of Penn

Castle Howard, Yorkshire: Carlisle MSS

Chatsworth, Derbyshire: Devonshire MSS

College of Arms, London: Earl Marshal's Books

Cumbria County Record Office, Carlisle

  Lonsdale MSS

  D/LONS/L Papers from Lowther Estate Office

  L1/1 Letters to Thomas, Lord Wharton

  L2/6 MSS of John Lowther, Viscount Lonsdale containing advice to his son

  L3/20/1/1 John Lowther, Viscount Lonsdale's Estate and Household Accounts 1693–1699

  L13 Papers relating to Parliamentary Elections

  D/LONS/W Papers from Whitehaven Estate Office

  1. Bound volume of letters from William Gilpin to Sir John Lowther

  2. 8 bundles of letters from James Lowther to Sir John Lowther

  3. 6 bundles of letters from James Lowther to William Gilpin

  4. Bundles of stray letters

Cumbria County Record Office, Kendal

  Levens (Graham) MSS

  Rydal Hall (Fleming) MSS

Durham University Department of Palaeography and Diplomatic: Howard of Naworth MSS

Hertfordshire Record Office: Cowper (Panshanger) MSS
Hoare's Bank, London: Account of third Earl of Carlisle
Leeds Archives Department: Irwin MSS
National Library of Scotland, Edinburgh: MS2911 Journey of Sir William Burrell
Northumberland Record Office: Woodman Collection
North Yorkshire Record Office
   Cholmley/Strickland MSS
   Feversham MSS
   Worsley MSS. (microfilm)
Petworth House, Sussex: Somerset MSS. (available via West Sussex Record Office)
Public Record Office, London: Shaftesbury MSS
Royal Library, Windsor: Constable's Warrant Books
Scottish Record Office, Edinburgh: GD 18/2107 Sir John Clerk, A Journey to London in 1727
Sir John Soane's Museum, London
   Manuscript Observations of a Traveller in England principally on the Seats and Mansions of the Nobility and Gentry from 1722–1745, attributed to William Freman of Hamells, Hertfordshire (A.L.46A)
Trinity College, Cambridge: Rothschild MSS
West Suffolk Record Office, Bury St Edmunds
   E2/44/1 Sir John Cullum, Journal of a Tour to Yorkshire 1771.
   941/53/6 Journals to the Hon. William Hervey to North America and Europe from 1755 to 1814
Yale Center for British Art, New Haven, Connecticut
   John Tracy Atkyns, *Iter Boreale*
Yorkshire Archaeological Society, Leeds
   MS328 Account of my Journey begun 6 Aug 1724
Historical Manuscripts Commission Reports
   13 The Manuscripts of Capt. J. F. Bagot, of Levens Hall (10th Report IV)
   19 The Manuscripts of the Marquess Townshend
   24 The Manuscripts of his Grace the Duke of Rutland, GCB, preserved at Belvoir Castle
   25 The Manuscripts of S. H. Le Fleming, Esq. of Rydal Hall
   29 The Manuscripts of the Duke of Portland, preserved at Welbeck Abbey
   36 The Manuscripts of the Marquess of Ormonde, preserved at Kilkenny Castle
   42 The Manuscripts of the Earl of Carlisle, preserved at Castle Howard
   63 Diary of Viscount Perceval, afterwards 1st. Earl of Egmont
   64 The Manuscripts of the Earl of Verulam, preserved at Gorhambury
   67 The Manuscripts of Lord Polwarth, preserved at Mertoun House, Berwickshire
   71 The Manuscripts of the late Allan George Finch Esq., of Burley-on-the-Hill, Rutland
   78 The Manuscripts of the late Reginald Rawdon Hastings, Esq., of The Manor House, Ashby de la Zouche

SECONDARY SOURCES

Barman, Christian, *Sir John Vanbrugh*, London, 1924
Beard, Geoffrey, 'Castle Howard', *Connoisseur Year Book*, 1956, pp. 3–12
– 'On Patronage', *Leeds Art Calendar*, no. 46–7, 1961, pp. 4–11
– *Georgian Craftsmen and their Work*, London, 1966
– *Decorative Plasterwork in Great Britain*, London, 1975
– *The Work of John Vanbrugh*, London, 1986
Borenius, Tancred, 'Two Venetian Pictures of Queen Anne's London', *Apollo*, vol. 3, no. 16, [1926], pp. 207–209
– 'Venetian Eighteenth Century Painters in England', *Studio Fine Art*, April 1931, pp. 49–61

# SELECT BIBLIOGRAPHY

– 'Castle Howard and its Lost Treasures', *Burlington Magazine*, 78, 1941, pp. 3–9

Brogden, W. A. 'Stephen Switzer: "La Grand Manier",' *Furor Hortensis: Essays of the History of the English Landscape Garden in Memory of H. F. Clark*, ed. Peter Willis, Edinburgh, 1974

Campbell, Colen, *Vitruvius Britannicus, or The British Architect*, vol. 1. London, 1715, vol. 2. London, 1717, vol. 3. London, 1725

Cast, David, 'Seeing Vanbrugh and Hawksmoor', *Journal of the Society of Architectural Historians*, XLII, December 1984, pp. 310–27

*A Descriptive Catalogue of the Pictures at Castle-Howard*, Malton, 1805

*The Illustrated Hand-Book to Castle Howard, the Yorkshire Seat of the Right Hon. the Earl of Carlisle*, Malton, 1857

Colvin, Howard, and Craig, Maurice (eds.), *Architectural Drawings in the Library of Elton Hall by Sir John Vanbrugh and Sir Edward Lovett Pearce*, Roxburghe Club, Oxford, 1964

Croft-Murray, Edward, *Decorative Painting in England, 1537–1837*, vol. 1, *Early Tudor to Sir James Thornhill*, London, 1962; vol. 2, *The Eighteenth and Early Nineteenth Centuries*, Feltham, 1970

Davies, J. H. V., 'Nicholas Hawksmoor', *Journal of the Royal Institute of British Architects*, October 1962, pp.368–75

Dobrée, Bonamy (ed.), *The Complete Works of Sir John Vanbrugh*, vols. 1–3, *The Plays*, London, 1927

Downes, Kerry, *English Baroque Architecture*, London, 1966

– *Hawksmoor*, London, 1969

– *Vanbrugh*, London, 1977

– *Hawksmoor*, 2nd ed. London, 1979

– 'Vanbrugh's Heslington Lady', *Burlington Magazine*, vol. CXXIV, March 1982, pp. 153–5

– *Sir John Vanbrugh, A Biography*, London, 1987

Gent, Thomas, *Pater Patriae: Being, An Elegiac Pastoral Dialogue Occasioned By the most Lamented Death of the Late Rt. Honble, and Illustrious Charles Howard, Earl of Carlisle*, York, [1738]

Goodhart-Rendel, H. S., *Nicholas Hawksmoor*, London, 1924

Gunnis, Rupert, *Dictionary of British Sculptors 1660–1851*, London, n.d.

Hardwick N. (ed.). *A Diary of the Journey through the North of England made by William and John Blathwayt of Dyrham Park in 1703*, Gloucester, 1977

Harris, John, *William Talman: Maverick Architect*, London, 1982

Hawkesbury, Lord, *Catalogue of the Portraits, Miniatures & c. at Castle Howard*, Hull, 1903

Hunt, John Dixon and Willis, Peter, *The Genius of the Place: The English Landscape Garden 1620–1820*, London, 1975

Hussey, Christopher, *English Gardens and Landscapes 1700–1750*, London, 1967

Ibbotson, Henry, *The Visitor's Guide to Castle Howard*, Ganthorpe, 1851

Irwin, Lady Anne, *Castle Howard the Seat of the Right Honourable the Earl of Carlisle*, London, 1732

Laing, Alastair, 'Foreign Decorators and Plasterers in England', *The Rococo in England: A Symposium*, ed. Charles Hind, London, 1986, pp. 21–45

Lang, S., 'Note on Castle Howard', *Architectural Review*, vol. 108, 1950, pp. 129–30

– 'Vanbrugh's Theory and Hawksmoor's Buildings', *Journal of the Society of Architectural Historians*, XXIV, May 1965, pp. 127–51

– 'The Genesis of the English Landscape Garden', *The Picturesque Garden and its Influence outside the British Isles*, ed. N. Pevsner, Washington, 1974

Lees-Milne, James, *English Country Houses: Baroque 1685–1715* Feltham, 1970

Loveday, John, *Diary of a Tour in 1732 through Parts of England, Wales, Ireland and Scotland*, Roxburghe Club, Edinburgh, 1890

McCarthy, Michael, 'Sir Thomas Robinson: An Original English Palladian', *Architectura*, 10:1, 1980, pp. 38–57

Paulson, Ronald, *Emblem and Expression: Meaning in English Art of the Eighteenth Century*, London, 1975

Pevsner, Nikolaus, *The Buildings of England, Yorkshire: The North Riding*, Harmondsworth, 1966

Rogers, J. E. Thorold, *A History of Agriculture and Prices in England, 1259–1793*, 7 vols, Oxford, 1887–1902

Saumarez Smith, Charles, 'Battle of the Giants', *Building Design*, 16 October 1987, pp. 38–9

Story, Thomas, *A Journal of the Life of Thomas Story*, Newcastle, 1747

Summerson, J., *Architecture in Britain 1530–1830*, Harmondsworth, 1953

– 'The Classical Country House in 18th Century England', *Journal of the Royal Society of Arts*, vol. 107, July 1959, pp. 539–87

Switzer, Stephen, *Ichnographia Rustica: Or, the Nobleman, Gentleman, and Gardener's Recreation*, 3 vols., London, 1718

Tipping, H. A. 'The Outworks of Castle Howard', *Country Life*, vol. LXII, 6–13 August 1927, pp. 200–208

Tipping, H. A. and Hussey, Christopher, *English Homes Period IV*, Vol. II, *The Work of Sir John Vanbrugh and his School, 1699–1736*, London, 1928

Waagen, G. F., *Art Treasures in Great Britain*, 3 vols, London, 1854

Watkin, D. J. (ed.), *Sale Catalogues of Libraries of Eminent Persons*, vol. 4, *Architects*, London, 1972

Webb, Geoffrey, 'Sir John Vanbrugh', *Burlington Magazine*, vol. XLVII, November 1925, pp. 222–7

– (ed.), *The Complete Works of Sir John Vanbrugh*, vol. 4, *The Letters*, London, 1928

– 'The Letters and Drawings of Nicholas Hawksmoor relating to the Building of the Mausoleum at Castle Howard', *Walpole Society*, vol. XIX, 1931

– 'Baroque Art', *Proceedings of the British Academy*, vol. XXXIII, 1947, pp. 131–48

Wenger, Mark R. (ed.), *The English Travels of Sir John Percival and William Byrd II*, Columbia, Missouri, 1989

Whinney, Margaret and Millar, Oliver, *English Art 1625–1714*, Oxford, 1957

Whistler, Lawrence, *Sir John Vanbrugh, Architect and Dramatist 1664–1726*, London, 1938

— 'Unpublished Drawings for Castle Howard', *New English Review Magazine*, 1950, pp. 27–33

— 'The Evolution of Castle Howard', *Country Life*, Vol. CXIII, 1953, January 30th, pp. 276–9

— *The Imagination of Vanbrugh and his Fellow Artists*, London, 1954

UNPUBLISHED DISSERTATIONS

Beckett, J. V., 'Landownership in Cumbria c. 1680-c. 1750', PhD. dissertation, University of Lancaster, 1975

Brogden, W. A., 'Stephen Switzer and Garden Design in the Early Eighteenth Century', PhD. dissertation, University of Edinburgh, 1973

Duncan, Andrew I. M., 'A Study of the Life and Public Career of Frederick Howard, fifth Earl of Carlisle, 1748–1825', PhD. dissertation, University of Oxford, 1981

Ellis, E. L., The Whig Junto in Relation to the Development of Party Politics and Party Organization from its Inception to 1714', PhD. dissertation, University of Oxford, 1961

Hopkinson, R., 'Elections in Cumberland and Westmorland 1695–1723', PhD. dissertation, University of Newcastle, 1973

Kaiser, Wolfgang, 'Castle Howard. Studien zu Planungs und Baugeschichte', M.A. dissertation, University of Freiburg, 1979

– 'Castle Howard, Ein Englischer Landsitz des Fruhen 18. Jahrhunderts: Studien zu Architektur und Landschaftspark', PhD. dissertation, University of Freiburg, 1982

Murdoch, Tessa, 'Huguenot Artists, Designers and Craftsmen in Great Britain and Ireland, 1680–1760', PhD. dissertation, University of London, 1982

Saumarez Smith, Charles, 'Charles Howard, third Earl of Carlisle and the Architecture of Castle Howard', PhD. dissertation, University of London, 1986

# Index